THE PEACE GUIDEBOOK

How to
Cultivate Hope,
Healing, and Harmony
for the Good of
Humankind

Elizabeth Hamilton-Guarino and Dr. Katie Eastman

Foreword by The Rev. Canon Mpho Tutu van Furth,
Priest in Charge, All Saints Amsterdam

Health Communications, Inc.
Mount Pleasant, South Carolina
www.hcibooks.com

Library of Congress Cataloging-in-Publication Data
is available through the Library of Congress

©2026 Elizabeth Hamilton-Guarino and Dr. Katie Eastman

ISBN-13: 978-07573-2608-0 (Paperback)
ISBN-10: 07573-2608-0 (Paperback)
ISBN-13: 978-07573-2609-7 (ePub)
ISBN-10: 07573-2609-9 (ePub)

Publisher: Health Communications, Inc.
        1240 Winnowing Way, Suite 100
        Mt. Pleasant, SC 29466

Cover, interior design, and formatting by Larissa Hise Henoch
Elizabeth Hamilton-Guarino photo ©Peter R. Guarino
Hair styling by Kelly Giambra
Dr. Katie Eastman photo ©Ben Bender

Praise for *The Peace Guidebook*

"Once again, Elizabeth and Katie bring us what we all need, right when we need it, in an actionable and inspiring format. No matter where you are in your journey, this practical guide will help you practice peace and feel less alone while doing it."

—**Lizz Schumer,** books editor at *People Magazine* and author of *Biography of a Body* and *Buffalo Steel*

"This guidebook is a true beacon of wisdom in turbulent times. It reminds us that peace is something we cultivate, moment by moment, within ourselves. Every chapter invites reflection, compassion, and a deeper connection to life. A must-read for anyone ready to live with greater purpose and grace."

—**Ken D. Foster,** bestselling author, producer of the *Voices of Courage* and *Heal It* shows

"Peace is a soul-centered inside job. Your peace is easy as you read, study, and apply the principles herein."

—**Mark Victor Hansen,** international bestselling coauthor of the Chicken Soup for the Soul series

"*The Peace Guidebook* sets a real-world framework for understanding and actively participating in the aspects of your life that cause the most stress, anxiety, and pain. As a medical oncologist, I am often faced with the most difficult time in a patient's and their family's lives, and what is amazing is seeing in many of these families the ability to approach that challenge with peace, understanding, inquisition, and compassion. This work will help many faced with similar challenges develop a way to understand and cope with these events, not necessarily changing the outcomes but fundamentally changing the experience."

—**Dr. Bently Doonan, MD, MS,** medical oncologist, The Mayo Clinic Florida

"Having worked with Archbishop Desmond Tutu as an advocate for hospice and palliative care, during South Africa's transition from apartheid, I know the power of courageous leadership rooted in compassion. 'The Arch,' as we affectionately called him, would be so proud that his daughter's foreword to *The Peace Guidebook* honors and extends his legacy. In a world still shaped by injustice and division, this book offers an essential pathway toward peace. *The Peace Guidebook,* and helping to generate peace within individuals and communities, is aspirational, inspirational, and essential."

—**Joan Marston,** executive committee, PallCHASE, Palliative Care in Humanitarian Aid Situations and Emergencies

"As a full-time emergency physician for twenty-five years, I've seen the healing that comes with those who choose peace or who are blessed with an inner peace. The importance of searching within to achieve true peace and the emphasis on communication and sharing peace is critical. May we all embrace the pathways provided by Elizabeth and Dr. Katie with love and grace!"

—**Marcus Riccioni, MD,** emergency physician

"As a Ukrainian living through war, *The Peace Guidebook* has given me strength, perspective, and a path toward peace—both personally and professionally."

—**Mariya Vynnytska,** psychologist, cofounder of The NGO-The Soul

"A beautiful, inspirational book that brings peace to your soul. It allows you to journey through life with renewed gratitude, love, and understanding."

—**Karen Middleton,** publisher MyMaine

"*The Peace Guidebook* is an exceptionally valuable resource for anyone who desires not only greater peace, but greater understanding of how to sustain and ever expand that peace in the most extraordinary way."

—**Michael McGlone,** actor and musician

"*The Peace Guidebook* is a powerful companion for anyone ready to live with greater presence. It reminds us that peace is not passive—we must choose it. And that choice is life-changing. With clarity and heart, this book guides us back to wholeness, helping us cultivate true peace from the inside out—radiating into the world around us."

—**Kelly Browne,** bestselling author of *101 Ways to Say Thank You* and *101 Ways to Create Mindful Forgiveness*

"A truly interspiritual offering from Elizabeth Hamilton-Guarino and Dr. Katie Eastman grounded in the shared truths at the heart of every religious and spiritual path and in our universal longing for peace."

—**Karen Noé,** author of *We Consciousness: 33 Profound Truths for Inner and Outer Peace*

"*The Peace Guidebook* is a playbook for life. As a coach, I'm always looking for tools that help my athletes become not just better players—but better people. This book shows us how to lead with values, respond with grace, and build peace from the inside out. Elizabeth and Dr. Katie have created something powerful, practical, and deeply needed in today's world."

—**Coach Edwin Thompson,** head baseball coach, Georgetown University

"In competitive sports, we often talk about mental toughness and the impact it can make on the performance of individuals and teams. While I subscribe to the importance of mental toughness, self discipline, and prepa-ration, *The Peace Guidebook* also reminds us that real strength comes from patience, presence, compassion and mentorship. The book is more than simply pure philosophy—it's a strategy for becoming your best self on and off the competitive field or arena. I highly recommend *The Peace Guide-book* to coaches, leaders, and anyone who believes in the power of personal growth and development."

—**Al Bean,** commissioner, Little East Conference, director emeritus of athletics, University of Southern Maine

"Peace isn't passive; it's an active choice, just like showing up with heart and joy. *The Peace Guidebook* offers a powerful, practical reminder that when we lead with humanity, we change the energy of every room, every field, and every community. This is a guidebook the world needs right now."

—**Vincent Chapman,** The Dancing Umpire, Savannah Bananas

"At Maine Academy of Gymnastics, we teach that strength begins with emotional safety and trust. *The Peace Guidebook* beautifully captures how creating calm, respectful, and connected environments allows people, especially young people, to grow with confidence. This book is a powerful resource for anyone shaping a culture of care, resilience, and belonging."

—**Paul and Alyssa Amundson,** owners, Maine Academy of Gymnastics

DEDICATION

For everyone, everywhere,
Pave your path to peace.

CONTENTS

FOREWORD

Peace is not the absence of war. It is not simply quiet, nor is it a lack of conflict. True peace is presence—presence with ourselves, with one another, with the Divine, and with the sacred breath of each moment. It is wholeness made visible. In *The Peace Guidebook*, Elizabeth Hamilton-Guarino and Dr. Katie Eastman offer us not a lofty ideal but a living, breathing path—a deeply personal and profoundly practical invitation to become makers of peace in our own lives.

Reading this book, I am reminded of the African wisdom of Ubuntu: "I am because we are." Peace is not something we achieve alone; it is something we become together. This guidebook is not only a manual; it is a companion, holding your hand as you navigate the terrain of hurt, hope, and healing. It reminds us that the journey to peace begins not on distant battlefields but in the inner landscapes of our hearts and homes. Peace is nurtured in how we speak to our children, how we forgive ourselves, and how we return again and again to love when fear tempts us to retreat.

Elizabeth and Katie write with the kind of authenticity that can only be forged in the fire of real life. They do not pretend that the road to peace is easy. Instead, they tell the truth: that peace is a practice. It is a decision we make in the middle of disruption, a breath we take when we feel like screaming, a step toward compassion when judgment would be easier. They speak as mothers, daughters, survivors, and truth-tellers—offering the rare kind of wisdom that is both vulnerable and empowering.

In a world where fear shouts louder than love, and violence is often mistaken for strength, *The Peace Guidebook* is a sacred rebellion. It dares to believe that presence can be revolutionary, that kindness can be transformative, and that our stories—especially the ones laced with grief, imperfection, and grace—can be seeds of healing for others. Through each Peace Point and reflection, you are called not just to read but to live. Not just to hope, but to act.

You do not need to be perfect to practice peace. You do not need to have it all figured out. As my father, Archbishop Desmond Tutu, often said, "God needs only your willing heart." This book is a call to offer just that—your heart, your honesty, your longing for wholeness—and in return, you will find a road map to a new way of being.

May this guidebook serve you as a balm, a compass, and a mirror. May it remind you that your peace matters—not just to you, but to the whole human family. And may it lead you ever deeper into the truth that we do not walk this road alone. We walk it together, and together, we can Percolate Peace into every corner of the world.

Amen. Makubenjalo. And so it is.

—The Reverend Canon Mpho Tutu van Furth

Percolate (verb):

To filter gradually through a porous surface or substance.

Spread gradually through an area or group of people.

—Oxford English Dictionary

Percolate Peace

We believe the world is craving peace.

We believe divisions can heal.

We believe humanity is capable of oneness.

We are searching for hope—and for the courage to live it.

When peace and hope align with compassionate action,
the possibilities for humankind are endless.

We are in this together—one humanity, one Earth.

Imagine a world where we allow ourselves to be peaceful—

where we can travel safely, honor every culture and faith,

and give each person the space to be who they truly are.

Imagine lifting the world instead of tearing it down.

Imagine choosing oneness over separation.

Cultivate inner calm.

Share it with others—

in your family, your neighborhood, your community, and the world.

Pause for peace.

Create peace.

Percolate Peace.

With love and oneness,

—Elizabeth Hamilton-Guarino and Dr. Katie Eastman

INTRODUCTION

A Global Invitation to Percolate Peace

Compassion is the heartbeat of peace. You are a living expression of peace.

It starts with you, with all of us. When you commit to practicing compassion, you promote peace.

That's not just a sentiment. It's a truth we've seen echo through lives, across communities, and within every courageous heart that chooses connection over chaos, grace over judgment, and hope over hate.

Welcome! We're Elizabeth Hamilton-Guarino and Dr. Katie Eastman. We're so glad you're here!

Your path to peace is to become a guiding light in the world, and *The Peace Guidebook* is here to show you how. If you're exhausted by daily headlines and feel helpless in the face of mayhem and confusion, even in your own life, it's time for a new, transformative approach. When we choose to lead our lives with love, destinies can change, movements can arise, wars can cease.

1

Are you tired of waiting for the world to change? Are you ready to *be* the shift that so many only hope for? It doesn't start with someone else. It starts with you. Right now. Peace is not reserved for diplomats only. It doesn't sit behind podiums or wait on governments to legislate it into existence. Peace begins in real life. At the breakfast table. In the hospital room. On the sidewalk. On social media. In the pause between a reaction and a response. In the silence that follows the question *What really matters now?*

We're not world leaders seated at summits. We don't hold titles in government. We're leaders of the human heart. And that's where peace takes root.

As women, mothers, professionals, survivors, coaches, and storytellers, we've spent decades walking beside people as they've navigated life's most difficult moments, such as times of loss, change, success, and growth. We've seen firsthand that the longing for peace is not abstract. It's visceral. It's urgent. More importantly, it's possible. If there's one truth we've come to know with certainty, it's this:

Peace is not something we wait for.
It's something we practice—every day, in
every interaction, in every breath.

This book is here to help you do just that and is created from our own discovery of peaceful practices.

Having also written several bestselling and award-winning resources, such as *The Change Guidebook, Percolate: Let Your Best Self Filter Through, The Success Guidebook,* and *Uplifting: Inspiring Stories of Loss, Change, and Growth,* we feel a tremendous need to help readers and students of life Percolate Peace. *The Peace Guidebook* builds on these resources and our years of work with individuals, communities, and organizations around the world, offering a unique approach to personal transformation through the Ten Principles of Peace. *The Peace Guidebook* offers the next step: a deeply practical, soul-shifting map to help you create peace, not just in theory, but with action.

So, if you've ever asked, *Where do I begin?* it is here. This is your beginning.

We're Here with You

Before we dive into the chapters, we want to make one thing clear: We're on this journey with you. In this book, we take the time to show you how to apply everything to your real life. This isn't a book of fluff or empty optimism. In fact, we call it a no-fluff zone because peace doesn't ask for perfection. It asks for presence. It asks you to show up in your humanity, with courage, compassion, and the willingness to grow.

This book is written from the trenches of real life, both in our experiences and of the people you will meet. It is based on times of navigating change, overcoming loss, and learning to lead with love instead of fear. It comes from decades of helping people transform their pain into purposeful and meaningful living, their division into unity, and their struggles into personal growth.

We have studied peace, not as an abstract concept, but as a daily practice. We know it because we have fought for it in our own lives. We wrote this guide because we also needed it. We are all still learning to choose peace over pressure, calm over turmoil, and compassion over fear. We have learned how to cultivate peace when it is challenging, in times of triumph and in the face of adversity, and we believe that it is something that can be taught, shared, and spread by one person at a time.

We also know that waiting for someone else to bring peace to our world is not enough. If we leave it solely in the hands of politicians, activists, or religious leaders, we risk missing the most important truth: Peace starts with us. It starts with how we treat one another. It starts with how we choose to respond to conflict. It starts with how we heal from our past, how we forgive, how we let go, and how we extend love, even in moments of great challenge.

We are here to remind you that peace is not some far-off ideal. It is something we can build right now, in our homes, our relationships, and our communities. It is the quiet revolution that begins with the ways we speak, listen, and show up for ourselves and for one another.

We believe in the possibility of personal peace, collective peace, and a world that heals through love instead of divides through hate. That world starts with each of us. And it starts now.

How This Book Will Help You

The Peace Guidebook offers a practical, transformative road map for individuals, leaders, and organizations seeking to cultivate personal and collective peace while also creating positive change in the world. In a time of deep division and global unrest, this guidebook delivers ten actionable principles: a tool kit to help you heal, strengthen relationships, and foster peace within and around you. These principles, when practiced, will unlock and harness the power of your most peaceful, aligned life.

The Ten Principles of Peace will help you

- Heal what's unresolved within you.
- Navigate conflict with courage and grace.
- Create partnerships rooted in values and vision.
- Lead from love, even when the world forgets how.
- Build real, resilient, peace-filled communities.

You'll read powerful stories. You'll be invited to reflect, journal, and act. And most of all, you'll learn how to Percolate Peace and how to let it rise up from within you and spread outwardly in powerful, tangible ways. You don't need to be famous, flawless, or fearless to change the world. You just need to be willing to show up, as you are, and choose peace when it matters most.

Peace is often thought of as something external, like a distant hope for a world free of war, conflict, and suffering. In *Falling Upward: A Spirituality for the Two Halves of Life,* Richard Rohr states that the journey toward peace begins within each of us. True peace is not just the absence of turmoil; it is the presence of harmony, a sense of wholeness that transcends the circumstances around us. It is both an inner state and an outward practice, a continuous process of aligning our hearts, minds, and actions with the highest good for ourselves and the world. We agree! We want the world to expand the limiting definitions of peace.

What Qualifies Us to Write a Book with Global Implications?

Yes, we know, and you might have asked yourself this when you saw this book.

We're two women who've walked with thousands of people through their darkest moments and helped them find light. We've sat in hospital rooms, coached in boardrooms, stood on stages, and whispered hope to those who thought they couldn't go on.

We are credentialed professionals, and through our work in psychology, leadership, coaching, and personal development, we have guided people through the most difficult moments of their existence. We have supported them in their grief, listened to their deepest fears, and helped them rediscover hope when they thought all was lost. We have built communities that inspire and uplift, fostering spaces where people can find their voice, reclaim their power, and step into their best selves. We've made peace our practice. We've fought for it in our own lives. And we believe it is *teachable, transferable,* and *transformative*—one human being at a time.

We Are at a Turning Point

Hate is loud. Division is trending. Judgment is profitable. But underneath it all, there is a rising ache—a longing for something more meaningful, more humane, more kind.

You're in the right spot with us if you've been searching for peace, maybe without even realizing it. It's the quiet ache beneath the noise, the question that lingers when the world feels too loud, too divided, too unsteady. This isn't just a book. It's an invitation to step into a new way of being, where peace is no longer a wish, but something you actively create.

How to Use This Book

The Peace Guidebook is structured for clarity and action. Our intention in the format of this book is to offer you useful tools to improve your capacity for living peacefully. It's divided into three focus areas—Hope, Healing, and Harmony—and grounded in Ten Principles of Peace:

1. **Presence**—Being peaceful
2. **Potential**—Believing in peace
3. **Patience**—Trusting the pace of peace
4. **Practice**—Practicing peace
5. **Passion**—Fueling peaceful action
6. **Purpose**—Embodying peace
7. **Positivity**—Exuding peace
8. **Perseverance**—Persisting for peace
9. **Partnership**—Uniting for peace
10. **Peace**—Claiming peace

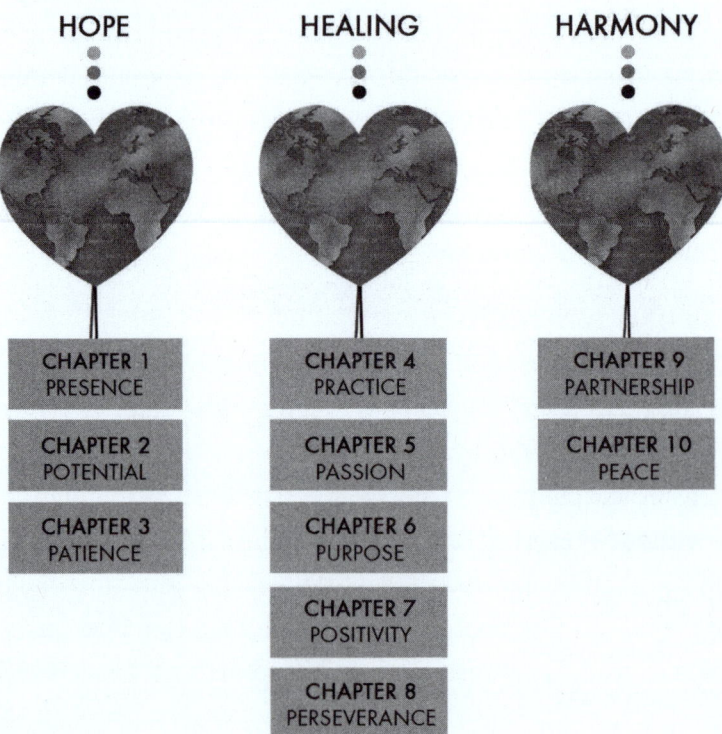

Each chapter is followed by original exercises, reflection prompts, and real-life stories from people just like you, because transformation isn't just a concept here. It's a practice.

The Movement Has Already Begun

Please Join The Percolate Peace Project

The Peace Guidebook is more than a book. It's a movement—a global call to action. It's a blueprint for change and an invitation to become part of something greater than yourself.

Through The Percolate Peace Project, we are uniting one million people to help create a world where compassion, understanding, and healing lead the way.

So, here's our bold request:

Find one moment in this book that moves you and share it.

Read it aloud at the dinner table.

Send it in a text.

Post it.

Speak it.

Live it.

Start conversations that matter.

Be the reason someone feels hopeful again.

Be the one who ripples peace outward.

If every person who reads this shares it with just one other person, we'll reach one million hearts faster than you think—at the speed of love. And if you keep going? You'll help spark something even bigger—a global wave of healing and harmony.

Don't just read this book. Live it. Share it. Be it.

What Can You Do?

- Visit PercolatePeace.com to officially join the movement. Add your message, connect with others, and explore tools to help you live and lead more peacefully.
- Post your moment of peace directly on the website or in social media using the hashtag #PercolatePeace. One post, one comment,

one ripple of kindness can inspire another—and another—until we become a wave.

- Want to engage in real time? Join our growing Facebook community: @PercolatePeaceProject, a safe, welcoming space for insight, encouragement, and shared action.
- Together, we're creating a peaceful world!

Let's Percolate Peace!

PART 1

HOPE

CHAPTER 1
PRESENCE

In the first principle of peace, Presence, we commit to a new way of living: living peacefully. Presence is where peace begins. We pause, become fully aware of any issues that may prevent us from being peaceful, and quiet any external noise, listening to the intuitive voice that speaks to us when we are still. In this quiet state, we explore and clarify what we value and whatever changes we need to make to fully embrace peace. Self-awareness is the key to reclaiming peace. Are you able to clearly recognize what prevents you from being peaceful? This is the heart of a peaceful presence, and compassion is its steady beat.

Peace begins with your everyday, real life. It is something you *practice*. This chapter is your invitation to begin this practice with these small steps: Gently introduce peace practices to your daily routine. Stop abandoning yourself when the world feels loud. Reclaim as holy ground the small, ordinary moments.

We are going to begin and end each chapter with personal stories of our own struggles to maintain peace in everyday situations. We are both empathic and intuitive. One of our greatest challenges is that we are both deeply affected by other people's pain.

What keeps us up at night are the same things that probably weigh on your heart. We worry about the world and feel helpless to create meaningful change. The world is big. The problems feel enormous. But that's why *The Peace Guidebook* is about small, lasting change that each of us can make through daily commitment. That kind of change is powerful. It allows us—and you—to move through helplessness into hope.

For example, we also share a common bond that when we see or hear anything about children being mistreated, it sends us both into a tailspin. It rattles our peace. The mama bears in us show up with a fierce desire to do something to protect the cubs of this world. We want to do something and do it now. We want to protect children. This sensibility disrupts our peace and has taught us that by supporting adults in becoming peacemakers, we ultimately create a more peaceful world for children.

That is one of our deepest, shared motivations for writing this book.

We learn and relearn daily that peace is not something that external circumstances dictate. Peace is an intentional way of living differently from what we may be experiencing now. It's about shifting perspectives. Taking time to pause, reflect, and redefine what peace means to all of us, both individually and collectively, and not as something to chase, but as something to embody.

So let's pause for a moment, take a deep, collective breath, and begin exploring a definition of peaceful presence that works for you and maybe even all of us. Give yourself a quiet moment right here and right now to listen to your intuition, your inner wisdom, and your truth. Why is peace important to you? How can you bring peace to the world? Breathe in the answers that arise.

Next, let's call in some raw honesty.

PEACE POINT 1: Peace Begins Where You Are

You cannot create peace in the world if you are at war with yourself. Self-compassion is not self-indulgence. It is self-restoration. It is the choice to learn, to heal, and to move forward with grace.

There are times when the idea of any aspect of peace feels beyond comprehension. Before we can create peace in any form, we must first come home to ourselves. Peace of mind begins with us, here and now.

You might be thinking, *I'm so worried about real life, and you want me to focus on peace, being calm, or helping humanity?*

- I'm worried about my bank account.
- I'm worried about my kids.
- I'm worried about my health, my home, my work, my parents, my marriage, my future.
- Sometimes I can't even remember if I ate lunch.

We're right here with you. Honestly, there are moments we feel like we're about to break and the thought of choosing peace feels like a luxury for other people. As we wrote this chapter, Dr. Katie and her husband, John, are battling a round of fleas in their house, Elizabeth and her husband are looking outside in their backyard at a septic disaster. Seriously, what a candid moment, when we definitely don't have our peaceful-presence acts together.

Depending on your circumstances at any given moment, it can be really challenging to just ask you to show up with a peaceful presence anyway. However, this is exactly when peace matters most. Not when life is perfect. Not when the bills are paid or the diagnosis comes back clear. Not when your to-do list is done or your heart isn't breaking. Peace isn't the reward for getting your life together. It's the *foundation* that helps you live through it. There is power in your presence.

Presence is the antidote to distraction. It's where the stories you tell yourself soften, and the truth of who you are becomes audible again. In presence, you remember that peace is not found in the past or the future. It lives here, in your body, in your breath, in the sacredness of now.

It is not a performance or a posture—it is the quiet return to the here and now. It's choosing to be fully awake in your own life, without numbing, rushing, or escaping. In a world that constantly pulls our attention in a thousand directions, presence is a revolutionary act of love.

We recently posed the question "What brings you peace?" to our friends on social media and a group of elementary school students performing a peace concert. The responses from adults poured in:

"My pets."

"Photography."

"Nature."

"My religion."

"My family."

"Food."

The children, however, answered differently. More than once, they told us:

"Peace is being kind."

"Peace is making someone feel good."

"Peace is doing something peaceful."

The children seemed to understand what adults were missing: Peace comes from within. This difference fascinated us. While the children recognized peace as a state of being, the adults externalized it by associating peace with things outside themselves. Not a single adult mentioned their responses, reactions, or choices as sources of peace. That gave us a pause. Why do children intuitively understand that peace is something within them, while adults think it is the result of something they do, create, or *experience*—dictated by external events?

In her book *Uplifting*, Dr. Katie quotes an eight-year-old boy who tells his mother, "There is love everywhere inside all of us and the purpose of life is to make a difference." When his mom questions why he knows this, he responds, "You knew it too, but you grew up!" This realization helps us all rediscover the peace that already exists within us; it helps us return to our presence, that peaceful place we once understood when we were younger.

PEACE POINT 2: Pause for Space and Grace

Implement the pause. Allow yourself and others in your presence the space and grace to just be.

In a world that moves at lightning speed, it's so easy to get caught up in the rush. On autopilot, you may tend to react instead of respond, speak before you think, and push forward without truly being present. Peace isn't just about what you do; it's also about what you choose not to do.

Sometimes, the most powerful step toward peace is simply stopping or pausing long enough to reconnect with yourself, your intentions, and the energy you bring into each moment. Pausing even for thirty seconds allows your brain to reset and your thoughts to recenter.

The act of pausing for peace and allowing for space and grace is one of self-awareness and responsibility. It allows you to break cycles of stress, frustration, and impulsive reactions and to create space to breathe and reset your mindset. In these moments you have an opportunity to choose a response aligned with your values and your emotions.

Pausing is a crucial step in this process. When you slow down, you create space to recognize what brings you calm, clarity, and ultimately joy. Once you identify your true sources of peace, you can intentionally integrate them into your daily life. This then becomes a lifelong practice instead of an afterthought or a one-time discovery. Identifying sources of peace requires curiosity, meaning asking important questions to guide you purposefully yet calmly. Curiosity is a key peace tool for peaceful communication. It helps you notice what truly nurtures you and your willingness to evolve, so that you understand that what brought you peace in the past may no longer serve you today. The key is to remain open, to listen to yourself, and to honor what truly nurtures your well-being.

When you pause, you make room for wisdom, understanding, and compassion to guide you through the tension and urgency. This practice is especially vital in moments of conflict or challenge. Instead of reacting immediately to a difficult conversation, a frustrating situation, or even your inner doubts, you can take a breath, step back, and ask,

"What does peace look like in this moment?"

Pausing is not about avoiding or ignoring challenges. It is about intention: creating liminal space to respond with clarity and purpose versus reacting, driven by impulsivity. *Liminal space* is a term that anthropologist Victor Turner originated. He explained that human behavior exists between two states. Liminal space is the pause between who we were and who we are becoming. As Turner observed, these thresholds hold the richest potential for transformation. His theory reminds you that you don't have to be swept away by the pace of the world. You can choose to slow down, reflect, and move forward with intention to become a more peaceful you.

PEACE POINT 3: Acknowledge What Isn't Peaceful

It's important to understand what disrupts your peace. When life speeds up or spirals, peaceful people anchor into the now. They don't bypass their emotions. They breathe into them. They don't escape the discomfort. They meet it with curiosity. This kind of presence isn't always quiet or still, but it is rooted. It says, "Even if I don't have the answers, I belong in this moment."

Ask yourself, *What pulls me out of presence?* Is it your phone? A familiar fear? The need to control or fix? Then ask, *What brings me back?* Is it a breath? A hand on your heart? A step outside? Move beyond distractions to seek true peace. In a fast-moving world, it is easy to sacrifice your peace. You may find yourself endlessly scrolling, binge-watching, or filling every quiet moment with noise or activity. These all may offer temporary relief, but they don't bring the deep, lasting peace that your soul craves. Move beyond the noise to reclaim true peace. We find real peace when we slow down and listen within.

True peace isn't discovered in escaping reality. True peace is found in connecting more deeply with what restores and strengthens you. It's bound up with the intentional exploration of what makes you feel aligned, present, coherent, and whole in all areas of your life.

Peace doesn't ask that you tiptoe through life avoiding the potential for conflict, like the time you were startled by your neighbor's 6 AM leaf blower. It asks that you meet what disturbs you and choose not to hand over your power.

Let's get this out of the way: Life *will* disrupt your peace. That's not a flaw in your design. It's the curriculum. Disruption looks like a passive-aggressive text, a bounced check, your child melting down at the exact moment your Wi-Fi crashes. It can also be the quiet storm of loneliness, uncertainty, or grief creeping in at 3 AM. The real skill? Knowing how to pivot from being derailed to being recentered. Not reactive, but responsive. Not chaotic, but calm. Not perfect, but present. The biggest myth we're told is that peace is about perfect stillness—that if you're disrupted, you've somehow failed. Real peace isn't the absence of noise; it's the presence of navigation.

So how do you manage the havoc?

First, *know your triggers.* You can't disarm what you refuse to name. Triggers aren't just dramatic traumas from childhood. They're often subtle: a look, a tone, a late response to a text. They can be physical too—shoulders tightening, jaw clenching, stomach fluttering. These aren't annoyances; they're alerts. Your nervous system is talking to you. Learn its language.

Second, *install an internal pause button.* Seriously. Engrave it in your mind like it's the most sacred object in your mental toolbox. The pause is where power returns. Take a deep breath in through your nose and breathe out through your mouth. After you exhale, ask yourself,

- *Is this reaction helping me or just giving my control away?*
- *Am I about to escalate or elevate this situation?*
- *What would a wiser, calmer me choose right now?*

A peaceful presence begins with a reset. When you pause and return to your wiser, more authentic self, peace percolates through your choices and into the world around you.

However, for many of us it's not that easy.

From childhood, many of us learn that peace is fragile. You may have grown up in a household filled with tension or unpredictability. Maybe you faced adversity such as loss, instability, or trauma that shook your sense of security. Those memories may trigger your response to current situations.

Your life story may continue to challenge you, often making peace feel distant, even impossible. It's important to reclaim your peace. When peace is disrupted, it's easy to feel powerless and believe that the weight of past wounds will always define you. You are not powerless. Your story is not finished!

Peace is not about pretending pain never happened or ignoring the past or forcing yourself to simply move on. True peace comes from acknowledging your struggles, processing them, and creating something meaningful from them. In their powerful book *The Book of Forgiving: The Fourfold Path for Healing Ourselves and Our World*, Mpho Tutu and her father, the peacemaker Desmond Tutu, remind us that turning pain into purposeful peace begins when we tell the truth, name the hurt, and dare to forgive—even when it feels impossible.

It also means recognizing that while you may not have control over what has happened to you, you do have control over how you move forward. It means *repeatedly* choosing compassion.

It means choosing to heal unresolved resentment and understanding that peace is not the absence of pain, but the presence of resilience, wisdom, and strength. The people who embody peace are not those who have never faced hardship. Rather, they are those who have faced it and chosen not to let it define them. They have turned wounds into wisdom, setbacks into growth, and painful circumstances into purpose. They do not wait for peace to be handed to them. They build it within themselves and bring it to the world!

PEACE POINT 4: Choose Peace and Embody Compassion

A few years ago, Elizabeth asked her son Cam what the world needed more of. She asked him to think about his college baseball team and think about something to teach for the year on her platform BestEverYou.com, to provide personal and professional development tools. Now, mind you, he was all of around eighteen at the time. His response: compassion. He went on to say that his team was very "I and me" focused instead of "we and us" focused, and these types of teams don't win championships. He was right. When people shift from individual success to collective success, something powerful happens: Trust deepens, communication strengthens, and every person rises. This became a lasting lesson for Cam. Now he is a college baseball coach who implements it.

His insight became a reminder that true peace and true success begin with compassion, belonging, and the courage to care about one another.

Compassion starts with awareness. It requires you to recognize that everyone is navigating unseen battles—some are heavy, some are quiet, but all are real. Choosing compassion means choosing understanding over assumption. It does not mean ignoring harm or excusing wrongdoing; rather, it is the decision not to let pain define your responses. It is about breaking the cycle of hurt instead of adding to it. True compassion does not waver based on convenience or circumstance; it is a steady commitment to seeing and honoring humanity in ourselves and others. Yet, in a world that often rewards bravado and speed, compassion can feel like a quiet, unspoken language. You may forget to embody compassion and instead allow stress, pain, or fear to take over.

Instead, we're suggesting you extend warmth to those you love, and when faced with those who challenge you, practice peaceful presence. Beginning with yourself, let peaceful presence guide you. Whether with a coworker, friend, neighbor, or family member—and even furry family members—offer that same gentleness and kindness to all you encounter. It's important not to take out on anyone else our frustration from what we experience in unrelated stressful situations.

Compassion comes from within. Often we replay our own missteps, voicing self-critical comments with words we would never say to someone else. We may even label our actions as failures instead of stepping stones—or, worse, call ourself a failure.

Both of us have made some spectacular, if not comical, mistakes. One time, Elizabeth baked a ham for Easter for her family with the packaging still on it. Dr. Katie once left eggs boiling on the stove when she went to pick up her daughter and returned home to find eggs exploded all over the ceiling. In each case, we attempted to provide our families with a nurturing experience, but we weren't paying attention. Our noble efforts were negated by our inattention. How often do you have great Martha Stewart–like visions only to have them sidetracked by real-life distractions and responsibilities? If you are like most people, probably more than you want. Remember, Martha Stewart has a team!

Instead of ruminating over what could have been, change your perspective. Missteps are learning opportunities that bring us closer to understanding how we can become more peaceful. It's time to stop holding onto regret or shame as if punishing yourself can change an outcome or somehow lead to peace. Stay in the present. We have both learned to pause and pay attention to the details. In this case, Elizabeth triple checks the ham and Dr. Katie has a fancy egg timer.

When you embody compassion, you transform the energy of every space you enter, creating ripples of peace that begin within and extend outward to others and the world. Consider how you speak to yourself when you make a mistake. Do you offer kindness, or do you lean toward criticism? Reflect on whether the patience and understanding you extend to others are the same gifts you grant yourself. True compassion starts from within; by nurturing it in your own heart, you build the capacity to share it more fully with those around you. Compassion is not a weakness. It is strength in its purest form. It is the foundation of inner peace, connection, and lasting change.

PEACE POINT 5: Share Your Story

Our stories can be as simple as a misstep or as profound as trauma. Each and everything in between matters because of the lessons we learn about ourselves and how to remain peaceful.

When Dr. Katie first received her doctorate, she was driving from Boston to Maine to present at a workshop. Before leaving town, she needed to stop by her apartment to change clothes. In a rush to get on the road, she grabbed a cup of coffee and proceeded to spill it all over herself. There was no time to wash and dry her outfit, so she went across the street to a thrift store to purchase the first thing she could find that would be professional enough to work for the presentation. She found a suit, but it was orange—bright orange—the shade that hunters wear to keep themselves safe in the woods from getting shot by other hunters. It was also a size or two to three too small. After her first words at the presentation, the front of the jacket split open, exposing her bra and other assets to the audience. While such a situation could have easily rattled her, she peacefully picked up her notes and placed them strategically in front of her chest. Maintaining presence and eye contact with the audience, she calmly told the audience what had happened. The room broke out in laughter, and she continued on with her presentation without missing a beat. This became a benchmark for future presentations. Things sometimes happen at the least opportune times, but what you do when the unexpected happens speaks volumes.

Remember, regardless of the intensity of the situation, *you matter* and you are significant and unique. Please read that sentence as many times as you need to until you believe it. Your story holds power. It's time you don't dim your light. Let it shine. There are times when you have a choice: to feel humiliated or to laugh at yourself and move on. Some moments may call for laughter, tears, or both or something in between. They are opportunities.

Every experience, every challenge, and every triumph shape the unique narrative of who you are. Yet, too often, we silence ourselves. We downplay our struggles, believing they are too small to matter. We tuck away our pain, fearing that vulnerability will be mistaken for weakness. We convince ourselves that our experiences are not significant enough to share. But when you hide your stories, you rob yourself of healing and deny others the gift of connection. Peace is built on understanding, and understanding begins with sharing.

When you bravely tell your real story—unpolished, unfiltered, and unedited—you permit others to do the same. You remind one another that you are not alone and that grief, resilience, loss, and hope are not solitary struggles but shared human experiences. Your story has the potential to become a bridge where a wall once stood. Our stories collectively are transformational and inspiring, encouraging us to lift ourselves to discover greater peace with wisdom, purpose, and unity.

Sharing your story is not just about speaking; it is about being witnessed and feeling heard. In modern trauma theory, author Judith Herman emphasizes the vital role of storytelling in healing, particularly the act of telling one's story in the presence of an empathetic listener. This process, she explains, is essential to reestablishing personal agency and dignity after traumatic experiences. In her seminal work *Trauma and Recovery*, she writes, "The first principle of recovery is the empowerment of the survivor. She must be the author and arbiter of her own recovery. . . . The first task of recovery is to establish safety . . . and the next is remembrance and mourning—done through the presence of a witness."

Peace unfolds and healing and growth progress when you listen as much as you share. It is found in the space between words, in the quiet validation of "I hear you, and you matter." That is where true healing begins.

PEACE POINT 6: Do the Best You Can with What You Know at the Time

Peace is the deep breath when your hands are shaking. It's the choice to put your hand over your heart and whisper, "I'm doing the best I can." It's calling a friend instead of suffering in silence. It's saying "no" when you're overwhelmed. It's sitting in the car for ten extra minutes just to cry and be still before walking back inside. Peace isn't ridiculous. Peaceful presence is revolutionary and, for example, is what allows you to care for your sick parent and still care for yourself. It's what helps you carry your stress without becoming it. It's what reminds you that you don't have to save the world today—you just have to meet this moment with love. And, yes, it's okay to be angry. To be exhausted. To feel over it.

Don't forget, you can always choose peace. Even if it's messy. Even if it's one shaky moment at a time. You don't have to get it all together before you practice peace. In fact, peace is how you hold yourself together when the rest of life feels like it's falling apart. If you're reading this, overwhelmed and teary-eyed and tired of trying, please hear us:

Peace is not a performance. It's your permission to rest, feel, and breathe and to keep going one peaceful choice at a time. You don't have to fix everything to believe in peace. Start with you. Start here. And let that be enough for today.

Keep in mind that peace is deeply personal. What soothes one person's soul may not resonate with another. Explore what brings you peace. It's not what society tells you should bring you peace or what others expect will bring you peace. It's what genuinely nurtures our spirit. Some find peace in nature; others in music, movement, quiet solitude, and a multitude of other ways.

Peace is often mistaken for comfort, and the two are not always the same. Something may feel familiar, yet that doesn't mean it's truly peaceful. True peace is not merely the absence of conflict; it is also the presence of well-being when faced with challenges. It's about recognizing what genuinely nourishes your soul rather than what merely numbs your stress. This is where reflection becomes essential.

Exploring diverse sources of peace can lead to unexpected insights. But exploration without clarity can leave you feeling scattered, perhaps unsure of what sustains you and maybe even feeling like you're lost. Taking the time to clarify what truly brings you peace allows you to be more intentional in every aspect of your life. It also helps you align your actions with what genuinely grounds and restores you. With this, you move beyond temporary distractions and make a move toward lasting inner peace. This clarity empowers you to create a life where peace is not accidental and is instead cultivated with purpose.

PEACE POINT 7: Listen to the Messages of Peace

Continuously mine your wisdom. If you listen carefully, whispers of guidance come from your body, mind, emotions, and spirit. As humans, we are most aligned with our truest, most important values when we make choices rooted in these inner signals. When you pay attention, and when you respond with intention, you create a ripple effect of peace within yourself and in the world around you.

For example, your thoughts shape your reality. The more you focus on what truly matters, the more your brain reinforces messages of peace that reflect your authentic self. The act of prioritizing these thoughts and aligning them with meaningful action is how peace takes root in your life.

We also love this translation by Eknath Easwaran of a quote by Buddha:

"We are what we think. All that we are arises with our thoughts. With our thoughts we make the world."

The great news is that we all have pathways to peace. To fully embrace them, your intentions must align with your actions. If you want to cultivate inner peace, you must be mindful of the signals you receive from your physical, emotional, mental, and spiritual sources of wisdom. Everything is connected. When you commit to choices that nurture your well-being, you activate four interconnected pathways to peace. These concepts are based on the innovative work of Dr. Elisabeth Kübler-Ross's adaption of the Four Quadrants model. She applied this powerful framework to describe the four dimensions of being human. It was part of her later work in teaching whole-person care and personal transformation, particularly in her workshops and training retreats.

Here's a summary of the Four Quadrants:

1. **Physical (Body):** Your body communicates through sensations, symptoms, and responses.
2. **Mental (Perception):** Your thoughts influence how you interpret and engage with the world.
3. **Emotional (Passion):** Your feelings shape what you care about most deeply.
4. **Spiritual (Purpose):** Your sense of meaning guides how you respond to life's challenges.

Let's look at an example of two people receiving equally valuable messages from two different values-based perspectives. These two people are navigating their personal pathways to peace after an election:

- The first person feels physically drained and exhausted, with tears welling up from a deep place of uncertainty. Despite her legal status, she fears for her future as a woman of color. Rather than staying in that fear, she leans into her passion for diversity and inclusion and takes action. She finds peace by volunteering at her local school, using her gifts to uplift and empower others. Through this act of service, she reclaims her sense of purpose.

- The second person feels physically energized, relieved that his financial security is intact. His thoughts are centered on his ability to provide for his family, and his passion for ensuring his children's future gives him a sense of peace. Knowing that his loved ones are safe and stable affirms his sense of purpose and strengthens his commitment to building a secure future.

These examples highlight how perceptions of challenges and outcomes can shape the path to peace in vastly diverse ways. If you choose peace, you must embrace the full experience. You cannot rush or bypass the deep reflection and self-awareness needed to cultivate lasting peace. Instead, you must allow your thoughts, emotions, and physical responses to guide you toward clarity. You also must recognize what you value most and how it influences your choices and align your intentions with actions to create a sustainable sense of peace.

Pathways to peace offer a powerful concept to change your life and share your story with others of how you perhaps turn a negative into a positive or pave a path through a challenging situation.

●●●

Our Pathways to Peace with Elizabeth and Dr. Katie

Throughout the book, we share personal stories that have shaped our understanding of peace, resilience, and the power of transformation. We also introduce you to many other people who will share their experiences and revelations. Through moments of challenge, growth, and discovery, we invite you to walk alongside us as we explore what it truly means to cultivate peace in our lives and in the world.

Elizabeth: Chaos

To write a book about peace, I feel like I must first show you that I've known the opposite. I am an early witness to dysfunction.

My first memories are a mixture of peace and pain. Like many of you, I am the product of a once-beautiful marriage gone sour. It eventually rotted into contention, addiction, emotional and physical trauma, and fear.

My mom says it was heartbreaking to watch a man she loved turn into someone she didn't even recognize. The shift happened after a vehicle accident. Something changed in him. Substance abuse and domestic violence followed. My mom is a survivor. My parents divorced, but it wasn't simple. As a child, I was caught in the middle of contentious court battles.

There were moments of fear that etched themselves into my memory. There were times when we didn't feel safe. There were long days of not knowing what would come next. And there were turning points, critical ones, where my mother made choices that saved us.

I remember more than I sometimes wish I did, and writing it all down for a book makes me nervous. It's one thing to hold a memory. It's another to release it into the world.

What I remember more than anything is how strong my mother was. She still is—fiercely independent, protective, and brave. I've always been proud of her for pulling us out of that terrible situation and standing up for both of us.

When I was around three, my mom met the man who would become my true father, James F. Hamilton. He adopted me, and together we began to unlearn fear and abuse and learn love. My mom and I started over. I found my footing again in dance, in gymnastics, ballet, and tap dancing; in books and in solitude. I was the girl who helped others read. I was quieter than most. I liked calmness. I found peace in books, movement, and stillness.

There's an unspoken bond between my mom and me. After all we'd been through together, sometimes we only need a glance to communicate. There's history there. Safety. An agreement between souls.

When I was around four years old, we drove to our new home. The windows were down. Our hair was blowing in the wind—freedom. We were both coping in our own ways: my mom stress-smoking, me biting my nails so badly they were bleeding.

"You've got to stop biting your nails," she said.

I looked at her and replied, "Well, you've got to stop smoking."

And that was that.

We made a pact on the side of the road, mid-move, two souls in a car carving a new life. If I stopped biting my nails, she'd stop smoking.

We both kept our promise.

To this day, fifty-one years later for me and seventy-six for her, we've never gone back. It was more than a deal. It was a vow. A silent, steady commitment to each other and to the peace we were trying to find.

That moment shaped who I became. As a mother of four sons now, I understand just how powerful that agreement was. It taught me that accountability is love in action. That mutual reliance builds trust. That peace starts with tiny choices honored over time.

Others have told me I have a calming presence. That I'm strong in storms. That I help others feel safe and seen. I believe that part of me was born in that car, with the windows down and a future being rewritten between a mother and daughter who refused to repeat the past.

That's where peace began for me, in the decision to live differently. To listen. To lead. To offer others the steadiness I had once longed for.

Peace isn't just something we find. It's something we create, and sometimes, it's written into the quiet pacts we keep for a lifetime.

That's why I'm writing this book, not because my life has always been peaceful, but because I've spent my life choosing peace anyway.

Dr. Katie: War of Words

It was a war of words that stole my peace as a child. Words hurt children, especially when they are desperately trying to be liked. I was one of those children—heavier than most and awkward, deeply impacted by bullies who left me feeling threatened, small, insecure, and less than.

Even in my home, my supposed safe space, there was frequent arguing. I can still remember cowering under my blankets, covering my ears with a pillow to drown out the yelling. Peace was something I yearned for desperately.

Like Elizabeth, I learned to drown out the noise, the negativity, and the toxicity by focusing on kindness with Pollyannaish optimism. I became a Walt Disney addict, obsessed with happy endings and wishes coming true. My mother would confide in me about her frustrations with my father—inappropriate, yet this became the source of one of my greatest strengths as a listener, eventually leading to a successful career as a psychotherapist.

I also became a dreamer, a visionary, someone who always sees potential. Why? It is likely because of my Disney addiction. I wanted happy endings and perfect families who didn't fight. I saw positivity in everything, and as an adult, I learned to transform anything that might otherwise be considered a loss into a gain. Pollyanna was my heroine, and to this day my family jokingly says, "It's a Katie moment," when something nauseatingly perfect and unrealistic occurs in a show or movie.

At an incredibly early age, I started imagining myself helping others see themselves with loving acceptance. In many ways, I transformed my lack of external peace into a drive to help others discover their inner peace. Even as a child, I listened to people's problems and offered advice. It's no surprise that I'm writing this now, with over thirty-five years of professional experience helping others transform their losses into growth. This book represents a childhood dream coming full circle.

If just one child can live more peacefully because one parent chooses to better understand their own triggers, then I will have accomplished what I always imagined. "Percolating peace" is the vision of a six-year-old girl who once told her parents that a homeless individual living on a park bench in Central Park deserved respect and that his home should be left alone as his sacred space. A social worker from birth, I am grateful to have risen from the pain of feeling small to harness and percolate my peaceful power. I hope that you, regardless of your circumstances, will do the same.

Presence is a powerful tool for practicing peace. Like Elizabeth, I learned that remaining present could make a profound difference, especially in moments when safety is a priority.

At thirteen, I found myself being followed home by a group of bullies. An unfortunate accident had marked me as a vulnerable target. After school, they surrounded me, taunting me with insults and threats. My heart raced with every word. Terrified, I was faced with a choice, and I chose peace.

Despite their intimidating comments, I decided to respond calmly. I remained silently present in a state of quiet kindness, turned my back to them, and began walking home. I could feel their presence, their bodies and energy following close behind. The insults—"fat," "ugly," "dumb"—kept coming. Their words stung deeply. Yet my focus was to stay grounded in love. I visualized light and held space for compassionate connection. I refused to let fear take over, staying steadfast in my commitment to peace.

As I walked, they began throwing rocks that landed inches away from me. Again, I had a choice: to defend myself or to hold onto my message of kindness and continue. For three long miles, I held that peaceful space, and I made it home safely.

Do I know if my energy made a difference? I choose to believe it did. When we remain present in mind, body, emotions, and spirit with compassionate presence, we stand in our personal peace power.

I'm not suggesting that someone should never defend themselves in the face of abuse, but there are countless moments during nonviolent conflicts where practicing peaceful presence can diffuse angry energy. Compassionate communication starts with the choice to remain calmly present. When one person makes that choice, it becomes harder for the conversation to escalate. There can't be a power struggle when one person stands in peaceful power and releases the need to be right. I often illustrate this visually for my clients by asking them to grab one end of a pencil and pull; when I let go, the tension between us dissolves.

As painful as my memory of bullying is, it became an opportunity to practice peace gifts that continue to shape my life. As a psychotherapist, coach, and in my daily relationships, compassionate, calm presence is a fundamental strength. It allows me to connect with others and foster peaceful exchanges that enhance both my life and the lives of those I support.

From an early age, my life experiences led me to wonder how things could be more peaceful and how we could cultivate a more peaceful presence with ourselves, those around us, and the larger world.

Stories from the Heart

Next, please meet Christopher Radko and Santosh Govindaraju, among our twenty contributors to the book who share their powerful stories with us. We have selected stories throughout this book that provide you with the opportunity to heal by bearing witness to the lives of others while reflecting upon your own experience as you complete the exercises and writing prompts. The stories and contributors were carefully selected to honor this process.

Christopher Radko—My Peace I Give You

I'll never forget the day I was visited by an angel.

I was only six years old, walking home from school. Steel-gray clouds parted after heavy rain, and the sun's silvery sun rays blessed the land. A sidewalk puddle shimmered with prismatic colors. I stopped to admire the delicate light dancing on the water, wishing I could dive into its rainbow world. Suddenly, something strange happened. The sounds of street life faded around me; traffic and pedestrians vanished from view. A beam of sunlight touched my cheek, and my ears tingled. Then, a soothing deep baritone voice enveloped me and began to speak.

"Christopher," it started, sounding like Charlton Heston's Moses in *The Ten Commandments*, "remember who you are. Others may not see or understand you yet. Keep your own counsel. You have worth. In time, you will come into your own—more than you can ever imagine. For now, have patience! You have value. Remember."

What could I do with this? I was in awe, but I knew sharing it would make me seem crazy, so I hid the experience deep in my heart to guide me through future tough times. The event taught me two lessons: I can thrive, not just survive, and I'm not alone; the Universe, God, or a loving guardian angel walks with me.

Due to my parents' financial struggles, I lived in a foster home. Often, I was lonely. The local kids viewed me as just another transient child from the system. However, I found companionship and a family of sorts in TV characters like Elroy, Scooby-Doo, the Thunderbirds, and Captain Troy Tempest. I also spent hours playing under century-old oak trees, where nature felt like home. Even before I could read, I felt the spirit of St. Francis and Walt Whitman. Though life was isolating, I sensed a bigger world out there and stuck with it.

Eventually, my parents saved enough money to bring me home from foster care, but their tumultuous marriage disrupted the calm I had known. I felt a chilling distance from my father and was thrust into the pain of domestic violence and abuse. This situation could have crushed me, but I already felt like I didn't truly belong to this family. My earlier years of solitude had fostered a sense of resilience and independence. I learned to avoid most of my father's anger and misplaced rage. My mother was not so lucky.

It would take years for me to understand that my dad's explosive rage stemmed from his own traumatic beginnings. He was rejected by his father at birth and suffered abuse as a slave laborer under the Nazis during World War II. He never emotionally recovered from these experiences, and he lacked the self-awareness to seek the healing he so desperately needed.

Each year, one bright moment broke the tension: Christmas! During this season, my parents seemed to get along better. Instead of wandering the siren-filled city streets, which somehow felt safer after school, I'd want to come home. After completing my homework by the soft light of the Christmas tree, I'd slide under its lowest branches and gaze up at the twinkling lights and glistening ornaments. I'd spy a sparkling space Santa on a rocket, or a glass snowman on a sleek sliver of a moon. Bing Crosby's soothing voice filled the air as the jewel-toned tree lights cast rainbow patterns on the wall. Inhaling the fresh scent of the pine tree, I was transported to another world, one free of strife and filled with peace. How I longed to stay there!

Sadly, Christmas always seemed too brief, and soon after, life's challenges would return like a bad rash.

As I grew older, our Christmas trees grew taller, always needing to be taller than me. By my early twenties, after my parents' divorce, I was responsible for bringing home the tree. One year, I picked a hefty twelve-footer with a shiny red and green aluminum stand that promised to support it. Unfortunately, it didn't.

The morning after we finished decorating the tree, one of the flimsy metal legs gave way, causing it to crash onto the wooden floor. Hundreds of cherished family heirlooms shattered, creating a sound that brought my grandmother running from the kitchen. She surveyed the shards of glass beneath the heavy pine branches and, shaking her head, dourly proclaimed, "Christopher, you've ruined Christmas forever!"

And she meant it. Each ornament held a cherished Christmas memory. Unfortunately, now those memories seemed lost. A visit to New York City department stores revealed only mass-produced plastic and Styrofoam decorations made in Hong Kong.

The following spring, while visiting a cousin in Poland, she mentioned, "I got a letter from your grandmother about your Christmas tree crash. We still have glass ornaments, and I can introduce you to a glassblower." Excited to make amends with my grandmother, I produced sketches of her favorite ornaments, and the artisan crafted them for me!

I brought home these glass wonders and shared them with my coworkers, who excitedly reminisced about similar ones from their childhood. In need of extra money, I started selling ornaments during my lunch hour. To my surprise, I made nearly $25,000 in the first year and over $100,000 in the second year. And so, I discovered my purpose. I reintroduced the world to something I had once lost—beautiful, hand-painted memory-makers created from glitter and glass. These art pieces connected us to our loved ones and Christmases both past and future. I was helping myself and others also. This would become my way of making a meaningful difference.

Everything went well for nearly twenty years. I was a Christmas phoenix rising from shattered glass and glitter, growing my company to 130 employees, collaborating with over 3,000 European glassblowers, and enjoying sales exceeding $60 million. However, as work consumed my life, I had to hire a CEO, unaware that apparently my CFO aspired to that position. The CFO's failure to meet loan regulations led the bank to call my company's loan, and I didn't have the cash to meet their demands. My magical world came crashing down again, and in more ways than one.

On September 11, 2001, at 9 am, while I was in my showroom near the Twin Towers, two bank representatives informed me that they were taking over my company. As a native New Yorker, I felt doubly under siege. My beloved city was under attack by terrorists, and my beloved company was being taken over by ruthless bankers.

For several years, I struggled to rebuild my life, but it became overwhelming. I developed stress-related vision issues, and my doctor warned me that I needed to find balance or risk permanent blindness. For the sake of my health, I sold my company to a local investment group. What a mistake that turned out to be! "It's nothing personal," I was told, "it's just business." Disagreements quickly arose, which led to my being fired. This led to a costly and horrific four-year lawsuit that resulted in a ten-year noncompete clause. For a second time, I lost nearly everything I had.

If I was no longer "Mr. Christmas," then who was I?

Though I could have never guessed it, those ten years turned out to be a blessing in disguise. I returned to my roots, embracing the outdoors and the rhythms and beauty of nature, the ultimate teacher. I embarked on a Franciscan pilgrimage to Italy, guided by St. Francis to hidden gems that the guidebooks overlooked. I became an organic lavender farmer and launched a spa collection. I also reunited with old friends whom I had neglected while climbing the career ladder. Ultimately, I grew emotionally stronger and developed a deeper spiritual connection. From lemons, I made lemonade!

My early resilience continued to guide me through numerous challenges. I was thrilled to launch a new brand, now called the Ornament King. But my former company sued me again! Despite feeling battered and abused, I chose to move forward and reclaim my peace. Since then, I've let go of excessive worry about the future, realizing it solves nothing and only holds us back. This is act 3 of my life, and there's no telling what wonders are yet to come. Journeys don't always start with a clear destination, and life's full of uncertainties. So, I'm committed to living more fully in the present, as that's all we truly have.

After nearly sixty-five years of life, I'm confronting my mortality, seeing how quickly time passes. I think we're all passersby—sailors and comrades through the Universe, pausing for a moment on spaceship Earth. I hope to enjoy at least twenty-five more good years, but I understand there are no guarantees. That's why I make an effort to make each day count.

Life has certainly been a roller coaster for me, filled with ups and downs, twists and turns. Along this wild journey, I've stumbled upon some valuable life principles that I believe could make your path a bit smoother. Let's explore them together!

1. I stay actively involved with a community of friends. I am eternally grateful for their support, as they lift me up when I'm down, help me find my center, and warm my heart. Our friendships are reciprocal, and my friends don't care about my fame or wealth, they care about me. We are each a thread, more resilient than we often admit, supporting and strengthening the world's fabric.

2. I stay involved with creative activities, like ceramics, writing, photography, baking, and gardening. I also enjoy calisthenics and taking long walks with my dog, Ariel. I believe creativity is inherent in everyone; all our daily actions—from waking up to how we interact with others to activating our intentions—are each forms of creation. And you don't have to be Picasso to express it!

3. I look at strangers as potential friends I haven't yet met. While learning to distinguish love from attachment, I keep an open heart. Being loving and kind are gifts I can give for free. After all, life's a work of heart.

4. I avoid toxic, fearmongering headlines that can paralyze us. Instead, I focus on my own backyard, where I can take action and make a difference to others—being a candle in the darkness. My actions and responses are my only true belongings.

5. I have a purpose; we all do. Our purpose is centered around what we love doing and how we use this passion to serve others. While money, fame, and possessions can be enticing, let's remember the words attributed to Mary, the mother of Jesus: "All we take with us is all we have given and all we have loved." I view creation, people, and nature as interconnected and as part of a greater whole. Einstein spoke of this interconnectedness years ago, and I believe in his wisdom.

6. I cultivate my direct connection with my copilot, God, Source, Jesus (insert your name for a higher power here), and my long lineage of Polish, French, and Scottish ancestors. I know I am never alone. None of us are. Don't let your egos fool you into thinking otherwise.

Last and most importantly, I choose to forgive. Each of us, including those we may consider our "enemies," must answer to an inner conscience. The person I see as my captor also holds the key to my freedom. It's reciprocal; I forgive to be forgiven and reclaim my freedom. Hatred and resentment act like chains that bind us to those we struggle against. We can't dwell in the light while keeping others in darkness, nor even ignoring our own inner shadows. It's a choice: personal imprisonment or liberation. Would you rather be bitter or better? Forgiveness has been a difficult lesson for me, but the reward is freedom, and the ultimate prize is the ability to truly shine as a light in the world.

These are my sources of inner peace, and now, this peace I give to you.

Santosh Govindaraju—Just Do as You're Told

Om Shanthi, Shanthi, Shanthi. A consistent ending to nearly every prayer in Eastern religions is the seeker hailing peace. From a young age, I was obligated without a choice, without the ability to ask questions, and to do just what I was told in the recitation of ancient mantras and the practice of various rituals. The mantras were all about seeking peace, but I never saw that peace around me. I saw fear and compromise and asking questions was synonymous with defiance. "Just do as you're told."

I wrote in my diary that I was surrounded by a world of hypocrites. Do as I say, not as I do. My family and the community around me claimed we were peaceful people, but it confused me because all I could observe in action was fear. My intuition had been telling me that these people did not understand the meaning of peace. I often recited those words in a state with eyes closed, and my instincts told me that that these words were not meant for the external world, but an individual's inner world. However, everyone around me was focused on the external world and managing the appearance of peace, while as an insider who understood the nuances of culture, I could observe that nothing akin to peace was on the inside of the people around me.

Instead of following the blind path without question, somehow I developed a deep trust in my inner instincts. My instincts understood the principles and constantly found conflict with the actions of the community around me. My journey to peace, a state of mind rather than what the senses perceive to be as harmony in the external world, has been a journey in inner exploration.

I love studying history, not just American or Western European history, but the history of world civilizations. While researching various wars, I was able to discern that the same person who is a terrorist to one person is a freedom fighter to another. This dichotomy initiated a journey into exploring the concept that my five basic senses can never understand what peace is. From one point of view, a revolutionary is an individual who is disturbing peace, and from another point of view, that individual is seen as someone fighting for peace through a different form of justice. For example, were the revolutionaries who gained America's independence from the English monarchy terrorists who disturbed the peace, or were they heroic freedom fighters trying to establish peaceful equality for all, as the inhabitants of a new land?

I quickly understood that the mind determines which narrative you want to believe and what can be understood as peace. This sparked a spiritual journey toward finding eternal peace. Studying the principles of what I later learned are known as the *shat sampat* or the six virtues, and practicing them vigorously, I arrived at the mental state known as *vairagya*. This included (1) practicing a state of single-pointed focus in all of my actions; (2) conscious awareness of every thought in my mind, catching each one, analyzing it, and then deciding whether the thought was allowed to continue or should be extinguished; and (3) developing strong faith that whatever outcome may arise, it was fated for some meaning that I would eventually learn. As the state of *vairagya* opened up, my consciousness shifted from what my five senses perceived to what I perceived from my inner blissful spirit.

This shift empowered me with a constant state of peace, and the only action that my consciousness focused on was my own. Dispassion began to emerge toward the actions of others, and I learned that things and activities outside of my control need not distract me. Instead, I focused day and night on purifying my heart, and making sure every action that I took was conscious and purposeful.

While dispassion rose, I also found that my compassion grew as well. Purification of my heart allowed it to expand. With this expanded heart, I set off to serve others. I quit my job on Wall Street and began serving youth in Queens, New York. I worked side by side with young children to create a pathway toward their dreams. In those efforts, I learned the power of presence. The children could feel the joy, and they could understand that, even in the midst of hardship, they could find joy in themselves.

I had many debates with friends and colleagues after these experiences. The first was questioning the purpose of the existence of conflict. Conflict is not necessarily the absence of peace. *Pax Romana* was not necessarily a peaceful state. I have always tried to reframe concepts and look at the same situation from a different perspective. In these exercises, I found that the real test of peace is whether one can be in a full state of peace horrific experiences of civilians in Russia's war against Ukraine, I decided to depart the quietude of Florida life to serve in humanitarian efforts in Ukraine.

In the six months I spent in Ukraine, I experienced the most beautiful aspects of human nature. I worked alongside worldwide teammates banding together for the sole purpose of bringing humanity to internally displaced Ukrainians. We aimed to provide dignity to ordinary citizens who had been forced out of their homes and were now living in shelters. We built showers, bathrooms, and kitchens to give them mental comfort. We engaged in art, music, and dance and found ourselves reveling in our shared love. I felt connected. I laughed, and I cried. Together we found joy with our new Ukrainian friends, a unique experience that can only be found in the midst of tragedy—the joy from seeing that people from other countries could show their fellow human beings that they care. Through the power of compassion, I found peace even in the middle of war. It was a shared state of peace, which gave some sense of comfort to people who had lost so much.

Each of my actions have built on past actions and thus led to a constant flow of ever-increasing effort and impact. Things have happened along the way that have stumped me. I couldn't always understand why strange events occurred that required extra effort on my part. Eventually, with time, sometimes after many years, I was able to see how all the dots connected and that the extra effort placed in my path had a purpose. As I became more and more aware that the hurdles in my path were just signs directing me, I found solace and embraced the connectedness.

A wise mentor told me something disturbing once: "Remember that peace is just the period between two wars." That statement threatened what I thought I knew about peace. However, I soon realized that such wisdom could be construed as a lesson in the ephemeral nature of joy, which is often confused as peace.

To combat an addiction to joy or blindness that could have led me to believe that it was equivalent to peace, I found even deeper peace in the practice of gratitude. Deeply contemplating and expressing gratitude took me to a more profound state of peace. It increased my awareness of the elated feeling that I am not alone. Connected to this universe of kindred spirits, peace felt real, permanent, and thus highly empowering.

Despite this feeling of the permanence of peace, I remained wary of my mentor's earlier words. The monster of the mind can easily emerge and remove that peace, so I developed daily practices to maintain it. The most important activity was a daily purification of heart. In this practice, I vigorously identify all the thoughts that may be seeking to tarnish my pure-hearted nature. The work in the real war is to pluck out the thoughts and burn them with the fire of a truth rooted in faith. This inner peace that I have found could possibly come during a period between two wars within my mind. Daily practice, constant awareness of thoughts, and lighting a fire every time a thought could poison the peace are required to maintain the permanence of this peace.

During the journey of this daily practice, I have found that laughter is a great medicine. When thoughts appear that may possibly jeopardize the peace, genuine and bona fide laughter help me realize that these are tests to my conscious awareness of existing in a true state of peace. The laughter shakes my spirit and vaporizes the thoughts, and fire is no longer necessary to burn the thoughts that have diminished.

My parents had two sons and named them Prashant and Santosh. Prashant means peace (*shanthi* in the opening sentence), and *santosh* in Sanskrit means contentment (originally, I was told it meant happiness). In my adolescent years, I fantasized that my parents were real hippies in the spirit of peace, love, and happiness. Over time, I learned that my parents were spiritual capitalists.

In some of my spiritual reading, I learned that the wealthiest person is the one who has *santosh*. Finding the path to inner peace and then embracing unconditional love in all situations is the path to the eternal and ultimate wealth of contentment. Peace is eternal, peace is divine, and inner peace is the only real peace and the path to immense wealth.

We feel blessed to bring you this book and our stories. In the chapters ahead, more stories appear just like these from people all over the world.

So, are you ready for your own peace assessment? On these next pages, you'll find heart-based exercises titled "Points to Ponder." Two exercises, which create reflection points, are at the end of each chapter, and all exercises compound and continue to the end of the book, playing off one another as we work through peace. In these first exercises, you'll read a relaxation statement and then take a peace assessment. In the second exercise, we collaborate with you to explore the language you use with yourself and give you some tools to help you be confident, peaceful, and kind in your approach with yourself.

This personalized Peace Action Plan transforms the insights from *The Peace Guidebook* into real, daily practices. By taking small, intentional steps, you become an active participant in hope, healing, and harmony— both for yourself and the world.

POINTS TO PONDER

Think. Write. Talk. Action. *(Because practice makes us do our best.)*

EXERCISE 1: Let's Begin! *The Peace Guidebook* Assessment

Let's take an honest assessment of what is going on in your life in multiple areas. In the areas below, please give yourself a score of 1 to 10 (with 1 being the lowest rating and 10 being the highest). For each area, please place notes or comments to briefly explain your score.

Here's an example:

Relationships

Score: 5

Reason: There are conflicts that go unresolved, leading to strained relationships that affect my ability to have peaceful conversations.

Before you begin, take a moment to get centered in your heart. This is an exercise of love. Love yourself and give an honest evaluation of where you are in your life now. You may want to take a moment to read this relaxation statement once or twice. Focus your energy on your heart center.

RELAXATION TUNE-IN

Begin by taking several deep breaths. As you take a deep breath in and then out, imagine beautiful white light coming into your energy field from the top of your head down to your toes. Move your attention into your heart. Feel love and peace within your body begin to vibrate through your entire being. Taking another deep breath in and out, allow the energy of gratitude to emanate throughout your body. Feel gratitude for everything in your life that has brought you to where you are today. Know that today you have the power of infinite possibilities for peace within you. Take a deep breath. Stay present in your heart center.

READ THIS RELAXATION STATEMENT TO YOURSELF OR ALOUD:

I now realize that I am very relaxed. In fact, the more I stop and take deep breaths, the more relaxed I feel. I am now aware that I am creating intentional peace every day in every way. Each and every time I stop and take deep breaths, I am already going beyond my normal experience, which causes me to recognize my infinite possibilities for peace. That's right! I now recognize that I am grateful for everything that has occurred in my life, which feels increasingly amazing. I now notice that my confidence has expanded exponentially. I am now ready to begin an honest assessment of my peacefulness today.

You are ready to begin.

The Peace Guidebook Assessment

A REFLECTION THROUGH THE TEN PRINCIPLES OF PEACE

Use this assessment as a compass to explore how peace flows through each principle of your life.

For each question, rate yourself from 1 to 10 and note the reason for your score.

(1 = rarely true for me | 10 = consistently true for me)

PRESENCE—BEING PEACEFUL

1. Mindful Awareness:

   Do I stay grounded in the present moment instead of getting lost in past regrets or future worries?

   Score: _____   Reason: _____

2. Peaceful Presence:

   When I walk into a room, do I bring calm energy that others can feel?

   Score: _____   Reason: _____

POTENTIAL—BELIEVING IN PEACE

3. Expanding Possibility:

   Do I believe peace can exist even in the midst of difficulty or conflict?

   Score: _____   Reason: _____

4. Empowered Response:

   When faced with challenges, do I choose growth and compassion instead of fear or blame?

   Score: _____   Reason: _____

PATIENCE—TRUSTING THE PACE OF PEACE

5. Grace in Waiting:

   Do I give life, others, and myself the time and space needed for growth and healing?

   Score: _____   Reason: _____

6. Calm in Chaos:

   When things don't go my way, can I pause, breathe, and respond instead of react?

   Score: _____   Reason: _____

PRACTICE—PRACTICING PEACE

7. Consistent Practice:

   Do I intentionally use peace tools—like gratitude, forgiveness, or compassion —each day?

   Score: _____   Reason: _____

8. Conscious Communication:

   Do I take responsibility for my words and tone, speaking from clarity rather than emotion?

   Score: _____   Reason: _____

PASSION—FUELING PEACEFUL ACTION

9. Purposeful Passion:

   Do I pursue what lights me up without losing sight of inner peace?

   Score: _____   Reason: _____

10. Aligned Energy:

    Is my work or service aligned with my soul's truth and done in a peaceful, sustainable way?

    Score: _____   Reason: _____

PURPOSE—EMBODYING PEACE

11. Meaningful Direction:

    Do I know what gives my life meaning, and am I living in alignment with it?

    Score: _____   Reason: _____

12. Service Through Purpose:

    Do I use my gifts to make a positive difference in the lives of others?

    _____

POSITIVITY—EXUDING PEACE

13. Mindset of Hope:

Do I focus on what's good and possible, even when life feels hard?

Score: _____   Reason: _____

14. Gratitude as Guidance:

Do I intentionally practice gratitude to shift perspective and nurture joy?

Score: _____   Reason: _____

PERSEVERANCE—PERSISTING FOR PEACE

15. Strength Through Challenge:

Do I remain steady and hopeful during difficult times?

Score: _____   Reason: _____

16. Peaceful Persistence:

When obstacles arise, do I find calm, creative ways to continue rather than give up?

Score: _____   Reason: _____

PARTNERSHIP—UNITING FOR PEACE

17. Reciprocal Relationships:

Do I foster relationships built on mutual respect, trust, and shared values?

Score: _____   Reason: _____

18. Collaborative Spirit:

Do I seek to uplift others and create win–win outcomes instead of competing or controlling?

Score: _____   Reason: _____

PEACE—CLAIMING PEACE

19. Inner Stillness:

Do I take time to connect with my soul and anchor myself in stillness each day?

Score: _____   Reason: _____

20. Ripple Effect:

Do my choices, words, and presence contribute to greater harmony in the world?

Score: _____   Reason: _____

EXERCISE 2: A Guided Exercise for Hope, Healing, and Harmony

STEP 1: REFLECT ON YOUR PEACE ASSESSMENT

Revisit your answers from *The Peace Guidebook* Assessment and pause for self-reflection.

Identify three areas where you already feel aligned with peace.

1. _____

2. _____

3. _____

Identify three areas where you'd like to cultivate deeper peace.

4. _____

5. _____

6. _____

STEP 2: CHOOSE YOUR PERSONAL PEACE FOCUS

Select one area from your assessment that feels most important to nurture right now.

_____

_____

Write down why this area matters to you. *(Example: "I want to release resentment because it keeps me stuck in the past and prevents me from fully experiencing harmony.")*

_____

_____

STEP 3: CREATE PEACEFUL PRACTICE

Choose a small, intentional action that aligns with your focus. This action should be simple, meaningful, and consistent, and something you can practice daily.

For example, if you want to bring more peace to your thoughts, start each morning with a calming mantra from *The Peace Guidebook*. If you seek peace in relationships, commit to active listening and speaking with kindness. If you want to bring peace to the world, engage in one mindful act of service each week.

Each day, I will nurture peace by

_____

_____

_____

STEP 4: CHOOSE DAILY PEACE

Keep a peace journal or use a simple daily check-in system to stay mindful of your progress. Each day, answer these three guiding questions:

What brought me peace today? _____

_____

What challenged my peace today?_____

_____

What's one intentional action I will take tomorrow to nurture peace?

_____

_____

After one week, reflect on what's changed. How do you feel?

_____

_____

Congratulations! You completed Exercises 1 and 2. Let's continue our journey.

As you now understand the power of presence in preparing you to envision opportunities to learn more about yourself and others, let's move to the next principle of peace, which is Potential.

CHAPTER 2
POTENTIAL

In the second principle of peace, Potential, we find a positive opportunity tucked inside even the most challenging situations. Each moment carries within it the seed of a peaceful exchange. When we pause, reflect, respond, and pivot, even difficult conversations can transform into shared healing experiences. We are confident that within every encounter there is potential for compromise. Potential is the invisible thread woven through every interaction. It's what glimmers beneath tension, waiting for us to choose compassion over conflict, grace over grudge, and harmony instead of harm. Peace begins where and when we believe it is possible. When a person dares to imagine that even the smallest moment holds the power to transform everything, there is potential for peace. Every breath, every word, every silence holds the capacity for a peaceful exchange. When you pause, reflect, respond, and pivot, even the most challenging conversations can become shared moments of growth, understanding, and harmony.

As we were writing this, we discovered a mutual obstacle that impacts our ability to remain peaceful. It's relationships. It's people. It's what we call "people problems." We are both empaths and fans of Dr. Judith Orloff, who helped popularize the term *empath* through her books such as *The Empath's Survival Guide: Life Strategies for Sensitive People*. Orloff describes empaths as individuals with very high sensitivity to others' emotions and energies.

We walk through the world highly sensitive to what's going on around us, and we both are recovering Pollyannas. We just don't understand a taking-versus-giving perspective. You might say we sometimes find ourselves feeling like dolphins living in a shark tank.

Elizabeth here, speaking of dangerous waters: Recently, a family member sold her truck to a "shark" disguised as a "dolphin." The truck meant a lot to her, and the buyer promised to care for it as well as she had. The family member felt good hearing this, and, in good faith, she kindly discounted the truck by a few thousand dollars. To her shock and dismay, she discovered the buyer had sold the truck a few days later for a big profit. Moments like this leave many of us bewildered, asking, "How can someone do that?"

The lesson to be learned from this is that you rob yourself of peace when you look outside yourself. When you do so, it becomes easy to categorize people and explain how they are responsible for your behaviors and circumstances. Any peaceful endeavor begins with recognizing that we all have the capacity to be compassionate or hateful, and most of us live somewhere in between. When we attribute anything in our lives to someone else and label them and blame them—as a shark or a dolphin, for example—we ignore our inner peace. We can't be peaceful and hateful. The fact is that we're all a little bit of both. Sharks can bite, but dolphins can be mean too! The rule of peace is to focus on the *potential* for compassion.

Both of us live near and value the ocean, and we both grew up watching and learning from stories that depicted animal behavior stereotypically, which in turn influenced how we saw the world. We both watched the television show *Flipper* (live or in reruns). *Flipper* ran on NBC from 1964 to 1967 and was a classic American family adventure show. Often dubbed the "aquatic Lassie," it centered on a remarkably intelligent bottlenose dolphin named Flipper, who lived near the fictional Coral Key Park and Marine Preserve in South Florida.

Flipper served as both companion and protector to the Ricks family: widowed park ranger Porter Ricks and his two sons, Sandy, fifteen, and Bud, ten. The dolphin was raised by a family that represented peace and harmony and valued lessons about how to live and work together, and how to do so despite our differences. The show always had a happy ending, usually when Flipper saved the day and brought everyone together to celebrate the goodness in life. In simplistic terms, good always won and good people always came out on top.

Real life, however, is not always so cut-and-dried. Some days, the peaceful choice feels effortless, like catching the perfect wave. Other days, it's like you're swimming upstream with seaweed in your fins. But no matter which direction the current is running, the possibility for peace is still there.

Potential is the wave you ride through all your interactions and how you choose to maneuver through and around them. It is the sacred energy that asks us to choose compassion over conflict, connection over reaction, and grace over judgment. It may seem difficult to think peacefully about your current situation, especially when you are overwhelmed, hurt, or afraid. But peace is not passive. It is the potential realized through presence, intention, and conscious action.

Potential isn't about perfection. It's about *possibility*. It's not a destination but a direction. And every choice we make, no matter how small, moves us closer to shore.

Which brings us to one of our favorite peace points for staying out of the riptides of life.

PEACE POINT 8: Have Dolphin Energy in a Sharky World

We both love ocean creatures such as dolphins, seals, whales, and even sharks! We had no idea how influential their characteristics would be until we started having a conversation about finding a place where we fit.

Some days, being a peaceful person in our society feels like being a dolphin doing water ballet in a tank full of sharks. We feel that way with all the judging, labeling, and criticizing going on in the world. We want you to explore your inner world for a minute and think about the dolphinlike, whalelike, and sharklike like parts of yourself.

Dolphins feel to us like the optimists of the sea. They frolic, flip, and play catch with seaweed. They whistle joyfully and glide in pods, looking out for one another. They are the embodiment of joyful intelligence and emotional depth. Dolphins are in it for the team. They're here for the connection, the communication, the collective good. And truth be told, dolphins can be really destructive and mean. They can take on sharks when they need to, and guess what? So can you!

Then there are sharks.

Sharks do not frolic. Sharks do not play catch. Sharks bite. Sharks circle. They look for weakness and prey upon it. They don't do community, they do conquest—but not all sharks! Sharks have a docile side just like dolphins can be aggressive.

So, what happens when you look at the world through the lens of a dolphin, with your soft heart and hopeful spirit, and find yourself surrounded by the dorsal fins of people who see your kindness not as a strength but as bait?

You start to wonder, *Am I in the wrong ocean?*

The world sometimes feels like it rewards shark behavior—sharpness over softness, competition over collaboration, power over peace. You begin to question your dolphin ways. *Should I be tougher? Meaner? Louder? Should I sharpen my own teeth just to keep up?*

**No. The reality is that you're not a dolphin or a shark.
You're human. And that's the gift.**

When we find ourselves feeling this way, it's time to pause and reflect on how we might hold both energies within us. What are the behaviors that leave us feeling frightened, powerless, or reactive?

We can feel like we're trapped in a situation we can't escape, blaming the person who takes advantage of us—like diving into deep waters without scuba gear, fighting the current, and cursing our guide for letting us jump.

If you ever find yourself thinking, for example,

I lost my job because of . . .

I can't pay my bills because of . . .

I can't get ahead because of . . .

We want you to be clear that ending those sentences with blame toward another person—or, even worse, a group of people—is going to disturb your peace. It's a waste of your energy.

You see, dolphins aren't weak. They're incredibly powerful. They protect their pod. They're fast, agile, and wildly intuitive. They can navigate stormy seas with grace. And when needed, they'll ram a shark right in the gills and keep it moving. (Yes, that's a real thing.)

Let us share an example. One of our podcast listeners, a teacher named Olivia, told us she felt completely out of place in her school's staff meetings. They were tense, political, and ego-filled. She's a total dolphin—upbeat, heart forward, always bringing snacks and sunshine. She said, "It feels like everyone's swimming in circles with their teeth out. And I just want to talk about how we can help the kids."

We told her, "Don't stop being you."

At the next meeting, she spoke up, gently but clearly, and said, "I know we're all under pressure. But we're a team. What's one thing we can agree on right now that supports the students?" The energy shifted. She didn't bite back; she brought the pod together.

That's dolphin energy. That's Percolating Peace.

When we Percolate Peace, we don't abandon who we are. We become *more* of who we are, and we ripple that strength outward—even in the shark-infested waters.

The magic of the dolphin is that it knows how to swim smartly. It knows when to glide, when to dive deep, and when to leap joyfully above the surface—not to impress the sharks, but to feel the sun.

So, what's the Peace Point?

Stay dolphin by using your shark aspects for good.

Stay playful. Stay graceful. Stay kind.

But also, stay alert and don't allow someone or something else to take away your power to share your dolphin energy. Not everyone deserves access to your swim lane.

Being peaceful doesn't mean being passive. It means knowing who you are, protecting your energy, and still showing up in this world with joy, even when others are circling.

If you feel today like you've been bitten recently, remember this:

- You don't have to match the bite. Match the *brightness*.
- You don't have to grow teeth to survive. Grow *boundaries*.
- You don't have to outswim them. You just have to *out*-joy them.

And if you feel out of place sometimes, good! It means you're not becoming what you were never meant to be. You've been disrupted, and maybe that pause or delay is grace in disguise, steering you away from what wasn't aligned and toward what's truly meaningful to you. How many of us have experienced not receiving a promotion? Was your immediate response, "It's because of . . ."? Do you make excuses and point your energy inward on your "not enoughness" or outward on another's fault? In the past month, Dr. Katie has had several clients who have gone through this process and learned that once they get past the pain of experiencing the loss, there is opportunity in discovering their gifts, talents, and strengths and a different ocean where they fit better.

There's power in your peace when you choose to see yourself as you are: talented, useful, and worthy of your own place in the ocean. You discover, once again, that level of peace that comes with recognizing your potential.

PEACE POINT 9: Understand People Problems

Moving out of the ocean and onto shore, let's talk about one of the biggest disruptors to peace. **People.** Yes, *people problems*.

Not world events. Not climate disasters. Not your Internet going down during a Zoom call. Just . . . people. Ordinary, everyday people who cut you off in traffic, ghost your texts, talk too loudly on speakerphone in public, say the wrong thing at the wrong time, or in more consequential and complex situations, completely betray your trust.

If you've ever thought, *I'd be so much more peaceful if people would just stop being so . . . people-y,* you're not alone.

People are wonderfully complicated. We are full of beauty, brilliance, flaws, and fractures. And sometimes the biggest obstacle to inner peace isn't *what's* happening *to* us; it's *who's* happening *around* us.

Even when we start our day with the best intentions—maybe we meditated and drank our green juice—we're often thrown off course by someone else's mood, actions, or energy. One passive-aggressive comment, one sideways look, one unexpected email—and *boom.* The peace we worked so hard to cultivate disappears in a puff of human behavior.

It happens in families. In friendships. In workplaces. In traffic. And let's be honest—even in line at Target.

That's why we coined the term *people problems.* Directing fault is not as important as taking responsibility to choose a peaceful response. See the potential in every interaction. Remove the judgment of right or wrong. Understand the question "Would you rather be right or happy?" You're reacting to disruptive energy. When two people are out of sorts, their energy becomes deeply out of balance, and now it is passing back and forth.

What do we do about it?

We get clear on one thing: Peace is not dependent on other people's behavior.

Yes, people may frustrate you and break your heart. But your peace—your deep, inner calm—belongs to you.

You don't have to make everyone happy. You don't have to fix people. You don't have to carry what isn't yours. And you certainly don't have to allow *their* issues to hijack *your* clarity.

Here's the advanced peace move: *Learn how to protect your peace while still loving people who upset you.*

Seeing potential requires setting boundaries, communicating clearly, and learning when to stay and when to walk away. That means accepting that some people won't change, and you don't have to wait for them to do so in order to feel better.

In fact, some people are simply in your life to teach you how not to be. And even that is a sacred gift.

- You are allowed to be the calm in the room.
- You are allowed to leave the room.
- You are always allowed to protect your peace.

The next time people problems pop up as they inevitably will, take a breath. Choose your response. And remember: You are responsible for your peace, not their behavior.

People are going to be people. But you? You're going to radiate peace.

Keep choosing peace. Over and over again. Because there is always potential for peace.

In every conversation and decision, and even in silence, you're always contributing to harmony or to discord. There's no neutral energy. It's time to get intentional about the energy you bring into every room, every exchange, every breath. Even when you're alone, your thoughts and self-talk are shaping your peace.

Real life doesn't always make space for what can feel like idealism. Sometimes peace feels a lot more like survival than serenity. What do you do when peace sounds like a fantasy and your real life feels like a disaster?

That's where the real work begins. That's where we call it like it is.

PEACE POINT 10: Swim Together

When you do jump back into the ocean from shore, it's important to remember that the potential for peace isn't a solo pursuit. Even dolphins are in pods.

While individual inner peace is vital, peace itself is not an individual game. It's collective. When you Percolate Peace, it doesn't stop at "I" or "me." It expands to "us" and "we." It becomes a ripple. One person's presence influences another's. It's the conscious energy that lifts a conversation, softens a room, and shifts the direction of a community.

True peace doesn't serve a self-centered agenda. It isn't about individuals chasing their own version of peace in isolation. Peace is expansive. It's a shared language, a shared breath, a shared choice. The potential for peace lies in our willingness to look beyond our own story and into the shared experience of humanity. It's beautiful in theory—until you have to share that humanity with, well, with other humans.

Choose your pod intentionally. Cultivate dolphin energy. Be someone others can move alongside with trust, ease, and joy. And when the sharks circle? Smile, glide deeper, and protect your peace with grace. Because peace doesn't mean avoiding the sharks. It means knowing how to swim smarter, stronger, and never alone.

Here's your buffer kit:

- A practice of daily grounding—whether it's a quiet moment, prayer, journaling, or just staring at the sky for sixty seconds
- Breathwork—because your breath is the most underused super-power you have
- Strong boundaries—say no without guilt and yes with a full heart.
- A gratitude lens—you don't ignore the mess, but you do keep your eyes on the meaning

Here's a bold reframe: *What if every disruption is a teacher? Every time you're thrown off, it's a call to go deeper into your self-awareness.* Instead of asking, "Why is this happening to me?" try, "What is this waking up in me?" And don't forget humor. When all else fails, laugh. At yourself, with yourself. Laughter is an underrated reset button.

Managing disruptions to your peace isn't about finding Zen 24/7. It's about remembering who you are in the middle of the mess. It's about reaching for your tools instead of your temper. It's about becoming the person who can sit with the storm without letting it become you.

Next time you find yourself unraveling at the seams over a burned dinner, an underhanded comment, or your own inner critic throwing a tantrum, remember this: You're allowed to *feel* it, but you don't have to *feed* it. Make your peace nonnegotiable—not because life will suddenly stop being hard, but because you've decided to stop letting everything shake you. Peace is a practiced posture. Stand in it. Grow into it. Return to it. Again and again. Because disruption is inevitable. So is your return to center.

PEACE POINT 11: Create a No-Fluff Zone

Whether you're in the ocean, at the shore, or on your own island, remember to be gentle with yourself, because living a peaceful life is sometimes hard. In our *Real Life* podcast, Dr. Katie coined the term "no-fluff zone," and it has resonated with our viewers. Real-life experiences can be unbearable. Discovering the potential for peace can seem unattainable. Real life is messy.

That's why we created the no-fluff zone. It's part of how we show up for our podcast audience, and it's how we wrote this book—with heart, honesty, and zero sugarcoating.

What does that actually mean?

It means that when things get hard, and they will, you don't need platitudes. You don't need a cliché. You need tools. You need truth. You need someone to sit beside you and say, "Yep, this is hard. But you're still capable. You're still powerful. And peace is still possible—even here."

It also means holding yourself accountable, especially when you start to slide into the land of "us versus them." It's easier to judge than to understand, and to assume rather than to ask. But the real peace practice? It starts when we call ourselves back to integrity. Back to awareness. Back to effort.

You might not be able to keep the peace in every moment. But you can work to keep your self-respect intact.

The self-help world is full of shiny promises and quick fixes, but nothing works all the time. There are no magic words, no flawless formulas. Peace is a living, breathing process. And it takes work. Daily. Hourly. Sometimes, minute by minute. No one can do that work for you. But you're never alone in doing it.

PEACE POINT 12: Recognize Potential Peace in Stressful Situations

When you imagine peace, don't envision a perfect life. See yourself showing up to your real life with your whole heart. Watch how life can change when you ask better questions. Imagine how your world might shift if you believed that every day held the potential for something beautiful, even if it's just the courage to keep trying.

We've identified what we call the "15 Major Disruptors to Inner Peace." These are the things that keep people up at night. They are the worries that take over the mind, hijack the nervous system, and make peace feel impossible. But naming them gives us power. Understanding them gives us tools. Working with them gives us a chance to create peace from the inside out.

We created this list of disruptors from our own experiences related to stress. Our definition of *stress* is any issue, event, or situation that disrupts our peace. Here we combine our own experiences as a master life coach and a psychotherapist along with psychological studies to offer you a road map, including a list of potential barriers to maintaining peace. Think of these as your daily reminders of obstacles to peace.

1: Financial Fear

Money stress is one of the most common and isolating peace disruptors. Whether it's worrying about not having enough, losing what you've worked hard to build, or just trying to get through another month, financial fear hijacks your calm. When basic needs feel uncertain, even the joy in your life can feel inaccessible. Peace begins when you acknowledge your financial fear without shame and take even the smallest stabilizing actions that help restore a sense of control.

Peace Tip: When financial stress takes over, it shrinks your perspective and heightens survival mode. The antidote isn't a magic solution; it's one grounded step. Write down what you *can* control today. Review one account. Cancel one unnecessary subscription. Make one empowering call. Small, stabilizing actions anchor your nervous system and remind you that peace starts with a plan, not perfection.

2: Health Anxiety

Your body is the vessel of your peace. When health feels fragile—whether it's your own diagnosis, a chronic condition, the care of a loved one, or the weight of a past illness—it disrupts everything. Peace can begin with a return to the present moment, and by honoring what your body is still capable of right now. Even in limitation, there is life.

Peace Tip: Fear around health—your own or that of someone you love—can make you feel powerless. But you're still here. Your breath still works. Your presence still matters. Try this: Place your hand on your heart and breathe deeply for sixty seconds. Ask yourself, *What can I do to support my body right now?* Then listen. Honor your energy. Peace returns in the present, not in the "what if?"

3: Relationship Strain

We are hardwired for connection. When relationships strain—a business partnership, a friendship, family issues, or a work dynamic—the emotional fallout can be enormous. Silence, resentment, blame, or just growing distance all fracture peace. Rebuilding begins with replacing accusation and judgment with love and boundaries. Healthy love honors both closeness and space.

Peace Tip: When a relationship feels tense, your instinct may be to fix it or flee. But peace lives in the pause. Next time you feel triggered, stop. Breathe. Ask, *Is this about now, or about something deeper?* Pausing allows you to ask important questions and can soften defensiveness. If it's safe, name your feeling. If not, journal it out. Remember, peace doesn't mean perfection; peace means preserving connection where possible and choosing healthy boundaries when needed.

4: Fear of the Unknown

From global headlines to personal transitions, uncertainty has a way of creeping into our lives. It loops in our minds, replaying worst-case scenarios. Peace doesn't come from controlling what's ahead. It comes from knowing that you can meet whatever comes next with strength, softness, and grace. Soothe your nervous system with presence, not prediction.

Peace Tip: Fear loves a blank slate. The unknown becomes a canvas for every worst-case scenario. Try this reframe: Say your concern out loud. Then follow it with, *And even if that happens, here's what I'll do. . . .* Naming your fear reduces its power. Peace lives in preparation, not prediction.

5: Identity Overload

Who are you supposed to be today? Parent, partner, professional, friend, caregiver, provider, all at once? When we shift roles constantly—or shape ourselves to meet everyone else's expectations—we lose sight of our core self. Peace begins when you give yourself permission to stop performing and start simply being. You don't have to be everything to everyone. You only have to be you.

Peace Tip: If you're constantly switching to meet expectations, no wonder you feel exhausted. You don't have to be everyone's everything. Set a timer for ten minutes. Sit with no role to play. Just be you. Write down three things you love about your unfiltered self. Peace grows when we stop performing and start remembering who we truly are.

6: Grief in the Quiet Hours

Grief doesn't follow a clock. It arrives in the stillness—perhaps after midnight, in the middle of the night, in the pause between thoughts, in the middle of a memory. Whether you've lost someone or something precious, grief often feels like it pulls the peace right out of you. But grief is not the enemy of peace. It is part of love. Peace begins when we stop trying to outrun grief and instead invite it to sit beside us, gently, as proof that something or someone once mattered deeply. Dr. Katie writes in her book *Uplifting* that grief is a holistic process that arises from any profound change—not just death—and unfolds in its own time. When met with self-compassion, it becomes a teacher, revealing what we value and guiding us through the tender space between what was and what will be.

Peace Tip: Grief wants to be witnessed, not fixed. If you're grieving, let that be part of your peace practice. Light a candle. Write a letter. Say their name. Tell the truth: *I miss you.* When we stop trying to outrun grief and invite it in as sacred, it stops screaming and starts whispering, *Love still lives here.*

7: Loneliness and Disconnection

Loneliness is one of the quietest disruptors to peace—and one of the most common. It's not always about being physically alone. You can be surrounded by people and still feel invisible. Disconnection from others (or even from your own purpose) creates a subtle, aching kind of unrest.

Peace Tip: Loneliness doesn't always need to be "cured"—sometimes it needs to be understood. Try this: Name your loneliness. Is it social? Spiritual? Emotional? Then take one gentle step. Text a friend. Join a group. Or reconnect with yourself. Sometimes the first bridge to peace is the one you build back to your own heart.

8: Comparison Culture

Social media. Life updates. Highlight reels. Everywhere we look, we're invited to compare our behind-the-scenes mess with someone else's polished version of success. Comparison is a thief and it rarely steals just joy. It also robs us of our peace, our confidence, and our presence.

Peace Tip: The next time you catch yourself spiraling into "not enough," pause. Replace the thought *Why don't I have that?* with *What do I already love about my life right now?* Gratitude and comparison can't coexist. For example, the second you start comparing yourself to other people, you block your own gratitude. Make peace by standing in your own lane and decorating it beautifully.

9: Burnout and Overwhelm

We live in a productivity-obsessed culture. Rest is seen as lazy. Hustle is glamorized. But when we chronically override our body's need for stillness, we deplete the very reservoir where peace resides. Burnout doesn't just exhaust you. It erodes your clarity, your presence, and your ability to enjoy what you've worked so hard to build.

Peace Tip: You don't have to earn rest. Rest is productive. Start small.

Cancel one nonessential thing. Close your laptop five minutes earlier. Breathe without multitasking. Refill before you deplete. You are not a machine. You are a soul in a body. Peace needs fuel. Let that be your new priority.

10: Self-Criticism and Inner Judgment

Your inner dialogue creates your outer world. If your self-talk is laced with guilt, shame, perfectionism, or pressure, no wonder peace feels distant for you. The harshest voices in your head often aren't even yours; they're echoes of expectations, past wounds, or fear trying to protect you.

Peace Tip: Replace critique with curiosity. When you catch a self-judgmental thought, gently ask, *Would I speak this way to someone I love?* If not, revise it. Begin treating yourself like someone worthy of peace, because you are. Self-compassion is a peace practice.

11: Guilt and Regret

The past has a way of following us: guilt for something said or unsaid, regret over a choice made—or not made. While the past can teach us, it can also trap us in a loop of self-blame that quietly drains peace from the present.

Peace Tip: You're allowed to grow beyond your past. Guilt is only helpful when it teaches. After that, it becomes emotional clutter. Ask yourself, *What lesson can I take forward?* Then let yourself move on. Growth is not betrayal. It's proof you've evolved.

12: Decision Fatigue

We make thousands of choices every day—from what to eat to how to respond to a text to whether to say what we're really feeling. Constant decision-making exhausts the brain and creates a low-grade hum of unrest that builds into mental burnout.

Peace Tip: Simplify your choices. Prioritize your decision-making to daily living necessities first: meals, scheduling, and responsibilities. Then give your mind room to breathe. Save the nonessential choices for when you are rejuvenated. Peace is sometimes found in fewer choices, not more. Create margin in your day and consider that space sacred.

13: Lack of Purpose

When we're unsure of our why, everything feels heavier. Tasks feel empty. Goals feel blurry. Peace can't land where meaning feels absent. This doesn't mean you need a grand mission—it means your life needs to feel like it matters.

Peace Tip: Purpose can be quiet. It might be raising kind children, being present with aging parents, or growing into your truest self. Write down one way you make the world softer just by being you. Then do it on purpose. Peace follows presence with purpose.

14: Digital Overload and Political Noise

Ping. Scroll. Outrage. Repeat.

We live in a world where notifications never stop, opinions come in hot, and politics floods every feed. One minute you're checking the weather; the next you're spiraling in a comment thread about something that wasn't even on your radar five minutes earlier. That's not information, it's inflammation.

Digital overload and political noise work hand-in-hand to keep us in a perpetual state of reaction. Our nervous systems—beautifully designed for presence and nuance—are now constantly bombarded by updates, algorithms, and agendas. It's not just mentally exhausting. It's spiritually depleting.

We need to discover balance between what we need to know to understand what is happening and to remain informed. Otherwise, we can find ourselves like the seals sunning on a rock—blissfully unaware that a predator is circling right below them. We are not seals, and we do need to remain prepared, aware, and conscious of how our world is evolving. The key is balance. How often and how we consume news is the focus of maintaining our peace.

Peace doesn't require total disconnection. Peace asks for discernment. Set digital boundaries that support your well-being. Silence the noise to amplify your truth. Then decide what you want to do with the information. Expressing emotion without action is a waste of your energy. Instead, try this: Turn off alerts and notifications. Turn down the noise. Take a walk without your phone and reflect on whether anything is worthy of your attention and time. If so, pick one thing you have learned about where you want to get involved. Then pick a realistic action. We aren't advocating ignoring; we are proposing that you take deliberate breaks and moderate your responses.

Peace isn't found in scrolling. It's found in the space between clicks where your own thoughts live.

Peace Tip: Choose where you want to enter discussion. You don't have to enter every debate. Choose, based on your values, where to put your energy.

15: Moral Exhaustion

Many people are quietly fatigued by the state of the world. The cruelty. The injustice. The polarization. The weight of feeling like you have to stay informed and make a difference but not knowing how. This can create a kind of spiritual burnout.

Peace Tip: You can care deeply and still take a break. You don't have to fix the world in a day. Choose one issue. One act of goodness. One place to focus your care. Let the rest be held by others for a moment. Collective peace is a relay—not a solo marathon.

Can you think of others? Let's be honest: It's one thing to acknowledge what's keeping you up at night, what's draining your energy, what's making you feel like peace is out of reach. But it's another thing entirely to start moving through it. That's why we're here.

The good news? Peace is for the weary, the worried, the overwhelmed, the grieving, the questioning. Peace is for all of us.

In *The Change Guidebook*, Elizabeth writes that change begins when you align your heart, truths, and energy—even when you feel like you have nothing left to give. That alignment is what allows you to pivot from chaos to clarity and move from avoidance into action.

Each disruptor you just read about has a doorway. A practice. A pivot point. And while it may not be easy or instant, the shift from disruption to restoration begins with a decision: to choose awareness over avoidance, softness over shame, and movement over stagnation.

PEACE POINT 13: Go Ahead, Worry, and Maybe Set a Timer

We all worry. This is a special peace point for all of us. We are with you. We both find ourselves worrying and have frequent check-in conversations with each other just to confirm that nothing is "wrong" with how much we worry—about our children, our families, the world, the neighbor's cat—whatever it is. As we are writing this book, we are both new empty nesters. You may think that when your children leave the nest, you stop worrying. Reality is, the worries just change shape. As parents of five adult children between us, all in their twenties and thirties, we find ourselves in unknown waters and worry about how our children are facing the creatures in their sea.

Dr. Susan Jeffers, in her book *Feel the Fear and Do It Anyway*, reminds us, "The only way to get rid of the fear of doing something is to go out and do it." She encourages action in the face of uncertainty. This is one of the most effective strategies in managing worry.

Worry is the mind's way of trying to control what feels uncontrollable. It's natural. It happens in the face of change, fear, or grief. But when it spirals, worry pulls us out of the present moment and into imagined futures that may never come.

For us, we are learning when to throw a life raft and when to let our children tread water. We have had some really challenging moments and interesting conversations about our role as they discover their own potential. When to take action and when to pause before taking action are fundamental aspects of understanding that potential.

Rather than judging yourself for worrying, as we sometimes do, it's important to meet the worry with compassion and curiosity.

When we are dealing with our family or working with others, we ask,

- What is this worry trying to protect?
- What does it need to feel safe?

We remind ourselves that by acknowledging worry instead of resisting it, we create space to recenter, reground, and respond to our children and other situations with peaceful intention.

Whenever you find yourself dwelling on the what-ifs, try this simple approach. Ask yourself,

- Is there any rational reason to be concerned?
- Why am I worried?
- Most importantly: What can I do right now to prevent, protect, or stabilize the situation?

This is your "preventive thinking cap." When you've done what you can, remind yourself, *I've taken the steps I'm able to.* Then let go. Until the worries sneak back in . . . and you then repeat the process.

A young cancer patient once taught Dr. Katie a profound truth:

"If you worry and nothing happens; you've suffered for no reason. If you worry and something does happen, you've suffered twice." Let that sink in. Let it guide you. Don't let the what-ifs manage you. Instead, manage them.

And if worry grows so big that it becomes unmanageable and it interferes with your ability to see potential, **please ask for help.** You don't need to navigate this alone.

●●●

Our Pathways to Peace with Elizabeth and Dr. Katie

Elizabeth—When the World Forgets Its Humanity

There's a unique kind of ache and worry that I carry. It's one that comes from watching the world forget its own humanity. It happens in moments both massive and mundane. In wars and headlines, yes, and also in traffic. In comment sections. In courtrooms and classrooms. In dinner conversations that spiral into judgment. In lives interrupted by cancer, grief, cruelty, or simply being overlooked.

I feel it when someone is cut off midsentence and no one bothers to circle back, when someone's suffering is ignored because it makes others uncomfortable, when cruelty is dressed up as humor, when ego screams louder than empathy. I think—quietly, inwardly—*How did we get so far from kindness?*

I know I'm not alone in this. I know many of you who are reading this also feel it. You're likely sensitive to it, even if you've never said it out loud. You absorb the world deeply. You notice the tone of a conversation, the mood in a room, the shift in someone's spirit. You're the one who pauses when others rush, the one who feels too much and sometimes questions whether that's a strength or a burden. Let me tell you: It's a gift, even if it doesn't always feel that way.

Some days the world feels loud and callous, and it's hard to imagine that peace is possible. Some days I've felt overwhelmed by how much needs to change and how often I've tried, only to wonder if it made any difference at all.

I've devoted my life and work to helping people navigate change, lead with love, and live with peace. I've written about it, coached around it, and built communities that reflect it. But I would be lying if I said it made me immune to heartbreak. It doesn't. It makes me feel it more.

Yet I still believe in peace. Fiercely. I believe in it not as a passive dream but as an active, daily practice. A way of being. A choice we make moment by moment to return to our own humanity and to recognize it in others.

For me, peace is disrupted when I see that recognition missing; when people are reduced to labels, statistics, and mistakes; when life becomes about winning rather than connecting; when systems prioritize control over compassion. It doesn't have to be this way. I think, deep down, that we all know that. That's why it hurts so much when we see it happening anyway.

We are all born with this inner knowing that life is sacred, that kindness matters, and that people deserve to be seen and treated with dignity. As children, most of us understood this without needing to be told. We helped each other up on the playground. We asked, "Are you okay?" without hesitation. We held hands without fear. Somewhere along the way, the world told us to toughen up, fall in line, grow up, and get over it. And slowly, the softness started to fade. But it doesn't have to be lost forever.

That softness, that humanity, is still inside us. It's the quiet voice that says, "Slow down." It's the instinct to reach out when someone's in pain. It's the catch in your throat when you see something unjust. It's the tears you wipe away in private when no one's looking, because you care that deeply. That, to me, is the real strength. When I think about the times I've been most disrupted in my own peace, it's not because something went wrong in my schedule or my goals. It's when someone I love is hurting. It's when kindness could have changed everything and wasn't offered. It's when I see someone being dismissed, denied, or dehumanized. And it's when I realize that I, too, have forgotten to offer grace and I have to come back to myself.

Coming back to ourselves: That's the work. That's the bridge to peace. And when we do it, when we come back, we don't just find stillness. We find strength. We find clarity. We find the capacity to show up again for others, for the world, and most importantly, for ourselves.

If you're someone who feels like you're carrying too much of the world, I want to say this:

You're not too sensitive. You're awake.

You're not broken. You're built for this.

And you're not alone. You're part of something bigger.

The Peace Guidebook wasn't written because peace is easy. It was written because peace is *essential,* especially when the world forgets itself and when we forget ourselves.

But we can remember. We can remember that peace is not the absence of pain. It's how we respond to it. We can remember that love, softness, and empathy are not weaknesses; they are the most revolutionary forms of strength. And we can remember that our humanity isn't something to be protected from—it's something to be lived fully.

The world will forget itself sometimes. But you don't have to.

You can be the one who remembers.

You can be the one who reminds others.

You can be the one who creates a pocket of peace, right where you are.

And from that small beginning, everything can change.

Dr. Katie—Overwhelm

People often ask me, "How can you, as a therapist, listen to so much pain and not get overwhelmed?"

The honest answer? I do get overwhelmed.

For as long as I can remember, people have come to me with their worries. Even when I was a child, kids confided in me. I didn't have formal training back then, but

I had what I now call Walt Disney optimism—a way of seeing every challenge as an opportunity, every fear as a doorway to deeper wisdom.

That part of me never left. I've always stood strong in the face of challenge—not because I learned to, but because it's simply who I am.

When people ask how I cope with hearing daily how life has disturbed someone's peace, I tell them: That's the very thing that challenges my peace.

In one single day, I might sit with someone who's been diagnosed with cancer, another who's lost their job, someone grieving the death of a child from substance use, and another navigating physical or emotional abuse. That's a typical day at the office.

The point is: We all carry reasons to worry. If we dwell too long in the what-ifs, it's easy to want to crawl back under the covers.

But, like Elizabeth, and like the others you're meeting in this book, I am tenaciously and passionately committed to living every moment I have. I don't measure life by how much better it should be. I measure it by how much better I can make it—for others, and for myself.

My mission is to help people rediscover the wisdom that lives beneath their worry. I guide them to ask, "What can I learn from this?" and "What will make me stronger, wiser, more compassionate?"

Every day, I live by a few simple words: *What can I do, and what can I learn, to make me better?*

Adopting a growth mindset in the face of life's daily losses doesn't make things easy. But it makes peace possible.

When I was a child, I used to take my dog out on a small Sunfish sailboat. He'd sit quietly at my feet, knowing not to move when a sudden gust of wind would force me to duck and adjust the sails.

Then there were the calm days. We'd glide across the lake under a gentle sun, making subtle adjustments, soaking in the stillness. Just the two of us.

That lake taught me a lot about life.

Worry is like the wind—sometimes sudden and overwhelming, sometimes gentle and familiar. But peace comes from knowing how to pause, pivot, and readjust.

To live.

Peace isn't always found in grand gestures. Sometimes it's hidden beneath layers of worry, overstimulation, and the heavy demands of daily life. In this chapter's Stories from the Heart, Christine Belleris and Jennifer Vaughn invite us into the deeply human experiences of striving for peace while navigating the weight of information overload and emotional burnout. Christine's story explores the presence of persistent worry and how it can both protect and derail us—until we learn to reset, reframe, and return to presence. Jennifer shares her raw, insightful journey of reporting on the world's most distressing headlines as a TV news anchor while learning to preserve her inner peace by intentionally detaching from the bedlam around her. Both stories remind us that peace doesn't require perfection. It requires practice. And the first step in unlocking our potential is learning to release what we cannot control.

Stories from the Heart

Christine Belleris—Worry

I have a companion I can't seem to shake. She wakes me in the middle of the night and spins thoughts in my head that keep me up, then she feeds me with more trouble as I doomscroll until the weight of my eyelids pulls me back to sleep. She haunts me nearly all of the six months of hurricane season (I live in Florida) as I hang on weather bloggers' interpretations of forecast cones and probability numbers. She makes road trips miserable as she taunts me with what-ifs of speeding cars in the next lane. Her name is Worry, and she definitely wreaks havoc on my personal sense of peace.

My kids laughed knowingly when we were going through boxes of my memorabilia recently and I found my high school driver's ed evaluation. The instructor wrote, "Will be a good driver, but she needs to relax." Wow, not much has changed in the intervening decades.

I guess I landed in the perfect career for someone with my semipermanent state of anxiety—I'm an editor of self-help books. I come to work in order to work on myself. I have experts guiding me from all over the country, but I'm still learning lessons even at my advanced age.

I once joked—well, maybe not—that bad things happen unexpectedly; the things that aren't on your watch list are the ones that sink their teeth into you. Hence, goes my twisted logic, if you have multiple focal points of worry, then you will be protected, like a cosmic force field dotting your emotional landscape. It makes me feel in control, to some degree.

We're bombarded with bad news and noise from the outside world that seeps into our thoughts from several fronts. If it's not the local or national news, then it's our cell-phone feed. Staying in touch and being an informed citizen are important, especially for us political junkies, but do we truly need a minute-by-minute account of everything that is happening? Does it help?

A therapist I spoke with once said I should ask myself a variation of those words when I start to feel anxious. "Is this helping?" This simple action makes you reframe and reset. She also advised me to pin my thoughts to gratitude. She said that when she reaches home every night, she takes a few deep breaths, closes her eyes, and says a prayer of thanks for getting her safely to her destination.

Solitude is also a good way to muzzle Worry. Today, as I was getting ready for work, I realized that I hadn't turned on the TV. The lack of background noise was refreshing. I could hear the birds welcoming the day instead of getting caught up on the latest overnight disaster. The routine of putting on my makeup and brushing my teeth was relaxing, almost meditative.

I once read a book called *The Artist's Way* about how to unleash your creativity. One of the exercises, as I recall, was called "Media Deprivation Week." You have a complete news diet for seven days. No TV, no newspaper, no radio (this was long before cellphones and the Internet). I spent more time reading, more time outside in nature, more time with my family, more time being in the here and now. At the end of the week, I felt a remarkable sense of calm and a renewed spirit.

Worry won't ever completely disappear. I need her sometimes. She is a protector, after all. But she doesn't need to be my BFF. Sometimes, it is best to let go of control. To listen to the breeze in the trees and the birds singing at daybreak. To have faith that the day will be good and that everything will work out for the best in the end.

Jennifer Vaughn—Determination to Detach

Peace is a lovely concept, and no one would argue it's not the master key to unlock a happier life. But what does one do to find peace when each day is spent presenting the exact opposite?

That's been my dilemma for over two decades.

When I became a TV news reporter, I wasn't naïve as much as altruistic. I thought simply by virtue of this profession, I would inform, lift, shine a light, and reveal what's wrong—so that it can be made right. I knew the subject matter was often lousy and the demands all-consuming, but I was enamored with the concept of storytelling and being the voice someone else needed me to be.

Did I anticipate the torrid emotional upheaval that comes with "being in the know"? Perhaps not as fully as I should have, because when you immerse yourself in the world's vat of problems, it should be no surprise when you come out with its residue stuck in all your nooks and crannies.

The news business is a twenty-four-hour, every-day-of-the-year endeavor, and that alone is a peace sucker. You're often exhausted, running on fumes, and the story still comes before your individual needs or woes. I have raced back to work after massive surgeries, with injuries requiring stitches and casts; the deaths of my parents, my mother-in-law, and my dog—because I had been programmed to believe the stories and my job were more important than my grief, pain, sadness, or recovery. No, I'm not blaming anyone except myself. It was the business I chose, the job I loved, and the career I'd built. But as I've aged with experience and depth, I have taught myself how to be more proactive in making my own life choices. In that, I am now determined to detach. Does that mean I have quit my job and now live on a tropical island with a strawberry daiquiri in hand? Well, no, at least not yet. I am still a TV news anchor, but when I detach, I can grasp my first glimpse of peace in this topsy-turvy human experience.

To start, when I became a mother, I automatically put my two children above all else. They, my husband, and my family are the first and foremost detachment protocol I follow. In that, simplicity is presented, and I will drop everything to attend to whatever they need. But beyond family, detachment doesn't mean walking away from a responsibility, deadline, or promise. Rather, it's the space and time after all of that is fulfilled—when I'm home alone, training my new puppy, working on my latest book, or helping a friend with a task or project. What I have developed in myself is a concentrated discipline to detach. It starts with purposeful actions.

First, I will never attain a shred of peace if I'm connected to the play-by-play of my job. It's so much broader than being on TV to anchor two hours of newscasts every day or digging into a challenging special report. Detachment, for me, is the absence of information, and my determination is to close the only spigot I can control—my access to the technology superhighway. Sure, my phone may be nearby, but in this detachment, I am simultaneously working out, going for a walk in my beautiful New Hampshire hometown, talking to a friend, laughing with my kids, or breathing in the air around me. Sure, the TV may be on in the background when I work on my books, but I am detached from that noise and drilling down on my characters, scene, and nuances of their stories and finessing their dialogue. My detachment may look different from yours, but I will tell you, letting go for just a moment in time is my sanctuary.

Peace will never be represented in the videos I see on TV from all parts of the globe, or in the wars, the financial disarray, or fiery political discourse I present nightly. I understand and respect this part of my life. I also realize it will never be quiet in my own head unless I force the silence back in. I had to teach myself to override the empathetic tug of what I report on, the disaster and decay, the sadness and strife.

The determination to detach is vital. It's preserving my soul. To have a life of my own—and in that, a shred of peace, it's truly the guiding light of what I hope you, too, can find. Detach when you can, even for a moment, every day. If your job, your circumstance, or the pressure of it all feels infinite and never-ending, do this one thing: Master a determination to purge, to preserve. Your peace is also your responsibility to cultivate.

POINTS TO PONDER

Think. Write. Talk. Action. (*Because practice makes us our best.*)

EXERCISE 3: Breaking Through Your Peace Barriers

Peace isn't just about what we invite into our lives. It's also about what we release. Before we can fully embrace peace, we must first understand what's blocking it. This exercise will help you uncover the obstacles standing in your way and begin the process of shifting them.

UNCOVERING YOUR BARRIERS TO PEACE

Close your eyes for a moment and take a deep breath. Imagine what peace feels like to you. Now think about the areas of your life where that feeling seems out of reach. What weighs on your heart? What situations or thoughts disrupt your sense of calm?

Write down three barriers that are currently preventing you from experiencing deeper peace. These could be anything: self-doubt, unresolved conflict, overwhelm, resistance to change, or something else entirely.

1. _____

_____

2. _____

_____

3. _____

_____

REFRAMING YOUR PERSPECTIVE

Choose one of these three barriers that feels most significant right now: the one that, if shifted, would create the greatest opening for peace in your life.

Ask yourself the following questions and write your responses below:

How does this barrier show up in my daily life?

_____

_____

What story have I been telling myself about this barrier?

_____

_____

What if I let go of this story? What new perspective would allow me to move forward with more ease?

_____

_____

What emotions come up when I think about releasing this barrier?

_____

_____

TAKING THE FIRST STEP TOWARD FREEDOM

Peace isn't just about reflection—it's about action. Small shifts in how we think, speak, and behave can make a powerful difference. Commit to one step you will take this week to begin dissolving this barrier.

The one action I will take to shift this barrier is:

The date I will begin: _____

My personal affirmation to reinforce this shift:

_____

_____

I am ready to release what no longer serves me and invite in greater peace.

(Signed) _____

EXERCISE 4: Forgiveness Exercise—Letter-Writing Method

This exercise is a private and powerful way to process your emotions and reclaim your peace.

Write three letters:

1. Write to the person who harmed you (whether alive or deceased). Say everything you need to say, without holding back. Remember, this letter is for your eyes only.

2. Write a response as if the person were replying to you—based on what they might realistically say. This may help you see the situation from another perspective.

3. Write what you wish the person would say—the apology, acknowledgment, or understanding you desire. This final step allows you to give yourself the closure you deserve.

Once you've completed the exercise, reflect on how you feel. You may choose to keep, destroy, or ceremonially release these letters. Whatever you decide, remember that this process is about your healing, not theirs.

As we keep saying, peace is a practice. It's not about being perfect or having everything figured out. It's about making intentional choices, one step at a time. Trust that as you clear space, peace will naturally flow in.

CHAPTER 3
PATIENCE

In the third principle of peace, Patience, we invite a radical new understanding. Let's move beyond the old idea of patience as mere waiting. Patience can be a challenge and impatience can be a gift. The art of becoming peaceful in relationship to patience means to wait until you can discern which message you need to be hearing while you seek to feel more peaceful. Patience can be the steady, grounded commitment to peace when the world around you feels fast, chaotic, or out of reach. And it can be a stirring, restless reminder that you need to take action. True patience is not about waiting quietly while your heart churns. It's about actively partnering with time to bring forward your best intention.

Believe it or not, one of the things we have in common is that we each have come face-to-face with dying. This has influenced our relationships and attitude about patience. We both keenly understand that we aren't entitled to time. Because of this attitude and approach, we practice revolutionary patience. We may slow down when the world speeds up and we may do the opposite of the crowd. For us, patience is a sensitive awareness of when to pause and when to be in motion while waiting for time and the external world to catch up. Patience has become our superpower, and here's why.

Each year, Elizabeth and her family celebrate April 10 and June 5. These dates are not a birthday or a wedding anniversary but rather the days she survived after nearly dying from an allergic reaction to food. On April 10, 1998, Elizabeth had a life-threatening allergic reaction after eating a small bag of almonds at a local coffee shop. She had an EpiPen in the car, which was used immediately and she was rushed to the hospital. When she arrived at the emergency room, however, her blood pressure was 65/38 and steadily dropping, so she was put on a resuscitation cart. When Elizabeth came to life, she was hooked up to a variety of machines and drips mostly designed to get her kidneys functioning again.

Not even a year later, on June 5, 1999, while six months pregnant with Cam, her third son, she unknowingly ate a chocolate chip cookie that had walnuts in it. Within seconds, she and Cam were fighting for their lives and rushed by ambulance to the hospital where they spent the next two weeks.

These experiences changed Elizabeth's perspective on life entirely, especially about time. It was then that she coined the phrase "We are not entitled to time." In the moments that followed that last episode, she knew she wanted to live her life differently.

Patience took on another level for Dr. Katie when, a year and a half ago, she had two expansive blood clots move from her leg to her lungs. After a long flight from Singapore, she began to experience pain behind her knee and difficulty breathing. Although she was admitted to a hospital close to home, she needed emergency surgery using a special procedure that could only be performed at a hospital in Seattle. As her breathing changed, the minutes ticked away as the staff diligently tried to find her a bed at the other hospital. Dr. Katie learned to understand revolutionary patience. She found herself peacefully asking the question: *If I live through this, have I lived my life with love?* She also asked, *Do the people I love know that I love them?*

The answer that came was that she wasn't sure. She knew what this meant: If she survived, she would need to be more openly loving. Of course, she did survive. An ambulance rushed her down to Seattle for the lifesaving surgery, and she immediately called her family and friends after the surgery and told them she loved them.

Much like Elizabeth, Dr. Katie lives differently now, taking nothing for granted about health and relationships, and she understands that patience requires trust in an unknown outcome. The event could have easily had a different outcome for Dr. Katie. Death was a real possibility. But even though she lived, the road to recovery has not been easy. It meant months of not being able to walk without pain and having to wait patiently and take small, slow steps toward recovery. She eventually reached her goal to once again hop on her bike and ride without pain. How? Because she waited and listened and slowly, methodically, practiced revolutionary patience.

Our time here is heartbreakingly brief. We are visitors, entrusted with a moment, a body, a voice—yet we too often forget. We are here to share stories, to marvel at how miraculous it is that we even exist in the same space. We are part of one breathtaking existence.

PEACE POINT 14: Practice Revolutionary Patience

From our experiences with nearly dying, we learned this about peaceful living: Patience is a profound, courageous, active choice. It is the art of building peace within yourself while the rest of the world still catches up. Waiting doesn't diminish you or your potential. It deepens your roots and strengthens your spirit. It gives you time to clarify what you value and how you want to live in this world. Waiting empowers us, gives us a sense of contribution and connection and moves us forward. Peace requires time, attention, and pausing to find answers or breakthroughs. Remind yourself that you are not stalled. You may be percolating something extraordinary.

Peaceful patience is *active engagement with the present*, not passive suffering. It's about creating tiny shifts inside yourself. If the first steps of peace are Presence and Potential, then Patience is the light bulb alerting you to pay attention to what is happening now that is leaving you unsettled. You cannot cultivate meaningful, lasting change without patience.

PEACE POINT 15: Practice the Art of Timelessness

Peace invites us to live fully in the moment, knowing that each experience, joyful or painful, is for now *but only for now*. When we practice the art of timelessness, we step out of the pressure of clocks and calendars and into the grace of presence.

Practicing timelessness also means extending that grace to others. Everyone moves through life at a different rhythm, and peace grows when we allow people the time and space they need to process, pause, or find their own way forward. Just as we release the demand to rush ourselves, we must also release the urge to rush others.

Offer patience instead of pressure. Let others unfold in their own timing, even when it looks different from yours. When we give one another that spaciousness—to rest, to think, to breathe—we cultivate a shared peace that honors our humanity and our inherent worth.

This is for now, but remember, it is only for now. Moments change, people evolve, and peace deepens when we give everything and everyone, including ourselves, the grace of time.

PEACE POINT 16: Percolate Peace

Waiting makes you either bitter or better. Percolating Peace means you don't sit passively in the discomfort of waiting, you transform it. You breathe into it. You gently envision hope, patience, faith, and trust. You turn waiting itself into a living meditation on possibility.

It's easy to let waiting ferment into resentment. But peace doesn't grow in soil hardened by bitterness.

Percolating Peace happens at a different pace than we are used to living. When you Percolate Peace, you become aware of patience and that stirring of impatience as your messenger. You know that change is happening, even when you can't quite imagine how. You believe goodness is still on the way, even if it's slower than you hoped. You trust healing is unfolding, even if it's invisible right now. You choose to savor the richness of *what is* rather than curse *what has not yet arrived.*

It's not naive. It's revolutionary.

You're not waiting for peace to be delivered like a package on your doorstep. The next time impatience rises in your chest, pause and ask yourself,

What peace can I percolate here? What right action can I take that aligns with my intention?

PEACE POINT 17: Change Your Pace of Peace

Ask yourself which situations require you to have the most patience. For us, this question brought rich dialogue about when to act and when to wait and explore what is in between.

We live in a world that confuses movement with meaning. It's easy to fill our days with motion, noise, and obligation and call it progress, yet in doing so we often miss the quiet invitations to pause. The art of patience is not about standing still; it's about learning to listen to what's unfolding before rushing to the next thing.

We both hear platitudes that make us gag, but at other times platitudes fit and provide us with peace. We have all heard the phrase, "I am not going to sit around the campfire and sing 'Kumbaya'!" We want to challenge this and say, "Why not?"

Ancient wisdom teaches the value of slowing down, being with nature and sharing ideas, and passing on thoughts and stories. Yet how willing are we to slow ourselves down long enough to patiently take the steps to do so? For example, Indigenous peoples' stories of gathering wood, building a fire, lighting the fire, and sitting in a circle are obvious moments of communal sharing. In modern times, we re-created something similar to this ritual in coffeehouses, book groups, or simply sitting around a table and having a conversation. How often do you have meaningful, uninterrupted conversations?

We want you to remember your ancient roots and bring back the sacred circle! You cannot heal relationships, build or rebuild trust, or reimagine a world of peace without patience. Come to the circle with compassion, and you'll discover that a patient understanding can bring about a magical outcome.

PEACE POINT 18: Trust Something Beyond Yourself

The world may still spin in perceived turmoil. But inside your stretched-out, intentional breath, you can remain sovereign, steady, and free.

Ask yourself: *In this moment, can I stretch the space just a little longer and choose peace?*

Even two extra seconds can save years of regret. Two extra seconds are sometimes enough to save a friendship, a dream, a future you didn't even know was on the line. You may desire control of the when and how in your life, but time often has a different plan—and it's bigger than us or our understanding.

We both believe in something beyond ourselves. Sometimes we give it a name: God, Source, Godwink, angel hit, Godsend, or the universe. We all have different ways of describing what we can feel but not explain. We like to believe in something working behind the scenes, and invite you to ascribe whatever label you want to it.

Understand that the most meaningful changes don't announce themselves with flashing signs. They emerge gradually, revealed moment by moment, in the everyday miracle of persistence. Life's finest gifts—whether relationships, dreams, healing, or inner peace—are crafted with patient hands and faithful hearts.

Ask yourself:

Can I trust that what I'm creating will be worth whatever time it takes?

Can I relax into the magnificence developing from me?

Right now, your life is percolating something extraordinary. Let it strengthen. Let it become everything you dreamed and more. You are making peace, just for you. Trust the process.

PEACE POINT 19: Create Peaceful Circles and Community

To create peace in this modern world, commit to the ancient practice of honoring yourself and others by slowing down, listening, learning, and empathizing.

Rather than sitting at a long rectangular desk that divides different groups of decision-makers, imagine metaphorically sitting and living your life in circles of compassion. A discussion around a circular table has a different energy; it reminds us of our ancient practice of fire circles, where the fire represents the inner flame: the drive to love, to live, to create, and to passionately share with others what is most important to us. In his work *Fire and Civilization*, Johan Gouldsblom reminds us, "Fire became the first focus of human social life. The hearth was the original gathering place, and the circle around it, the first form of social organization."

A circle does not allow hierarchy. It instead provides unity and encourages listening and honoring the now, being present and holding the energy of trust. The next time you have a difficult discussion to lead, consider coming together in a circle. We aren't linear beings.

We created an image to illustrate what we mean. We want you to place pairs of words into the left and right circles and insert "PEACE" in the middle. For example, insert "north" and "south" or "liberal" and "conservative" with "PEACE" in between, and become an advocate for creating circles of compassion and filling that space.

Our mission is to create a new alternative to old ways of thinking, to expand your beliefs instead of compartmentalizing them. To unify is to expand our understanding of someone else's belief, which takes incredible patience, persistence, and courage!

Peace and living peacefully constitute existing in a harmonious balance between ideologies that can pull us away from one another.

We encourage you to explore peace as a family! We want children to learn new ways of defining peace and end generational conflicts that promote conflicts. Come together and commit to one another that your family unit will live peacefully and be part of the change. Engage friends, create circles or book clubs, and ripple out to the world a new way of being! We are here with practical tools to guide you through this process.

Nature reminds us that regardless of where we live, our lives follow seasons and cycles and natural unfoldings and transformations. Yet we have become more linear—some would say more argumentative, more rigid, more competitive, less collaborative, and much less willing to sit in a circle compassionately. If we all perceived Earth as collective community circles, what a peaceful place it could be.

PEACE POINT 20: Practice Planetary Patience

War happens when patience leaves the room. Peace grows when patience remains.

Planetary Patience is the wisdom to stay seated when the conversation gets uncomfortable. It is the willingness to listen deeply, to remember that every voice, even the ones we find hardest to hear, holds some piece of the larger story.

Planetary Patience invites us to stay a little longer with one another. In your own life, and in the larger life of the world, practice Planetary Patience by trusting that

- Understanding is worth the time it takes.
- Healing happens.
- Even when it feels like nothing is changing, transformation is happening just below the surface.

If more of us choose to sit, listen, and stay in the circle of compassion rather than storming out at the first offense, perhaps the world would remember what it forgot:

We are not enemies. We are travelers. We are part of one delicate, breathtaking existence.

The next time you feel the urge to give up on unity, to label, to leave, to fight: Pause. Be willing to remain hopeful even when there seems little reason to do so.

This is Planetary Patience. And it might just save the world. When you pause before you push, you shift. Creating space between reaction and response can transform not only your personal peace but collective peace too. Empathy enters in moments of pause, when curiosity softens conflict and healing begins.

Let your best self filter through. The planet is waiting.

Next, we wanted to share two personal stories that reflect how patience is cultivated not in grand moments but in the slow, often unseen experiences that shape who we become.

●●●

Our Pathways to Peace with Elizabeth and Dr. Katie

Elizabeth—The Blank and Blink of It All

The Blank

The blank is the space between who you were and who you're becoming. It's that foggy pause when life changes and you don't yet know what comes next. It's disappointment. It's loss. It's grief in real time. It's watching the person who gave you life slowly leave theirs.

I've lived in the blank more times than I can count. I've paced hospital halls. I've stared at walls. I've rewritten reality on napkins and in journals. I've sat in waiting rooms with a silence so deafening it rearranged my DNA.

The Blink

And then—blink. It's over. The moment has passed. Your dad takes his last breath. The baby doesn't come home. The last word said can't be unsaid. Time moves, whether we're ready or not.

The blink reminds us: Life is precious, and nothing is guaranteed. You blink, and suddenly your toddlers are adults. You blink, and the person you thought would live forever is gone.

Between the blank and the blink is where patience lives. It's the space where we don't have all the answers, but we learn to stay. It's where presence becomes an act of courage. Not running. Not fixing. Not distracting. Just staying.

That's what I know now.

People sometimes describe me as calm, grounded, and patient. It makes me smile because I've lived a life that forced me to learn those things through storms, not sunshine. I've practiced patience when everything inside me wanted to scream and run. I've chosen peace when it would have been easier to pick anger. I've trusted the timing of life even when it didn't feel fair.

What changed? I did.

I stopped needing to control everything. I stopped rushing. I started listening—to my breath, to my body, to the small signs all around me that life is always unfolding in its own perfect, unpredictable way.

Looking back, I wasn't the most patient child. I'd turn ten and immediately want to be eleven. The moment a milestone passed, I was already looking ahead to the next one. My dad used to ask me, "What's your rush?" and I'd shrug, not really knowing the answer. But I think it had a lot to do with being such a sickly child. When you don't feel well, you just want to get to the next moment, the one where you finally feel better. It creates this constant longing for *What's next?* rather than being fully present in the now.

I still think, *What's next?* more than I care to admit. Maybe you do, too. It's human. We want certainty. We want clarity. But the blank and the blink rarely offer that.

In my twenties, I learned patience in even harder ways. My first pregnancy ended in miscarriage. That was a devastating lesson in waiting. Waiting to heal. Waiting to grieve. Waiting to trust life again. But eventually, life brought me four healthy sons—each two years apart. And no matter how much I wanted to fast-forward through nausea, backaches, and the awkwardness of nesting like a maniac, I couldn't. Pregnancy unfolds on its own timeline, no matter how many cabinets you reorganize.

My mom and dad were there for each birth. And then in 2004, everything changed. My dad had his first stroke. We began the long, winding journey of hospitals, rehabilitation, setbacks, and the slow goodbye that stretched across years. On October 19, 2018, the world lost an incredible man—James F. Hamilton IV. My dad. My mom's partner of forty-three years. A father to ten and grandfather to eighteen.

I've written about him in *Percolate*, *The Change Guidebook*, and *The Success Guidebook*. But nothing I've ever written fully captures what it's like to sit in the blank when someone you love is slipping away. There isn't a *new normal*. There's just change. Some people get stuck in the blank and live there, frozen in grief. Others plod along. Some charge ahead, burying their feelings under busy schedules and long to-do lists. We all cope differently, but the ache is universal.

And the blink? The blink is brutal. I blinked, and he was gone. The day after he passed, I sat with my mom and wrote his obituary. Tears fell on the keyboard, and even now, the keys stick from the salt and sorrow soaked into them. My siblings and I revised, contributed, and stared at words that could never do him justice.

The blank and the blink go together. And between them, we're invited to root deeper into love and gratitude, to soften into community, and to stay present—especially when it hurts.

Now that I'm in my mid-fifties, people say I'm mellow, peaceful, and patient. I laugh a little when I hear that. If you had met the younger version of me, the one who rushed through milestones and didn't know how to sit still, you wouldn't recognize me. What changed? Perspective. Gratitude. Abundance.

Rather than anxiously awaiting the future, I now notice what's in front of me. I find peace in the quiet mornings, the lingering hugs, the slow walks. I see the richness in places I used to overlook. I don't need to rush anymore. I trust that life is happening *for* me, even when I don't understand it.

Patience isn't about waiting for something to end. It's about learning how to be fully alive while it's happening. It's choosing to love when the timeline feels cruel. It's choosing gratitude when the outcome isn't guaranteed.

If you're in the blank, I see you. If you're in the blink, I honor you. And if you're somewhere in between—that's enough.

Peace lives there too.

Dr. Katie—Waiting

One of my favorite sayings is, "Life is what happens when you're busy making other plans." Sometimes life throws us a curveball when we least expect it—an unexpected diagnosis, a sudden job loss, or a life-altering event that shakes our very foundation. In those moments, our peace is tested, our patience stretched to its limits. The life we thought we had mapped out is suddenly unrecognizable, and we stand at a crossroads. Do we pause, breathe, and allow ourselves to regroup, or do we react in a way that compromises our inner calm?

It's easy to believe that peace is impossible in the face of upheaval, but what if we leaned into patience instead of fear? What if, in the waiting, something even greater was unfolding?

Nothing brought this lesson home for me quite like my journey with infertility. As for so many others, when I began planning for a family, it was just that—a plan. I assumed it would unfold effortlessly: try, conceive, carry, and give birth. After all, that's how it's supposed to go, right? Until it doesn't.

Miscarriages weren't part of our vision for parenthood, and each loss felt like a devastating storm, shattering every expectation we had. It was a relentless cycle of hope, heartbreak, and longing. The world around us continued as if nothing had changed, but for us, everything had. And beyond the grief of loss, there was another pain, the unspoken messages that left us feeling like we were somehow less than.

I will never forget the supposed friend who told me, "You don't know what it's like to struggle; you aren't a parent." Those words cut deep. They shook my confidence, chipped away at my self-worth, and made me question if I even belonged in conversations about family. Even in my friendship with Elizabeth, there were moments when my heart ached with jealousy over her four successful pregnancies. Instead of recognizing my own path to peace and motherhood, I spent too much time believing that something was inherently wrong with me.

Then, one day, a powerful realization washed over me: No one could take my peace unless I let them. If becoming a mother was my soul's deepest calling, then, to paraphrase Scarlett O'Hara, "As God is my witness, I will be a mother!"

So I chose patience. I chose to trust. I chose to believe that the family meant for me was still on its way. When John and I decided to adopt, the road wasn't easy. There were setbacks, disappointments, and moments that tested our resolve. But each obstacle wasn't a denial; it was simply a delay. It meant our daughter wasn't here yet.

I'll never forget, in the midst of our adoption process, the moment a friend offered us the opportunity to take in an infant from another adoption agency. Being so far along in our process already with China, we knew in our hearts that we needed to wait. Something in our souls told us our daughter was coming from China. My husband and I chose to be patient. Our instincts told us that we needed to follow through with the adoption process with the organization that was already seeking to connect us with whom they believed was destined to be our daughter.

And then, two and a half years later, she came.

I will never forget the moment I saw her photo for the first time. I sobbed uncontrollably, not from sadness, but from an overwhelming, soul-deep knowing. She was ours. She had always been meant for us. It was as if the universe whispered, "See? This is why you had to wait." After my tears subsided, I felt the most profound peace I had ever known.

And just when I thought my heart couldn't hold more confirmation, I discovered something extraordinary: Her birthday was my birthday inverted. For over twenty years, I had worn a bracelet inscribed with that exact date, a gift my parents had given me on my twenty-first birthday. It had been with me all along, a quiet, constant reminder that patience leads to miracles beyond our wildest imagination.

At so many moments I wanted to give up, when the pain of waiting felt unbearable, when the uncertainty felt too heavy. But something deep inside me whispered, *Hold on. Someone is coming.* And she did.

On the third day of being parents to a bubbly, lively, and curious sixteen-month-old baby girl, John turned to me and exclaimed, "Oh wow, now I have two of you!" We were a family united in love and a lot of laughter.

Patience isn't just about waiting. It's about trusting. There's a common platitude that well-meaning people often recite that is a real peace buster in these times: "Things happen for a reason."

I don't for a minute think babies are intentionally taken from us, and instead I say, "We use our reason to manage what happens."

Patience is about pausing, reflecting on what truly matters, affirming our desires, and opening our hearts to the endless ways they can be fulfilled. It's about believing that even when the path twists and turns in unexpected ways, something beautiful is unfolding.

When we embrace patience, we don't just find what we were searching for; we find the deepest kind of peace. And in that peace, we discover that the greatest joys in life sometimes come not in the way we planned, but in the way we learn to receive them with gratitude.

Next, meet Mariya, who is proof that even in the face of unimaginable pain, we have resilient human tools to face any life event with peaceful patience. Nothing demonstrates the power of peaceful patience more than Mariya's story. If someone impacted by war's devastation can practice patience, the rest of us can too.

Stories from the Heart

Mariya Vynnytska—The Soul

I am Ukrainian, and just a few weeks after the full-scale invasion of Ukraine in February 2022, together with a group of women who are my fellow psychologists, I launched an online psychology crisis center, The Soul, to provide free mental health support to those affected by the war.

As you can imagine, there was horror all around. Bombings were happening day and night all around us. We could hear explosions close by and see the smoke billowing from others in the distance. Tanks rolling through the streets appeared on social media, where we also saw people getting shot trying to escape, with those who did not make it lying in the street. We ourselves were constantly running to the bomb shelters, not knowing how much time we had left, but we came together to bring solace to those in need. When you don't know what to do, you do what you know. We knew how to provide psychological help, so that's what we could offer to our community.

This journey taught me more about patience than any book ever could. I learned firsthand how to navigate stress, fear, and the constant demand for action amid profound uncertainty.

I'd like to share some things that have helped me survive and continue supporting others.

Our cofounder of The Soul, Alexandra, and I both fled Ukraine but managed to keep our program going from different countries. I had to work various jobs in several locations before finally finding a longer-term position in Singapore, where I am now. As a lawyer and practicing psychologist, I took on teaching and consulting roles, packing my bags to move again whenever my visa expired. In the last two and a half years, I lived in eleven different places—among Singapore, Malaysia, and Japan—and all these places were new to me and the people I stayed with were complete strangers. I knew none of them before the war, yet they opened their homes to me. I am forever grateful.

Living out of a suitcase these last few years with few belongings and realizing my laptop, brain, and heart were my most precious tools, I've had to practice peaceful patience.

There are thousands of Ukrainians whose pain is much bigger than mine. I feel blessed in many ways, but I've also experienced loss. I lost safety in my home city, which has been bombed daily. I lost peace in my country, which is going through unimaginable torture, war crimes, and atrocities. I've been separated from family and friends. My brother was injured on the battlefield and is still fighting for his recovery. Projects, plans, the life I had envisioned—all swept away like leaves in a relentless wind. They are all part of "the package of losses"—tangible and intangible ones—that the war brought, including a sense of stability and future.

Does that pain kindle anger? Yes, at times it does. I am only human. But I ask myself daily: *Do I want that anger and rage to consume me?* No. I pray for God's grace to release it, not because my pain isn't valid, but because that anger is a poison that can destroy my spirit. It would drag me to a place where peace cannot take root, and it would rob me of the ability to love, to serve, to heal, to bring hope. The world is broken enough; I don't want to be another fragment of its shattering. I don't want to contribute to more hatred.

Do I feel my country's pain? Yes, of course. It is a part of me, a drumbeat that echoes through my veins day and night. But I am determined that this suffering will not anchor us to cycles of revenge. I want our loss to be seeds for growth, not chains for our children and future generations of Ukrainians.

I dream of a Ukraine reborn—strong, radiant, and free. I want my country to be able to protect itself in the future. But I choose to be a builder, not a dweller among the ruins.

The truth is, no one knows when this war will end, how many more lives will be cut short, how many dreams left incomplete. But life exists in this moment, fragile and precious. We must use it, create with it, breathe meaning into it.

In the deepest darkness, don't just seek the light in others. Search for that small, quivering flame within yourself. Maybe it's the faint glow of a single candle—barely more than a whisper—but guard it fiercely. Hold it up against the shadows. And if you're blessed to feel its warmth, share it. That is how light grows. Amid the chaos, amid the terror, hold fast to something bigger than yourself. For me, it was my family, my colleagues, and our mission to serve, to support, to hold onto each other as long as we could.

In the brutality of war, nurturing peace within becomes an act of defiance. It's a choice rooted in faith, connection, and honest surrender to life's fragility. Accept your limits, acknowledge the gift of each day and your own mortality, however uncomfortable that may be. You may not be able to change the entire world or even a piece of it, but if you have another day, you can change something. Even when you cannot do 3 percent of what you wish you could do, focus on what you can do. It's more than enough.

Sometimes the weight of the world feels too immense, too cruel to touch. But do not hide behind the enormity of helplessness. Do not hide behind this inability to change the whole world. You can always change something on your level, your scale. Touch one life, take that one step, do one act of kindness, and choose peace, hope, and compassion— even when everything around you looks like a war zone or you feel like the world has gone mad. You'll be surprised. When you make this choice, you will start meeting people who have made the same choices. And then you can change the world. Bit by bit.

Imagine seeing thousands of candles burning at the same time in the darkness. Can you see it? That light, multiplied, a promise whispered even in the deepest shadows: hope lives. And it begins with one choice—your choice. Isn't it beautiful? Aren't you powerful?

Be that light. Be that hope. For as long as you can.

These lessons aren't exclusive to wartime; they're universal reminders for anyone. Resilience is built through connection, purpose, and the courage to hope.

Mariya's story brings perspective to the extent we take for granted what challenges our patience. She once said to Dr. Katie, "I am so grateful for the times when I sit in a coffee shop with a friend and I am not afraid, knowing my friends back home are terrified."

When was the last time we were grateful for a cup of coffee and time spent chatting with a friend? Or walking in a park or simply looking at a tree? We are so unaware most of the time—but even when times are tough and life is the most challenging, choices present themselves about how we can cope. Practicing peace is a way of life, and our next story offers insight into how many of us can apply these principles when the inevitable occurs—when we become caregivers.

Lisbeth Cort—Gratitude Amid the Unthinkable

The unthinkable happened ten years ago. Out of the blue, without any warning late one Sunday, my healthy, happy, fifty-nine-year-old husband had a severe seizure. I thought he was having a stroke. In the ER, he was put into an induced coma. We boarded an ambulance at 10 pm, rushing two hours from the island where we lived to Seattle. Throughout the night, people came and went. They did MRIs and conducted tests. Nurses brought in a blanket to keep me warm while I tried to sleep on the recliner in his room. A nurse on the early-morning shift promised that a neurologist would be in very shortly to talk to me.

Several hours went by with no visit from the neurologist. I frantically and desperately peppered the nurse with questions: "Where is he? When is he coming? What was going on? How serious is this? *What* is this?"

She curtly replied, "You're going to have to learn to be patient on this neurology journey." If it was possible to be more stunned than I already was, my head snapped back and I thought to myself, *What? We're on a journey?* I just wanted to find out what was wrong, get my husband treated, get home, and get back to our lives.

Two weeks later, I anxiously sat in a neuro-oncologist's office next to my husband, who was now recovering from brain surgery to remove a tumor. The doctor reported that he had a glioblastoma brain tumor. These are always fatal. *Always.* They were right. He died less than a year later.

I was asked to write my thoughts for this book about how patience gave me inner peace as a caregiver.

Honestly, I don't remember patience being an overwhelming struggle as a caregiver. I guess that the best and the worst of this situation was that my husband only had months after his diagnosis, not years. Except for enduring monthly visits with his prickly neuro-oncologist, navigating his health care went pretty smoothly. He wasn't in physical pain, and I was kept busy managing his care and his transportation since he couldn't drive. So I took solace in knowing that, while not perfect, I was doing the best I could for him while trying to take care of myself as well. I remember thinking to myself at some point, *This is probably the greatest gift I will ever give anyone.*

The real test of patience came later—after he passed and I was plodding slowly through two-plus years of searing grief. My test came not as a caregiver to my husband but as a caregiver to myself. I needed patience in learning, and then trying to accept, the reality that it was going to take a very, *very* long time and a lot of hard work to get through the worst of this grief. Patience trying to keep faith that eventually I would reach a place where I could try to move on. Patience when the loss of friendships piled on top of this already unspeakable loss. Patience learning to endure gut-wrenching comments people naively said, such as "Everything happens for a reason," or "God doesn't give you more than you can handle," and even, "This isn't all about you." Patience when friends, even my former "tribe," instantly disappeared, presumably too uncomfortable and unable to figure out how to help or what to do.

I had no choice but to be patient and get through it. What's that saying? "Behind every strong person is a story that gave them no other choice." Ultimately, though, I think that gratitude gave me patience to do what I had to do to care for myself. I was grateful that I had been lucky enough to share life with my love. I tenaciously held on to gratitude for the grief counselor who gently helped me to the other side of tragedy. I was in no way being intentional—you know: "Look for one thing each day to be grateful for." Yet almost daily, I noticed how grateful I was for something that was getting me through this.

Sometimes it was friends who hung in there with me. In the darkest moments when I couldn't even get a breath, from somewhere came a tiny light of self-awareness, of gratitude, and a small level of confidence that I would get through this somehow. Being grateful in the face of the worst thing that could have happened ended up giving me enough patience and strength to get through another day—and later to move forward.

Next, in Exercises 5 and 6, we focus on developing patience as a foundation for lasting peace. True peace often begins within, requiring us to shift our mindset, challenge our responses, and actively engage in behaviors that cultivate patience. These exercises can help you recognize the moments that test your patience and the strategies that can strengthen it.

POINTS TO PONDER

Think. Write. Talk. Action. *(Because practice makes us our best.)*

EXERCISE 5: Expanding Your Capacity for Patience

STEP 1: IDENTIFYING PATIENCE BUILDERS AND CHALLENGES

Write three things that regularly require your patience. These could be daily occurrences (traffic, waiting in line) or larger life challenges (healing from emotional wounds, achieving career goals).

1. _____

2. _____

3. _____

Write three things that test your patience or cause you to feel frustrated. Be honest: What situations or people push you toward impatience?

1. _____

2. _____

3. _____

STEP 2: REFLECTION ON YOUR TRIGGERS

Look at your two lists. What patterns do you notice? Are there similarities between What requires your patience and what tests it? _____

_____

_____

_____

How do you currently handle impatience? Do you withdraw, react, or find ways to self-soothe? _____

_____

_____

_____

Write about a recent time when you handled impatience well. How did you maintain your composure? _____

_____

_____

_____

EXERCISE 6: Practicing and Strengthening Patience

STEP 1: THE POWER OF ASSESSING TIME

The next time you feel in a hurry to create urgent change, challenge yourself to pause and intentionally wait instead of rush. A sense of urgency and a fire within sometimes signal that we feel passionately about making some kind of change. In other situations, there is less importance on when we act than on how we move forward. In these moments, we want you to take a breath and discover right action.

A recent situation where I felt passionately rushed was _____.

I chose to _____.

How did it feel to wait and choose action carefully? (Circle one)

    Anxious

    Frustrated

    Calm

    Empowered

    Other: _____

One insight I gained from this experience was _____.

STEP 2: WRITING TO RELEASE FRUSTRATION

Think of a person or situation that often frustrates you. Instead of reacting, imagine writing a letter expressing your feelings. Be raw, be honest—but do not send it.

The situation or person that frustrates me is _____

_____.

If I could say anything without consequences, I would say _____

_____.

After expressing these thoughts, I feel (Circle one)

    Relieved

    More frustrated

    Clear-headed

    Unchanged

    Other: _____

STEP 3: TURNING FRUSTRATION INTO ACTION

Now reframe part of your response from a place of patience and understanding. If you were giving advice to someone else in this situation, what words of wisdom would you offer?

A more patient and understanding way to view this situation is _____.

One small action I can take today to practice patience is _____.

If I approached similar situations with patience, I might feel _____.

By engaging in this exercise, you are actively strengthening your ability to manage impatience and build a foundation for greater peace in your daily interactions.

PART 2

HEALING

CHAPTER 4
PRACTICE

In the fourth principle of peace, Practice, we employ the tools we provide to practice peace. We all have our whys that guide our conversations and communication patterns. Having an awareness of our most vulnerable pain points allows us to pay attention, commit to compassion, and discover shared values in every interaction. We then let go of our need to be right and instead focus on our greater need to connect. We learn to apply the art of compromise—intentionally integrating, adapting, and modifying our lives when we make changes—and learn more about ourselves and what prevents us from living peacefully. Practicing peace is a radical act of self-responsibility. It's a conscious choice that requires daily discipline.

We think the hardest practice for a parent begins the moment you become a parent. It's a passionate desire to lift a child up, to help them be their best and not get in their way. What interferes is fear. Learning when to intervene and when to let go is quite possibly one of parenting's most difficult aspects. It requires practicing peaceful approaches at every turn.

Between the last chapter and this one, we're skipping over twenty-five years of parenting stories, sparing you most of them. However, our grown children still need us to some degree, and we are navigating that challenging balance of when they enter their own adult life yet know the door is always open for them at home.

Let's talk for a moment about the challenges COVID presented to our five twenty-somethings. They didn't follow a linear path. It was more like a Maine country road with lots of twists and turns and unexpected changes.

Three of Elizabeth's sons, for example, were all in college and abruptly sent home to finish classes online. In one case, her son's college baseball season was canceled, and in Dr. Katie's case, her daughter's dancing, acting, and singing activities were gone overnight. Our five humans lost a lot of a special time in their lives and pushed through some very difficult moments.

The effects of this time period are ongoing. What Elizabeth notices most is that whenever there is world stress, her children feel like they have had enough. They are easily overwhelmed. They are learning, as we all do, that adult life has its own unique challenges and is filled with other adults who are unpredictable and don't necessarily have their best interests at heart or practice peace.

Two of Elizabeth's sons have careers that have been upended with layoffs and hiring freezes. For Dr. Katie's daughter, one of the challenges in her launching has been figuring out how to enjoy life and make a living. As we write, we realize that really is everyone's challenge.

Let's be honest, if peace were easy, we'd all be humming like tuning forks, and spreading a compassionate, world-changing vibe. Our kids would be happily settled, living their lives content and peaceful.

Peace isn't tested when life is easy. It's when you're looking for a job and the automated computer process reads and turns your résumé down instantly for lack of the desired keywords or because bots instantaneously overwhelmed the hiring website minutes after the job opened. It's when you can't pay your bills, when your child is sick, when you lose your job, or when you are diagnosed with a major illness. Peace is tested when real life happens.

PEACE POINT 21: Wake Up

Awaken. Before you can practice peace, you have to realize you're even a participant in the process. This is called consciousness. To practice peace, you have to first wake up. You're not a bystander. You're a full participant in every space you enter, which means showing up, not perfectly, but consciously.

This is Consciousness 101: becoming aware that your presence, energy, words, tone, and even your silence affect every moment of your life. You're not invisible. You're not neutral. You are influencing every space you're in, whether you mean to or not. Swami Vivekananda (1863–1902) was one of the first to translate the ancient Hindu *chit* (consciousness) and *atman* (self) concepts into accessible English. He framed consciousness as both the essence of the self and the ground of all reality, making it understandable and appealing to Western spiritual seekers. He said, "Consciousness is infinite, the universe is but a drop in the ocean of consciousness."

Consciousness is awareness. It's knowing what energy you're bringing into the room, checking in with yourself before you react, and taking responsibility for how you respond, instead of defaulting to defensiveness or blame.

Ask yourself,

- What's my tone right now?
- Am I practicing peace in or escalating this situation?
- Am I leading with empathy or ego?

When you're unconscious, you're on autopilot. You're reacting based on your old stories, old wounds, old defenses. You're not choosing. You're repeating. But when you're conscious, you become the author. You pause and breathe. You respond with intention, and you choose peace, even when it's hard. *Especially* when it's hard.

Peace starts before the conversation begins. It starts with the moment you decide who and how you're going to be. Peace is the presence of compassion. We are not pretending that the world is okay. We hope. We fully understand the existence of war, injustice, and despair.

Before you can practice peace, you must first acknowledge that you're a human being with emotions, stress, and the occasional (or frequent) tendency to hurl something at the TV when something doesn't go your way or to explode at someone who says something that infuriates you. We are not robots. We are imperfect creatures who stub our toes, argue with customer service representatives, and sometimes yell at inanimate objects like they personally offended us. So let's not pretend this is easy. The real world has Wi-Fi outages, flat tires, cold coffee, layoffs, disease, war, and plenty of moments that make you want to scream into a pillow.

In the face of all that chaos, we're called not to bypass it—but to respond with intention, choosing peace as a deliberate, courageous act. Remember, your level of intensity and another person's perception of your ability to do them harm defines violence. Violence isn't just physical; it can be emotional, verbal, or energetic. Often, violence emerges not just from what we do, but from how our actions and intensity are perceived. One of the greatest lessons from famous peacemakers is that of choosing nonviolence. We love this quote from Mahatma Gandhi: "Nonviolence is the greatest force at the disposal of mankind. It is mightier than the mightiest weapon of destruction devised by the ingenuity of man." (Of course, we want you to translate this into humankind.)

PEACE POINT 22: Recover When You Lose It!

Practicing peace often starts with losing yourself entirely, sometimes in spectacular fashion! "Losing it" is a thing. There's just no better way to explain or describe what it's like when all sense of control seems to escape our bodies, and this unknown, terrifying, Tasmanian devil–like creature emerges that wants to attack and get even and tell everyone what is right for everybody.

We've all been there. You start your day with the best of intentions—deep breathing, a gratitude journal, maybe even a few yoga poses. Then someone cuts you off in traffic, and suddenly you're in an expletive-laden rant instead of practicing deep breathing. You set a resolution to remain calm. Later that day, technology happens when the signal goes out in the middle of an important video meeting, and before you know it, you're waving your phone around like it's a magic wand that should summon a stronger signal.

We've had days where we've made a commitment to be more patient, only to later be in line at the grocery store behind the world's slowest person, the one who inexplicably waits until everything is scanned before digging through their bottomless purse for a coupon.

Peace isn't about never losing it. It's about how quickly you can recover after you do. It's about learning to manage your anger. There is nothing wrong with getting angry, even rageful, as long as you direct that energy toward your idea of peaceful, right action.

Recovery is where the real peace work happens—in that moment after the explosion when you realize, *Okay, that wasn't my best self,* and you choose to clean up the emotional confetti instead of pretending it didn't happen. Recovery is the practice of accountability wrapped in grace. It's an apology when needed, a breath before reacting again, and the decision to laugh, learn, and move forward more lightly. Each recovery teaches you that peace isn't about being perfect; it's about being willing to return to center again and again.

PEACE POINT 23: Remain Calm-ish

When we're triggered, our nervous system often overrides our thinking brain. Our amygdala lights up, throwing us into fight-or-flight mode, the kind that has us snapping, storming out, or sending the text we regret five minutes later. But peace isn't found in the impulse. It's found in the pause. This is where practice lives: in the breath between feeling and doing. In the moment when your heart's pounding and you *still* say to yourself, *Pause. Breathe. Think. Choose.*

Calm is not passive. It's a powerful, intentional decision—a commitment to consciousness. And, yes, it takes practice. Repeated, messy, imperfect practice.

So next time something sets you off, do a quick scan:

- Where is your body holding tension?
- Are your thoughts inflaming the fire or cooling it down?
- Can you feel your breath?

If not, slow it down. Breathe in for four, hold for four, breathe out for four. Give your brain a moment to pivot from reaction to response.

This is the spiritual muscle you're building: the one that lets you pause long enough to be proud of what you do next.

Let's talk about something we all feel but don't always name: the internal sense of overload that builds when your nervous system is overworked. You know the feeling: Your heart's racing, your chest is tight, your thoughts are spiraling. The noise outside (and inside) is loud. Maybe it's constant notifications, an endless to-do list, family tension, world events, or simply the exhaustion of doing things for everyone else.

Your nervous system is not your enemy; it's your messenger. It's the sacred part of you saying, "I need a moment." When your nervous system is overwhelmed by worry, stress, or outside forces, the path back to peace isn't to ignore it. The path is to respond with care.

One of the principles of practicing peace is learning to remain calm long enough to make a conscious choice about how to respond. When we are stressed or something is challenging our ability to think clearly, we become reactive, speaking without thinking or behaving impulsively. Whether in the midst of a traumatic event or managing the stress of daily living, patience is a vital tool in remaining peaceful and engaging in any situation by making conscious choices about what to do and say.

According to Daniel Siegel, author of *The Developing Mind*, the part of the brain that is activated is our amygdala, which immediately begins assessing our risk based on our fight-or-flight response mechanism. We are in protective mode when we feel overly anxious, which causes us to react from fear. If we take a pause and choose rationally to focus on what and why we want to respond to a situation, then we activate the prefrontal cortex, the part of our brain that allows us to reason, be empathic, and consciously choose our response.

Practice these steps:

Next time something occurs that leaves you unsettled, disgruntled, disappointed, or genuinely upset: *STOP!*

Allow your body to show you where you are holding the tension and consider your thoughts. Are they holding space for peaceful, compromising dialogue? Take a deep breath. Breathe in through your nose and hold it for four seconds, then breathe out for four seconds through your mouth. Keep repeating this breath work until your body naturally slows long enough for you to make a conscious choice in a state of calm. Ask yourself what you are feeling and how those emotions are leading your behavior.

Believe it or not, all of this can be done in fewer than thirty seconds, the time it takes for your brain to pivot from reactive to responsive mode.

By taking these steps, start committing to a different and more peaceful way of communicating. Teach others that anytime they find themselves experiencing a stressful moment, when something isn't happening the way they want it to: Stop, breathe, think, and respond.

**We believe that you can do five key things
when you feel agitated or out of control.**

1. **Pause and Breathe**

   It sounds simple, but it's profound. One intentional breath—in through your nose, out through your mouth—can begin to reset your entire system. Say to yourself: *This breath is enough. This moment is mine.*

2. **Remove or Reduce Stimulation**

   Turn off the phone. Dim the lights. Step away from the noise, physically or emotionally. Give yourself permission to unplug and power down, even if it's only for five minutes.

3. **Ground in the Present**

Place your feet flat on the floor. Feel the chair beneath you. Hold something soft or textured. Use your senses to bring your awareness back into your body. Peace lives in presence.

4. **Name What You're Feeling**

"I'm overstimulated." "I feel unsafe." "I'm holding too much." Naming your feeling gives you space from it. The feeling moves from your nervous system into your conscious awareness, where healing begins.

5. **Flip the Script**

Use the Gratitude Flip. Ask, What am I grateful for right now? Even in chaos, there's something. It might be as small as warm socks or a moment of quiet. That tiny flip is the beginning of calm.

PEACE POINT 24: Recover

You lost it. You yelled. You cried. Maybe you slammed a door or rage-cleaned the entire kitchen. Good. Now what?

This is where the practice begins—not in never losing your peace, but in how *quickly and kindly* you come back to it. Returning to center doesn't mean pretending that the blowup didn't happen. It means *not letting the blowup become your identity*. It means recognizing the rupture, and then choosing repair—with yourself, others, and your environment.

Sometimes you come back through breath. Sometimes you come back through apology. Sometimes it's a walk, a cup of coffee, a cry in the shower, or just five quiet minutes with your phone off and your soul on.

Whatever it takes, come back, because in this moment you redefine peace—not as a flawless performance, but as a sacred practice of coming home to yourself. Peace isn't lost forever when you lose it. It's waiting for you at the moment you're ready to return. Once we return to center, we're clearer. That clarity gives us the courage to connect—not with blame or assumptions, but with questions. And that's where the next peace point begins.

PEACE POINT 25: Ask, Don't Assume

Every angry statement you replace with a question is a step toward peace. Assumptions are shortcuts, and like some shortcuts, they can take us the wrong way.

For example, online etiquette and peaceful exchanges online begin and end with commitments to support curiosity. When anger shows up online and starts to escalate, that's a signal to pause, regulate, and express it more constructively.

Dr. Katie saw a fitting example of this the other day. After an unfortunate and extremely controversial incident, many people posted comments and images of support for one side of the issue. Someone who had a differing opinion, a less popular one, posted a question: "Can someone please explain to me what all these posts are saying? Why do you believe this perspective? What is your reason for holding this belief?"

Dr. Katie thanked her for the courage to speak out with curiosity, and what ensued was a flood of very kind, respectful, and thoughtful answers. Everyone on that thread walked away knowing more and connecting more authentically because someone asked a question: Why?

Dr. Katie had another experience with this type of curious approach. Someone she was speaking with professionally made disparaging remarks about several groups of people. This person seemed to be compassionate and kind, so these words didn't fit with Dr. Katie's impression of her. Dr. Katie had an instinct that this person was reacting to being told what she should believe versus being allowed a safe space to express her own opinion. By applying the principle of practicing peace, Dr. Katie asked a probing question to test out her theory. Sure enough, much of this woman's anger had nothing to do with her compassion as a person; rather, it was about not feeling heard, not having a voice, being forced to hide her perspective, and feeling like she didn't fit in.

Fortunately, the woman realized she didn't want to inflict harm on anyone. Rather, she was allowing her anger about being silenced to fuel her hate speech. In this situation, after only twenty minutes, a beautiful, supportive human appeared with greater compassion and understanding because of a peaceful curiosity.

PEACE POINT 26: Be Curious

Whenever there is an opportunity to practice peace, we encourage you to ask probing questions about why someone holds a belief and then open-heartedly listen to their response. Show a genuine desire to understand them and leave them feeling heard. Then you will have made an empathic connection, which is the foundation of a peaceful exchange.

When we assume, we act on incomplete stories. We fill in blanks with fear, judgment, and old wounds. We hear a tone and assume intent. We witness a reaction and assign motive. And just like that, we go from connection to conflict without ever stopping to ask:

"What's really going on here?"

"What did you mean by that?"

"Can you help me understand where you're coming from?"

"What do you need right now that would help?"

When we ask instead of assume, we open up a *we space*. And in that space, something powerful happens: Understanding becomes possible. Peace becomes possible.

In relationships, assumptions often stem from past pain. We assume someone will hurt us because another person did. We assume we're being left out, dismissed, misunderstood. But peace doesn't grow in a garden of assumptions. It grows in the sunlight of shared truth.

Asking also helps us find the bridge point of compromise. When you say, "What do you need?" and "Here's what I need," you create the possibility of a shared solution. Compromise is not about giving in; it's about meeting in the middle without losing who you are.

The next time you feel yourself slipping into assumptions, take a breath and choose a question instead.

Choose curiosity.

Choose courage.

Choose connection.

Because peaceful communication doesn't begin with knowing. It begins with *asking*.

PEACE POINT 27: Believe in Global Peace

How do you reconcile all the unrest—unpeaceful people, war, politics, neighbors fighting, divorces, family breakdowns, and the daily hustle—with actual peace? The turmoil just seems endless and, quite frankly, exhausting. Our twenty-somethings understandably feel maxed out by it all.

Elizabeth's husband openly shares that he lost quite a bit of faith in God when the kids were struck down at Newtown. As we were writing this peace point, Elizabeth mentioned this to Dr. Katie, and her response was, "My perception of God had to change in order for me to support people dealing with tragedy like Newtown." Dr. Katie and her husband, John, who are both psychotherapists, believe God does not cause cruelty; humans do, and God is there within each one of us to help us heal. God is the human capacity for love and compassion that lies within all of us. This belief helps them help others.

This is one of the most important and honest questions we can all ask at this moment, and asking it means you're in it. Practice living peacefully. Don't just talk about it.

What do you need to do to feel that you are doing all you can to promote peace?

- Do you need to calm down and find a way to protest peacefully?
- Do you need to engage in a letter-writing campaign with peaceful language that allows your anger and rage to provide motivation for your right action?
- Are you someone who is less driven to public action and better at individualized tasks that allow you to make a difference quietly?

Peace isn't the denial of what's wrong. It's the decision to stay rooted in what's right.

Don't reconcile the unrest by pretending it's not there. Reconcile it by being willing to live as a counterpoint to it in your own way.

PEACE POINT 28: Discover Your Peace Perspective

Your peace perspective is the lens through which you understand and approach your peace practice. It asks that you deal with your unfinished business, emotional issues, and pain patterns.

If you don't deal with your pain, your patterns, and your past, you will pass that pain onto others—not because you're a bad person, but because you're human. We carry unresolved pain until we consciously choose to identify it, understand how it impacts our behaviors, and gently begin to shift.

When we deal with our own stuff, we stop making it somebody else's problem. We stop blaming and shaming. When we heal, even a little, we pass on peace instead of pain. We can't truly practice peace if we don't recognize this part of ourselves. We are messy, magical, wounded, extraordinary beings, and peace invites all of that to the table.

We also know that some pain runs deep. If you've experienced trauma, loss, or overwhelming grief, this peace point may feel heavier. Your healing will look different at different times in your life. Practicing peace may simply mean making one gentle choice that gets you out of bed. It may mean giving yourself permission to just *be* without the pressure to perform. Peace is not one-size-fits-all. Your beliefs, your lived experience, your history, and your capacity in this moment shape how peace shows up for you.

PEACE POINT 29: Use This Formula for Peace

Peace = (Presence + Compassion + Connection) × Action
Let's break that down:

● Presence

"Peace begins with awareness."

We can't create peace if we're distracted, disconnected, or reactive. Being fully present—with ourselves and others—is the gateway. Presence allows us to observe without judgment and to respond with wisdom.

Compassion

"Compassion is the heartbeat of peace."

Compassion shifts us from ego to empathy, from judgment to understanding. It's the emotional foundation of peaceful thoughts, words, and actions.

Connection

"There's a light in you that burns in me."

Peace is not a solo endeavor. It's rooted in relationship—to self, to others, to the Earth. When we see ourselves as interconnected, we become more invested in protecting one another's dignity.

Action

"Peace isn't passive—it's a practice."

The multiplier. Without action, presence, compassion, and connection remain ideas. Action means living peacefully out loud. Listening instead of judging. Helping when it's easier to walk away. Voting. Speaking up. Hugging. Showing up.

●●●

Our Pathways to Peace with Elizabeth and Dr. Katie

Elizabeth—Practicing Peace in a Quieter Nest

Being married for over twenty-seven years while raising four boys taught me that if peace is a practice, we've had plenty of opportunities to master it.

Peace is an art form when raising four boys. Each stage presented new challenges, from toddler tantrums to teenage debates about why cereal counts as dinner. Our house sounded like a football stadium on game day: shouts, laughter, and the occasional thud of someone testing gravity.

We learned that peace sometimes means embracing chaos, knowing someday we'd miss the noise. Now, as they have finished their master's degrees and launched, the house is noticeably quieter. The dogs still bark at nothing. The cats maintain their usual mild disapproval. But the boy-induced decibel level has decreased significantly.

Peace didn't come in the form of silence. It came in learning when to step in and when to let things be. It was accepting that bedtime never actually meant bedtime and that cereal for dinner was perfectly acceptable on game nights.

They each made one last loop back home before fully launching, filling the house with energy, big ideas, and an endless supply of protein powder. Practicing peace in this phase means embracing the beautiful unpredictability. My peaceful morning coffee always includes a cat knocking something off the counter or a dog staring into my soul, hoping for a bite of my breakfast.

That's the thing about peace. It's not about perfection. It's about finding humor in the imperfections, grace in the awkward moments, and understanding that life is messy, unpredictable, and more fun when you learn to go with it.

Peaceful living allows for grace and space, giving one another time to unwind or recognizing when someone needs the last piece of cake more than you do (even if you really wanted it). Peace is compromise, love, and choices.

As we watch our boys fly while keeping the nest warm, we know that practicing peace isn't about reaching some final destination. It's about continuing to choose joy, laughter, and patience, no matter what life throws our way.

Here's to twenty-seven-plus years of marriage, four incredible sons, and a lifetime of choosing peace—one chaotic, hilarious, love-filled moment at a time.

Dr. Katie—Compromise

One of the most crucial areas of life is practicing peace in our closest relationships: our family. Having been married for over twenty-five years and raising a twenty-two-year-old daughter, I have had plenty of practice!

This is what worked for us.

My husband and I are counselors, so we started with honesty and transparency as the foundation for our relationship. That meant we had to work through challenging moments about who liked what and how to manage our household. Peaceful compromise became essential when it was clear early on that we had different ways of doing things: One of us liked to hang towels one way, the other differently; one of us preferred mayonnaise while the other chose Miracle Whip; and one of us brought three cats into a tiny apartment. Challenges ensued. Like everyone, we had to figure out the fine art of peaceful compromise.

When you first start, the solutions are simple—adding extra bathroom hooks and buying both condiments. But over the years, challenges become more significant, sometimes resulting in voices rising to the point that the cats scatter. We all have trigger issues where compromise is toughest. Those complex exchanges are vital to a peaceful home—the "I want this, and you need this, so what's the middle choice?" conversations. When I work with couples, I always explain that we all have needs and wants. Needs are vital to our well-being while wants are negotiable. My husband I learned early on to hash everything out until we found a compromise. Sometimes the cats leave for a while, but eventually there's a calm, peaceful resolution.

We have a helpful metaphor to describe any partnering relationship: It's like a bridge, and every time a conflict goes unresolved, it puts weight on the bridge. If one of us holds onto an issue, that adds weight. If we allow that weight to build, the bridge eventually collapses, so we consciously try to keep the weight off. That is how we practice peace as a couple.

As parents, we taught our daughter the same peace principles, though it was more challenging when she was going through hormonal hell. It required us to gently remind her to pause and take a break, and when she was able to have a peaceful, calm dialogue with us, we figured out the compromises.

Well past this stage now at twenty-two, she tells us she knows how to manage compromise and engage in honest, calm dialogue in her relationships. That's the best feeling as a parent.

We always need to keep trying—and yes, if we argue, the cats still fly out of the room when we lose it, but we keep practicing. Peace in our home is a priority, and we work at it constantly. We have images with the word *Peace* throughout our home as reminders of what we value and how we commit to live. Living peacefully isn't easy because it requires practice, but it's worth it—and the cats genuinely appreciate it.

Peace isn't just a lofty concept reserved for sacred places and times. It's something we live, wrestle with, and rediscover in the quiet moments when no one's watching, and in the loud, life-altering seasons when everything breaks open. The stories that follow are not just stories of survival, they are stories of awakening. They show us that peace is not perfection. It's a choice to come home to ourselves, again and again, with more truth, more clarity, and more compassion.

Jennifer and Chad take us into the raw, unfiltered terrain of midlife transformation—the painful unraveling of roles and relationships, and the courageous rebuilding of self-trust and self-worth. Their honesty gives us permission to be human, to name what hurts, to release what no longer fits—and most of all, to believe that peace is possible, even after we've lost ourselves. Especially then.

These are not just stories of healing. They are proof that the most powerful kind of peace is the one we create from within.

Stories from the Heart

Jennifer Drews—Finding Peace at Fifty: From People-Pleasing to Powerfully Me

I've been chasing peace my entire life.

I don't just mean the kind of peace that shows up on meditation apps or Hallmark cards. I mean real peace, the kind that anchors your soul when the world feels chaotic. The kind that lives inside your bones. I didn't find it until I turned fifty. And when I did, it was like a switch flipped in my brain.

From the time I was a little girl, I was a people-pleaser. I wore different versions of myself like outfits, trying to be who I thought others wanted me to be. If someone was funny, I cracked jokes. If someone was cool, I mirrored their tone. I thought maybe if I dressed like the popular girls, I'd become one of them. Spoiler alert: I didn't. I always felt like I was on the outside looking in.

I wish I had known then what I know now about self-worth and mindset.

As I grew older, I kept trying to fill that inner void. I followed the expected path: college, job, marriage. I fell for the first guy who showed me attention. Deep down I knew there were red flags, but I ignored them. I thought if I just molded myself into what he wanted, he would love me. I lost more and more of myself with each passing year.

I remember one pivotal moment vividly. Early in our marriage, I asked my husband to do a couple's journal with me. When I asked, "What's one word you would use to describe me?" he looked at me and said a word no woman wants to hear from someone she loves. He called me a bitch. At that moment, so many emotions went through me, from shock and anger to disappointment. And still—I stayed. That's how desperate I was to be loved. To feel safe. To find peace, even if it meant walking on eggshells.

Twelve years of marriage to a narcissist took a toll. I tried leaving him twice, but he convinced me to stay. Eventually, he filed for divorce—and it was like someone lifted a thousand-pound weight off my shoulders. The pain was deep, but so was the relief. Even so, I was extremely broken. While waiting for the divorce to finalize, I cried more in those seven months than I did in the twelve years we were married. I cried for letting myself be so weak, for the woman I wish I was, for the failed relationship, and for wanting to be loved.

That's when my real healing began. It took over seven years to work through the pain and learn that being in a relationship didn't define who I am. My personality, my character, and how I make others feel are what define me.

At a key point in my career and personal success, just as I was finally starting to feel some peace again, I became a victim of cyberbullying. A group of people I thought were my friends turned against me out of jealousy. One created a group message just to attack my character. My body shook with disbelief and shock over the betrayal. Then I began receiving anonymous messages—bullying, threatening, cruel. I didn't know who was behind it at the time, but the cyberbullying cut deep. I was left feeling worthless and alone.

One Labor Day weekend, I sat in my condominium, feeling depressed and having little purpose in life, when I made a decision: I was done feeling powerless. I was ready to take my life back.

So I googled, "How to find purpose." "How to find peace." "How to overcome depression." I also started journaling on a regular basis about my feelings and what I was going through. It was extremely therapeutic.

I threw myself into self-development and enrolled in a coaching certification program through Best Ever You. I knew I was not the only woman to be going through COVID depression and feeling like life had no purpose. As I became stronger, I started sharing my journey in a Facebook group I created, the Love Your Life Tribe, specifically for women who are struggling with similar issues. My message: You can bloom into your true self no matter how murky the waters of your life have been. That message was me. I was the lotus, rising from mud.

But even with all the tools and personal growth, old thoughts still crept in.

Am I good enough? Will people follow me? What if I fail?

Another turning point came as I approached a milestone birthday in 2024: my fiftieth. I asked myself, *What would I love?* And the answer surprised me: To live life on my terms. That meant letting go of roles that drained me.

To celebrate I looked inside and asked, *What would I love?* The answer came back: to go on a vacation somewhere special. That meant booking my first real vacation in twenty-three years—a solo vacation cruise to the Mexican Riviera. As I walked on the ship, I was almost in tears—not sad tears, but happy tears. I was doing something so out-of-the-box for myself that I felt strong and free. No one on that ship knew me. I could just be Jen. Not Jen the achiever, not Jen the people-pleaser. Just me. And for the first time in decades, I realized I really liked her. And so did the new friends I made on that trip. It felt so free to feel at peace with myself.

When I got home, I started making even more serious changes. If something wasn't a yes, it became a no. I started questioning the nonprofits I was volunteering for and whether they aligned with my values. I released relationships where I couldn't be my authentic self. I stopped explaining my choices. I gave myself permission to live freely and unapologetically.

Then menopause hit.

Like so many women, I didn't see it coming. My weight crept up. Anxiety and depression returned. I felt exhausted but couldn't sleep through the night. I stopped going to the gym. I stopped wanting to socialize. I felt like a stranger in my own body.

And I didn't tell anyone.

But I knew I couldn't stay quiet anymore. After one particularly stressful episode that left me burned out and snippy at work, I realized it was time to prioritize my health. I scheduled blood work with a holistic women's health nurse practitioner. The results were shocking: hormonal imbalance, hypothyroidism, iron deficiency, even stage 2 chronic kidney disease from stress.

That was my wake-up call.

I started supplements. I cleaned up my calendar. I stepped down from a leadership role in one of three nonprofits I was part of, even though I had six months left on my term. And for the first time in a long time, I put my peace over my people-pleasing and felt like another weight had been lifted.

Two weeks into this new routine, something changed. I felt stronger. Lighter. More like me. I was the Energizer bunny, bouncing off the walls.

I went back to the gym. I started fitting into the clothes that used to make me cry. Being able to shop in my own closet became fun again. I finally made time for the things I love. I even became—wait for it—a mall walker. Every Sunday morning, I walk with my girlfriends through the mall in Scottsdale. It's our own girls club where the only boys allowed are ones with four legs. We talk, laugh, and celebrate being women in our fifties. Unapologetic. Alive. At peace.

And I've kept asking myself the same question: *What would I love?*

I continue journaling every day, and now instead of writing down my past feelings and how everything is wrong, I write about the future I want to live. I reflect on what's working and what needs to shift. I use sound meditations. I read my vision statement aloud. I've learned that peace isn't a destination, it's a practice. A choice. A series of small, powerful steps back to yourself.

At fifty-one, I am finally at peace with who I am. Not because everything is perfect—but because I've decided I don't have to prove anything to anyone anymore.

I am strong. I am whole. I am healing.

And most importantly, I am me.

Chad Stillwagon—Journey to Finding Peace

I've been struggling to find inner peace for most of my life. It hasn't always been a conscious struggle, more of a quiet awareness that something felt off. Even as a child, I sensed that something inside me was missing. That feeling never had a name. It wasn't depression or anxiety, although it sometimes resembled both. For the most part, I've been a happy, positive person with a zest for life. I have all the things that one would generally attribute to happiness: family, friends, career, pastimes, and a comfortable living. I have many, many things to be grateful for—yet that deep, unsettled feeling remained . . . until recently.

I'm the proud father of three phenomenal young adults, a well-respected pharmacist in my community, a U.S. Army veteran, and a fortunate colon cancer survivor. By all accounts, I've lived a very good life so far. Despite all of those blessings, however, something within me still felt incomplete.

I began to truly examine where that lack of peace might be coming from when I went through a serious health crisis. While battling colon cancer, my treatments led me to a number of serious complications. A surgical error left me with a leak in my colon and a long string of setbacks: bowel obstructions, infections, sepsis, nine surgeries, feeding tubes, catheters, drains—you name it. At one point, I had lost over fifty pounds, and I wasn't sure if I was going to survive.

Eventually I did recover, and remarkably I've returned to living a fairly normal life. After all of that, my outlook on life shifted dramatically. I felt more grateful than ever. Every small moment seemed bigger. Every ordinary day felt like a gift. But still—despite everything I had survived—I noticed that the lingering sadness hadn't gone away.

That's when I realized something important: Joy and gratitude are not the same as peace. I had plenty of reasons to be joyful. I was truly grateful for my life. But I still wasn't at peace.

I started digging. I dug deep. I reflected on every aspect of my life. I had to understand what had led me to live so long with that unsettled feeling. That meant going back to my childhood, looking at who I was before everything else was added.

Growing up as an only child, I was shy and often unsure of myself. I didn't push myself academically, afraid if I tried something too hard that I might fail. I was involved in bowling and martial arts—nontraditional sports—which I loved and excelled at, but they didn't exactly connect me to the larger social scene at school. That added to the feeling of being different, and it fueled my insecurity.

I remember wanting so badly to drive my dad's 1969 Corvette Stingray in high school. One day, he told me I could—if I got straight A's. Something finally clicked in me, and I rose to the challenge! This success instantly changed the way I saw myself. Encouraged by that momentum, I joined the army, where I found my calling. I became a combat medic and a pharmacy technician, graduating near the top of my class. I went on to pharmacy school, where I also excelled. Very early on as a pharmacist, I was promoted to pharmacy manager, which is where I've been for the majority of my thirty-year career. In my earliest years of practice, I developed a deep passion for helping others. I loved what I was doing, and my confidence soared.

But even as I thrived in school and in my career, I continued to make decisions in my marriage from a place of insecurity. I didn't always listen to my gut. I often prioritized comfort over connection and feared being alone more than I feared being unfulfilled. I told myself that if I worked hard enough, things would improve on their own. But that's not how peace works. You can't force peace. You can only create space for it to grow.

Going through my medical crisis shifted everything. I had no choice but to pause. To heal. To reevaluate. That forced pause gave me a new perspective. I realized how many of my choices in life, particularly in my marriage, had been driven by fear, insecurity, and lack of confidence.

But the truth is, I had already been through the hardest thing imaginable. I had looked death in the eye and come out on the other side. So why was I still afraid to live fully?

That realization changed me. I started standing taller. I began honoring my needs and my voice. I became more decisive. I stopped waiting for permission to choose joy. I began to trust myself—not just professionally, but personally. I stopped settling.

After years of reflection and personal growth, I finally came to the decision to end my marriage. It was not a decision made lightly or with resentment, but one rooted in the understanding that we had grown in different directions and that peace, for both of us, required change. Letting go was an act of compassion—for myself and for the life we had built together. It was time to step into a new chapter with clarity and the hope of finding a deeper alignment with who I've become.

The most important discovery came when I finally understood why I had spent so many years feeling incomplete. It had nothing to do with anyone else. It had everything to do with me. It basically all stemmed from a lack of confidence. I had carried a quiet belief from my childhood that I wasn't quite good enough, smart enough, social enough, or athletic enough. I felt that no matter how well I was doing in life, I still needed a confidence crutch. In my mind I needed someone to lean on. I didn't have the belief that I could handle life all by myself. I was basically scared of being alone. That belief led me to minimize myself, to prioritize other people's needs above my own, and to confuse loyalty with self-sacrifice.

But not anymore.

I've done the work. I've looked back, I've asked the hard questions, and I've stopped making fear-based decisions. I've also stopped resenting the past. Every step I've taken, every hardship I've endured, brought me here—to this new chapter.

Would I love to find a deep, lasting connection with someone? Of course. But for the first time in my life, I don't need it to feel whole. Peace is no longer something I'm chasing. It's something I've created—through clarity, courage, and self-trust.

I now understand that peace isn't about avoiding loneliness or fixing the past. It's about choosing, every day, to live with intention. To wake up knowing that I no longer settle. That I no longer carry the weight of not feeling good enough. That I no longer wait for life to feel better. I go out and live it.

This journey has changed me. It's taught me that peace doesn't come from comfort zones or survival mode. It comes from honoring yourself fully, forgiving yourself honestly, and walking forward with hope, even when the path is uncertain.

Peace is here now, and I choose it every single day.

POINTS TO PONDER

Think. Write. Talk. Action. *(Because practice makes us our best.)*

EXERCISE 7: Re-Create Your Peace

OBJECTIVE: To identify where peace actually exists in your real life—not with unrealistic expectations but that one magical moment where no one was yelling and the Wi-Fi worked.

INSTRUCTIONS: Think about a moment when you actually felt peaceful. It doesn't have to be dramatic. It could be three minutes of alone time in your car, or when everyone left you alone for five blessed minutes.

Describe the situation. What were you doing? What *wasn't* happening?

_____

_____

Why did this feel peaceful to you? Environment, emotions, silence, control?

_____

_____

How did your body feel? What did peace feel like physically?

_____

_____

Could you re-create a version of this today? Even just a sliver of it?

_____

_____

What's one small way you can invite that kind of peace again this week?

_____

_____

EXERCISE 8: Chaos Check-In—The Peace Reset

OBJECTIVE: To practice responding consciously (not reactively) in real-life stress situations by breaking the autopilot cycle.

INSTRUCTIONS: You're not expected to be Zen-like when everything's on fire. This is about not becoming the fire.

What was your last "tsunami moment"? (A minor or major chaos—describe it.)

_____

_____

What story were you telling yourself in that moment?

_____

_____

How did your body respond to the stress? (Tense jaw? Racing heart?)

_____

_____

Now reframe. If you could rewind and take a thirty-second reset, what would you do differently?

_____

_____

What's your personal peace strategy for next time? (Breath work? Mantra? Escape to the laundry room?)

_____

_____

● Bonus Reflection: Own Your Shift

Each week, check in with how you're *actually* doing—not just how you wish you were doing.

Where did you catch yourself reacting? Where did you pause, breathe, and respond? How can you practice peace more often—on purpose, not just by accident?

_____

_____

_____

_____

CHAPTER 5
PASSION

In the fifth principle of peace, Passion, we remain focused and committed to purposeful passion to make a difference and change not only our own life but also the lives of others. The power of transformative, compassionate change begins within us. It starts when we choose to re-create ourselves. As we become better, wiser, and kinder individuals with a greater ability to use our skills, gifts, and talents, we create a more compassionate world. This becomes the reason we get up in the morning and our why behind the choices we make daily.

The energy of passion is what makes the impossible possible. Peaceful power comes when peace and passion intertwine with authenticity.

We live our lives fueled by the energy of passion. There's not a day when either one of us doesn't make a decision, make a choice, or take an action energized by the emotional drive to make a difference. It's what gets us up in the morning and motivates us. Aside from writing books and managing our careers and families, and while weaving in our hobbies and other interests, we surround ourselves with visual reminders of peace.

For example, Dr. Katie's signature clothing item is her collection of bright-colored scarves, an uplifting reminder of what she values. Elizabeth finds peace in baking and donating thousands of chocolate chip cookies across the United States. Together, even though we live across the country from each other, we surround ourselves with shared, visual reminders of connection and joy. From bright flowers and holiday decorations to the colors turquoise and vibrant yellow, and the jewelry we've exchanged—including a heart-shaped necklace from Dr. Katie to Elizabeth as a reminder to Percolate Peace, and a butterfly bracelet from Elizabeth to Dr. Katie—each piece symbolizes our friendship and the spirit of peace we practice.

We are driven by passion. What does "driven by passion" look like?

We believe that the opposite of passion is complacency. When we are living peacefully, our values align with our actions, and we are naturally drawn to create change in ourselves and the world around us. We generate peace from the power of our passion, especially the kind we would pursue even if no one applauded, noticed, or paid us for it. That's how we know it's real.

Passion is one of the most misunderstood forces in life. It's not just ambition or excitement. It's the deep inner fire that stirs your soul and fuels your purpose, yet it's often met with resistance—not only from others, but also from the parts of ourselves that fear being seen or judged. But true passion doesn't need permission. It burns anyway. Quietly, steadily, relentlessly. And when that fire is rooted in peace, it becomes unstoppable.

PEACE POINT 30: Tune In Across Four Levels

The messages that alert us to our passions don't always come as lightning bolts. More often, they arrive quietly, through our bodies, emotions, thoughts, and spirit. We've come to understand that these messages live within us all the time. We just need to slow down enough to notice.

- Physically, passion can feel like energy rising—a flutter in the chest, a sense of warmth, or a quickened pulse when something feels aligned. At other times, it may show up as discomfort or restlessness in the body when we've drifted away from what truly matters. Emotionally, passion can surface as longing, awe, or even frustration, especially when the life we're living doesn't fully match who we are.

- Mentally, passion-related messages show up as thoughts or ideas that we can't shake. That recurring vision or dream? That's not a distraction; it's direction. We may find ourselves revisiting possibilities, imagining scenarios that stir excitement or clarity.

- Spiritually, there's a sense of quiet knowing. A call that rises from within. A voice—not always loud, but persistent—that reminds us we are here for something more. Passion lives there. It's not about chasing something outside us. It's about listening to what's already speaking inside.

When we tune in across all four levels—body, heart, mind, and spirit—we begin to hear the truth of who we are and what we're meant to bring into the world. That's where passion in action lives. That's where change begins. Sometimes, even the most profound transformations start with a simple gesture.

Mother Teresa reminded us, "Peace begins with a smile." She spoke often about peace, always linking it to love, service, and the inherent dignity of every person. In her 1979 Nobel Peace Prize lecture in Oslo, she said, "Let us always meet each other with a smile, for the smile is the beginning of love." This simple yet powerful truth captures her belief that peace starts within each individual and is expressed through the smallest acts of kindness—beginning with something as universal and human as a smile.

In *The Success Guidebook*, Elizabeth introduced us to Vincent Chapman, better known to millions as "The Dancing Ump" of the Savannah Bananas. His behind-the-plate antics make Vincent's story the perfect example of passion in action and how something joyful, playful, and seemingly small can create lasting peace and purpose.

"In 2008, working as an umpire, parents started bringing ice chests with built-in speakers to games," Vincent told us. "Between innings, I started dancing. It made the kids laugh. I just kept going."

If you have children in sports, you know that the games can be unnecessarily tense. While competition is natural, Vincent wanted to use his smile to lighten the mood and help everyone remember that baseball is still just a game and that kids just want to have fun. His dance moves brought joy to the field, lifted spirits, and created a unique bond with the kids and families in the stands. He quickly became known for his high-energy antics and infectious smile.

"When I heard about the Savannah Bananas' philosophy, I knew I wanted to be part of it," Vincent said. "Now I get to entertain and umpire in front of millions of fans. It's unbelievable that something I started doing nearly fifteen years ago just to help kids have more fun, I now get to do on a global stage."

Vincent's passion is more than a performance. It's peace in motion—joy personified. He reminds us that peace doesn't always look like stillness or silence. It can be movement, rhythm, laughter, and connection.

Later in this chapter, Savannah Bananas pitcher Andy Archer also joins us to share his personal journey with passion, peace, and perseverance—on and off the mound. Like Vincent, Andy shows us that peace can be practiced not just in quiet moments but in high-stakes situations, during fast-paced decisions, and in how we choose to show up every single day. His presence and mindset are a reminder that inner calm and outer performance aren't mutually exclusive; they're deeply connected.

PEACE POINT 31: Rise Above

Passion, pain, and joy are not separate experiences. They are often threads of the same tapestry. In our work and in our personal lives, we've learned that passion doesn't just come from what excites us; it often rises from what breaks us open.

Passion is the force that moves us toward what matters most. It's not always loud or fiery. Sometimes it begins as a quiet longing, a deep pull toward something meaningful. But the closer we get to it, the more it brushes up against our tenderness, fears, old wounds, and insecurities.

That's where pain enters. Not to stop us, but to refine us. Pain often reveals where we've been disconnected from ourselves. It shows us what we've outgrown and where we've settled for less. It asks us to feel deeply—not just to hurt, but to heal. Pursuing what we love often stirs grief for what we never had, or what we had to lose in order to grow. That's part of the process.

Then there's joy—not the fleeting kind, but the deep, soul-level joy that comes when we are fully aligned with our purpose. Joy often shows up not because everything is perfect, but because we are living from a place of truth. Passion leads us there, not by bypassing pain, but by walking through it with intention and courage.

When people ask us how to find their passion, we often say, "Start where your heart hurts, where your longing lives, and where your hope still flickers." There, in that sacred space, is where passion meets purpose. And in that place, pain becomes wisdom and joy becomes possible.

PEACE POINT 32: Begin Where Your Heart Hurts

We often think the biggest obstacles to pursuing our passions are external things such as time, money, and opportunity. But in our work, we've found that the real barriers usually live inside us. They're woven into our self-concept, shaped by past experiences, old narratives, and the deep-rooted fear of not being enough. Sometimes it's the quiet voice of self-doubt that whispers, *Who am I to do this?* Or the outdated internal message that says, *People like me don't get to live that kind of life.* These beliefs don't just appear out of nowhere. They are learned, inherited, or absorbed from environments that didn't see or support our potential.

Elizabeth here: When starting Best Ever You back in 2007, I registered the domain BestEverYou.com. Within a few days, a man called who said he owned all the domains that started with "Best" and that I needed to turn over my domain and ideas to him. I remember holding the phone away from my ear and cringing as he was talking. When I said, "No," he started yelling at me and called me a "forty-something washed-up soccer mom who would never amount to anything!" My response was, "Dude, my kids don't even play soccer."

I hung up the phone, caught my breath, composed myself, then went on GoDaddy and registered the domain BestEverYou.com for an extra thirty years. Fervor and devotion for the mission empowered me in that moment.

If I had given in to any insecure thoughts during this event, there may never have been Best Ever You and everything that followed. I made a conscious choice, despite triggered self-doubt, to rise up, face my fears, and let passion win.

Insecurity isn't a flaw; it's a signal. It points to the places where we long to grow but haven't yet given ourselves permission to do so. It's the bruise around a deeper truth: We want more, we're capable of more, but we fear what stepping into that truth might cost us.

Yet here's what we know: Our passion doesn't wait for us to feel ready. It waits for us to say yes, even when we're scared. The path to passion always asks us to meet ourselves with tenderness and courage, to question the old labels, to release what's been projected onto us, and to reclaim what we know, deep down, is possible. That's the real work, not pushing harder but softening toward what's true. Chances are that someone needs you, and by being available to them, you are contributing to a more peaceful world.

PEACE POINT 33: Hold Your Peace Power

Think about the last time you felt truly passionate about something. Not just mildly interested, not just intrigued, but deeply, undeniably, set-your-soul-on-fire passionate. Maybe it was a dream you couldn't shake, a cause that attracted you, or a vision that seemed to appear fully formed in your mind—that moment when inspiration hit, when you felt, *This is it, this is what I'm meant to do!*

Dr. Katie here: I attended Boston University seminary, and my desk in the library overlooked Fenway Park. At any given time on my desk, there were always books about loss, grief, and death, giving me the appropriate nickname of "Dr. Death," courtesy of my seminary colleagues. Imagine this

Debbie Downer persona being assigned to my passion for helping people grow from grief! Actually, I'm a very upbeat, colorful, creative, and fun person. One of the reasons for my positivity is that I am able to lift people up from the most unimaginable pain to experience a meaningful, purposeful life. That passion gives me great joy. It isn't necessary to reconcile the two.

That kind of passion is rare, precious, and powerful, yet it's often the very thing people try to talk us out of. Our peace power can often be the target of other people's attempts to sabotage our peace. I did not let them. I laughed it off and didn't let that title stick and instead enjoyed my perch over the Red Sox stadium.

The second you announce your passion to the world, the world may start testing you. People may doubt or question you. Some will roll their eyes. Others will tell you all the reasons it won't work or why you're not the right person for it. We have been on the receiving end of all these doubts, and you may have as well—phrases such as

- That's a nice idea, but how will you make money?
- Are you sure you're qualified for that?
- That's been done before.
- You should focus on something more practical.
- What if you fail?

Why do people say these negative things when you don't solicit their advice? Some do it out of jealousy, because your passion reminds them of their inability to believe wholeheartedly in the possibility of positive change. Some do it out of fear, because they project their own insecurities onto you. And some genuinely believe they're helping, because they think that "being realistic" is the kindest thing they can offer you.

Remember, no one else has to understand your passion for it to be valid. No one else must see your vision for it to be real. People always have opinions. They're entitled to their thoughts, just as you're entitled to ignore them. Your passion doesn't belong to them. It belongs to *you*.

Sometimes, however, your biggest naysayer is internal. Self-doubt is a sneaky thing. It disguises itself as logic, being responsible, or playing it safe. It whispers all the same things the external naysayers do:

- What if I fail?
- What if people judge me?
- What if I'm not good enough?

And before we know it, we've talked ourselves out of our own beliefs and efforts toward improving the world and generating peace.

You will be challenged. People will judge you. There will be moments of struggle, doubt, and uncertainty. That's part of the journey. But difficulty isn't the opposite of passion; it's proof that you're actually taking action. Effort counts.

And if you let it, all that external noise can drown out your inner voice, the voice that *knows* this passion was placed in you for a reason.

Many of us were also handed a list of "shoulds" that masquerade as wisdom but quietly limit our peace and potential. These are inherited rules we can lovingly retire, our "Thou Shall Nots":

- Thou shall not keep the peace at the expense of your own truth.
- Thou shall not measure your worth by productivity or perfection.
- Thou shall not stay small to avoid making others uncomfortable.
- Thou shall not confuse self-sacrifice with love.
- Thou shall not ignore your intuition just because someone older, louder, or "wiser" told you to.

Letting go of these learned shoulds isn't rebellion. It's healing. Each time you rewrite one, you reclaim a little more of your peace, your power, and your permission to live as your authentic self.

PEACE POINT 34: Follow Your Passion Path

One of the biggest obstacles to following our passion is the idea that we need permission or approval—that someone, somewhere, must validate our dream before we're allowed to pursue it. But that's not how passion works. Passion doesn't come with an application form or a permission slip.

Sometimes you have to temper it to accommodate rules, regulations, and laws, and sometimes you have to make up your own rules. Sometimes you color outside the lines. Doing what has never been done might require stepping outside current structures. Most people find themselves working with some version of both.

The world doesn't need more people to play it safe. Please don't be one of them! You may be denying the world of something that many people need. Peace and promoting peace require that all of us take time to discover something about which we can become passionate. What you do is not as important as that you commit to doing something to make the world better. Choose one passion and make it your focus.

Passion is what drives innovation and changes lives. Passion creates movements, builds businesses, writes books, paints artworks, discovers cures, and makes the impossible possible. As Apple founder Steve Jobs famously stated in his Stanford commencement address in June 2005, "The only way to do great work is to love what you do."

Imagine if every person who was passionate about something gave up the moment someone told them, "That won't work." Imagine if the Wright brothers had listened to the people who laughed at the idea of humans flying. Imagine if every musician, artist, author, or entrepreneur had let criticism stop them before they even began.

If you have a passion burning inside you, it's there for a reason. Your job isn't to seek permission. Your job is to honor it, nurture it, and protect it from the voices that try to extinguish it.

As parents, we have witnessed firsthand the dimming of our children's passions by critical adults who left them feeling like the walking wounded. If you read our other books, you'll find entire chapters written by our children about these adult dream crushers.

This can get complicated when that person is in a position of authority and has power over you, such as a teacher, family member, coach, or boss. It might be impossible or inadvisable to avoid them on your path to peaceful passion. Be very careful and teach your children to look out for these possibly well-meaning—but more often clueless—people who harm them by amplifying self-doubt, crushing dreams, and hampering passion rather than fostering peace.

PEACE POINT 35: Be a Passionate Parent to All Children, Including Your Inner Child

All it takes is one encounter with a significant adult to magnify your harboring doubts. Words and actions matter. Don't let anyone take away, diminish, undermine, or overpower any aspect of your or your children's hopes or confidence.

Have you ever wondered what kinds of coaching, teaching, and parenting truly support a child in developing their talents to their level of dreamed and perceived excellence? We believe there's a pivotal shift that happens when a child begins to think beyond the limitations of how they're *supposed* to live and starts to pursue what sets their soul on fire.

How does that shift happen? More importantly, how can you help make space for it?

As parents, we often feel boxed in—caught between our responsibility to teach our children the rules of right living and our desire to let them make independent choices that are meaningful and authentic to them. The way we were parented, and when and how we broke free from that dynamic, deeply influences the choices we make now—for ourselves and for our children.

We've all heard the stories—actors who moved to New York or Hollywood, athletes who trained in garages or on gravel, and people who followed their dreams despite impossible odds. What they had in common was that *they believed.* They focused their energy on fulfilling a dream and refused to be held back.

Yes, there's a place for rules and realism. But when you or your child feels that inner pull, that passionate drive, that undeniable call—you're tapping into something more powerful than limits.

PEACE POINT 36: Push Past the Doubt

Take time to reflect. What do you value? What strengths and gifts come naturally to you or your child? How might you apply those creatively to daily life? Just as an adolescent challenges their parent, we must challenge the internalized voices that hold us back. Ask yourself,

Who in my life makes me feel like I am stuck?

Another powerful step is to examine the quiet messages that creep into our thinking—those *yes, but . . . or I should . . .* thoughts that often stem from fear.

Instead, flip the narrative:

If I do this, I open the possibility for something meaningful to happen.

This simple shift invites imagination, growth, and alignment with *your* values—not someone else's.

It takes courage, trust, and community to live this way—outside the box. It's not easy to defy the fearful messages that surround us. But you do have the personal power to live—and parent—uniquely. Surround yourself with people who honor your willingness to challenge the status quo. That support is essential.

PEACE POINT 37: Trust Yourself

There's nothing quite as exhausting as the mental merry-go-round of second-guessing yourself. You take a step forward, then hesitate. For example, you start a project, then wonder if it's the right one, and then you might find yourself distracted or procrastinating. You get excited about an idea, only to overanalyze it until it crumbles under the weight of your own doubts. And just like that, you've turned your passion into a slow, painful game of what-ifs. Passion thrives on movement. Peace comes when you trust yourself enough to *go with it* instead of circling back a hundred times to question whether you should. Every time you hesitate, overanalyze, or seek excessive validation, you weaken your connection to your own intuition. Passion needs momentum, not hesitation.

So let's break the cycle:

- **Stop outsourcing your confidence.** You don't need fifteen opinions before making a move. If it feels right *to you*, that's enough.
- **Decide and don't look back.** Trust that the version of you *who made the decision* knew what they were doing. Don't undermine them.
- **Make for yourself a "no-going-back" rule.** Once you commit to a path, see it through before entertaining any creeping doubts.

Second-guessing is just fear wearing the disguise of logic. It tells you that if you analyze more, delay more, *think* more, you'll make the perfect choice. But perfection is a myth, and waiting for it will keep you stuck forever. Passionate people aren't the ones who never make mistakes; they're the ones who learn from them and keep moving forward.

So stop questioning yourself like you're on trial. Trust your passion. Own your choices. And most importantly: Keep going. Peace comes when you believe that no matter what happens, *you'll figure it out.*

PEACE POINT 38: Take the Risk

Your passion is worth the risk. One of the hardest things about following your passion is that it often means making changes—big ones. Maybe you must leave a job that no longer fulfills you. Maybe you have to set boundaries with people who don't support you. Maybe you have to carve out time in a schedule that already feels maxed out.

And sometimes that brings guilt. We feel guilty for pursuing what we love, what we believe in, what gets us up in the morning and gives our lives a sense of meaning. We feel guilty for choosing passion over practicality. We feel guilty for prioritizing something that others don't always understand.

You were not put on this earth just to check boxes and follow a script someone else wrote. You were meant to *live*, to create, to feel deeply, to chase what lights you up. Whatever lifts you will inevitably lift others. That's how a peaceful world is created, with all of us lifting one another.

Your passion isn't selfish. In fact, the world benefits *more* when people are passionate. A passionate teacher changes lives. A passionate entrepreneur builds something that helps others. A passionate artist inspires. A passionate activist sparks change. You following your passion isn't taking away from anyone else. It's adding *more* to the world.

Passion and peace must coexist. Think of peace as a verb. Peace and passion don't always need to be loud, hyper, or forceful. For example, introverts have plenty of peace and passion to go around; they are just energetically expressed differently than in someone who is more extroverted. Regardless of how much passion someone has or how it is expressed, the origin of our desired, passionate belief turned outward into authentic action unites us, fostering community and promoting passionate peace.

So if you're waiting for a sign, this is it. Go be passionate. Let them doubt you. Let them question you. Let them talk. Then prove them all wrong—not with words, but with action.

PEACE POINT 39: Shine Your Why

The world doesn't need more people dimming their light. It needs more people who are illuminating what they love. And that, my friend, is where peace truly begins. We all experience "passion pulls"—the energies that influence our behavior and responses. There is a reason the word *compassion* embodies this concept; it plays a vital role in helping us communicate with kindness and peace.

Where does this passionate energy originate? It comes from our why, which is the driving principle behind our choices and lives. By understanding our motivations, we can make more informed decisions and take control of our actions. When we harness this energy, our passion empowers us to live more peacefully.

Our Pathways to Peace with Elizabeth and Dr. Katie

Elizabeth—Overlooked and Objectified

As I share this story with you, please keep in mind that I am a mother of four boys, and they know these stories I am sharing with you.

There is a really painful moment in my life that challenged my ability to chase a dream. I was propositioned at work with the understanding that if I did not comply, I couldn't move forward with my dream. I didn't comply, and the result is that despite my qualifications, the incident freaked me out so much that I quit that career completely. I was young and didn't have the tools I have now to navigate constant threatening physical advances. A few movies have been made and a few songs have been sung that resonate with me to the point that, with Dr. Katie's help, I'm actually voicing this after decades of hiding it.

For many women like me, there's nothing worse than constantly being dismissed, overlooked, or objectified when all you're trying to do is chase your dreams. For me, I wanted to become a news broadcaster. However, from a young age, I felt it. Men telling me what I could or couldn't do. The eyes lingering too long, comments that made my skin crawl, and the frustrating reality that, no matter how hard I worked, some people would never take me seriously because I was a woman. It wasn't just an occasional experience; it was a constant presence, one that followed me from my teenage years into my early career, from internships to television studios to everyday life.

I wanted to be respected for my talent, my intelligence, my drive. But over and over again, I was reminded that, to many, I wasn't a person chasing a career. I was a woman navigating a world where some saw me as an object before they saw me as a professional.

Another moment—less creepy, but still impactful—occurred early in my television career. I was an intern at a station, bright-eyed and eager to learn. As I was entering the news business, I also quickly discovered the world of sports broadcasting, which I loved. Sports have always been a huge part of my life. As a gymnast, I knew competition, discipline, and the rush of being in the action. It made sense that I gravitated toward sports broadcasting. I wanted to tell the stories of athletes, break down plays, and be a voice in a space I loved. But the moment I voiced that desire, I was immediately shut down with the comment: "Women don't do that. It's a man's world. Stick to the news or better yet, go home, get married, and have babies."

That was it. A casual dismissal, like it wasn't even up for debate. I remember standing there, feeling the weight of those words settle on me. People weren't just telling me I couldn't do it—they were telling me I shouldn't even try. And the worst part? I let it get to me.

These two incidents caused me to not pursue television broadcasting despite the fact that it had been a lifelong dream, and I had a degree in journalism with honors.

For years after, I kept my head down. I avoided situations where I might have to deal with the endless comments, the inappropriate glances, or the feeling of being constantly sized up.

I made myself smaller.

It took me years to understand that true peace comes from alignment, standing in your passion and refusing to let anyone tell you that you don't belong. The voices of doubt and the naysayers will always be there. People always have opinions.

But slowly, piece by piece, I rebuilt.

And here's the full-circle moment: The very thing they told me I couldn't do—sports—I now do, boldly and unapologetically. I speak in front of collegiate sports teams, leaders, and coaches. I coach and mentor athletes. I write about them, promote them, and use my voice to empower their journeys on and off the field. My books are being read in athletic programs across the country. I have a seat at the table now—one I built myself.

The voices of doubt and disrespect still exist, but they no longer direct my path. The only voice that truly matters now is my own.

The day I gave myself permission to stop shrinking—to speak, write, lead, and *be seen*—was the day I found real peace. Not the peace of invisibility. Not the peace of avoidance. But the peace of *presence*. The peace of knowing I'm exactly where I'm meant to be, and I don't need anyone else's permission to stand tall.

So, if you've ever been told you don't belong . . .

If you've ever shrunk to feel safer . . .

If you've ever tried to make yourself invisible just to survive . . .

Hear this:

You are allowed to take up space.

You are allowed to follow your passion.

You are allowed to be loud, visible, talented, brilliant, and bold.

Peace isn't about keeping quiet.

It's about owning your space, standing in your truth, and refusing to let the world dim your light.

The world doesn't get to decide your worth.

You do.

Peace isn't about playing small. It's about owning your space, standing in your purpose, and refusing to let anyone make you feel like you don't belong. So go out there, chase your passion, and never let anyone make you second-guess your place in the world.

Dr. Katie—Bullied

When you grow up being bullied by women and men and feeling less than, it's not much of a stretch to think you will grow up into an insecure adult. And if you enter the competitive world of nonprofit health care as a young woman, passionate and mission-driven and insecure, there are plenty of opportunities to practice peace.

I have been hit on in an elevator, chastised in front of a hundred people for making a mistake, belittled, dismissed, and—my absolute favorite—ignored.

How do you practice peace in these kinds of situations?

When I was younger and naive about my power, I gave it away a lot—repeatedly. I thought that by continuously capitulating, I was taking the high road that would eventually gain me recognition as a "good person." In retrospect, all it did was lead to my feeling discouraged and unheard.

Until . . .

A fiery example occurred when I was in a meeting with a state-level healthcare executive. As the executive director of a children's palliative care and hospice program, my intention was to engage him, to use his influence and power to obtain resources and funds to support the needs of these seriously ill and dying kids. I told him stories about the needs of the children I advocated for and the evidence that our program, by caring for them in their communities, saved money by preventing unnecessary hospitalizations.

My business plan and strategies were solid. I was well prepared, providing the same information that had previously convinced members of the state legislature and the governor to provide us with funding. But this individual didn't hear me. He brushed me off and told me that my passion for these children would be my downfall. He patronized me and told me I was naive to think I could succeed. He then told me he did not have time for this and told me the meeting was done. My energy in that moment was building to Mount Vesuvius levels, and I could have erupted in a litany of very unpeaceful expletives. Instead, I did something that continues to help me today when I want to practice peace amid power dynamics. I left and to myself I muttered, "Watch me!"

When faced with someone whose ego is fragile and who needs to put you down to build themselves up, leave. They aren't interested, and you have more important things to do. Find your peaceful partners!

I had another similarly pivotal situation with a chief healthcare executive, who I imagine saw me as an irritating gnat that kept pestering him with my idea of collaborating on a pediatric program. He basically told me that if he liked what we did, he would do it himself—ego response! So I decided that if I engaged him in some way that stroked his ego, I would gain his respect. I said, "Teach me how you do it and then let's work together. Show me what you know, and I will show you what I know, and then we can decide what each of us can bring to the children and families." At that moment, there was a peaceful joining of two people. If I had become defensive and gone head-to-head with his ego, I would have been dismissed, but we came together because of my appeal to his heart and his desire to help children.

The peace that emanated from that one pivot continues to this day, providing children and families pediatric palliative care through educational programs worldwide. Why? Because I set my ego aside, appealed to his heart, and chose peace over power.

One of my favorite sayings is that being happy is more important than being right. This was the case when I made the choice to put my passion ahead of my ego and the result was greater peace for thousands of children throughout the country who benefit from the many professionals who learned from our model and training program. I didn't give in to the voices who tried to make me feel small, and I maintained my peaceful resolve.

For both of us, these experiences left us second-guessing ourselves but ultimately lit a fire from within to motivate us as advocates. Our message is clear: We want you to surround yourself with peaceful partners, friends, coworkers, and community that lift you up, support your dreams, and help you be your best.

● ● ●

Peace often reveals itself in the most unexpected places—in moments of quiet reflection or, in the case of Andy Archer, amid the thunderous cheers of 50,000 fans. And for David Lukov, peace blossoms not only in words but in service, through a lifelong commitment to compassion without division.

In this chapter on passion, we explore how purpose-driven energy becomes a force for peace. These two stories bring that idea to life in beautiful contrast. Andy, a pitcher for the viral sensation the Savannah Bananas, found his truest peace not in stillness but in fully stepping into his calling. His story is a radiant example of how passion, when aligned with faith and service, becomes a path to wholeness—even on the most unpredictable fields.

David, a funeral director and Rotarian, reminds us that peace doesn't always come from grand gestures. Sometimes it's found in the quiet discipline of community care and bridge-building. His decades of service through Rotary International show us how doing good work with good people, without needing to agree on everything, can create ripples of harmony in a fractured world.

These are not just stories. They are reminders that passion becomes peace when it is grounded in love, shared in service, and lived with intention. Each path is unique, but all share one powerful truth: When we follow what lights us up, we illuminate the world for others.

Stories from the Heart

Andy Archer—How I Found My Peace with the Savannah Bananas

Peace likely is the last word anyone would use if asked to describe seeing the Savannah Bananas play a game of Banana Ball. Over-the-top choreographed dance routines and celebrations, nonstop music, and even actual baby races on the infield between innings are among the common occurrences at these extravagant shows. As a matter of fact, a core principle of team culture for the Savannah Bananas is "If something is normal, do the exact opposite!" *Chaos, mayhem*, and *pandemonium* are words that objectively describe the Savannah Bananas more accurately than *peace*. Yet despite all of this, giving up my simple and quiet life on Oahu, Hawaii—where my days were spent longboarding the perfect waves of the south shore and working a corporate desk job for a small to midsize hotel chain—to go and play for the hottest and one of the most viral sports teams on the plane, was where I found my own peace.

I'll never forget the last day of my college baseball career. It was the final game of the regular season for my University of Hawaii Rainbow Warriors. We couldn't win our conference, and despite the fantastic season we had, we were unlikely to receive an at-large bid to the NCAA tournament. Additionally, it was Senior Day. Of course, I was excited and grateful to celebrate both my team's and my personal accomplishments with both my biological and *hānai* (adopted) families, but this day also marked the end of my athletic career. By the end of my collegiate career, I had amassed over 200 career innings, over 180 career strikeouts, and even a 121-pitch complete-game shutout win in the NCAA regional—successful by any measure, especially given the fact that my career began as a nonscholarship walk-on! However, after missing consecutive seasons due to reconstructive elbow surgery and the COVID year, my age did not make me a very attractive MLB draft prospect. It was time to hang up the cleats. I can still remember, like it was yesterday, taking off my jersey for the last time. I even strung my cleats together and threw them over the phone lines in the parking lot that overlooks Les Murakami Stadium on UH Mānoa's campus (anyone seen *Like Mike?*).

In hindsight, perhaps it was a little dramatic, but the genuine sorrow I experienced that day was unlike any other feeling I'd had in life up to that point. I *loved* baseball. Being at the field with my teammates, going to practice, and having the privilege of competition brought me pure joy. I believe this is why it hurt so much to know that my career had come to an end, because every ounce of my existence wanted to continue playing. Baseball taught me many lessons, created so many memories, and was the basis for so many friendships. It was what I looked forward to the most every single day, and now it was gone and I grieved its loss.

The next two years were quiet and uneventful, and life was actually great. I had a good job working in corporate finance for a hotel chain in Waikiki, Hawaii. Because of this, I had access every day to some of the most pristine surfing waves in the world, and I took full advantage of this perk! When I wasn't in the office or in the water, you could find me at my local church, where I had joined a men's discipleship group and become involved in junior high ministry. Despite not being born in Hawaii, I had found a home on the island of Oahu. After being *hānai*'ed, or informally adopted, by a local family, I experienced the aloha spirit in a way that so few outsiders ever get to do. Through serving the *keiki* in church, spending hours farming knee-deep in various *lo'i* patches around the island, and mentoring aspiring college and pro baseball players, I became part of a community. One day, however, I quickly realized that I didn't fully have the peace I thought that I had.

I had a turning point, and it came from one of my students, who was in seventh grade at the time. This young man served both on the worship team and as a peer leader for our weekend gatherings at church. His true passion, however, was baseball!

And on this particular day, he shared with me his desires to use his God-given abilities and passion for baseball to further the kingdom. He dreamed about going on to play for his hometown University of Hawaii Rainbow Warriors, where I played, and putting the team in the national spotlight. Further, he also dreamed about getting selected in the MLB draft and playing at the highest level in the world while giving God all of the glory, honor, and praise for blessing him with talent, opportunity, and motivation. While I was completely psyched to hear one of my students speak like this, I also felt like I had just had my heart ripped out of my chest. It became clear to me that I had not used *my* God-given gifts to the full extent in my own life. In reality, I had let them go to waste.

This is the reason I have found my peace playing for the Savannah Bananas. It's not perfect. I'm often nervous to pitch and perform in front of stadium crowds of up to 80,000 people. I'm constantly sleep-deprived and away from home for ten months out of the year. But, by faith, I have stepped into what God has called me to do, despite being unqualified, unworthy, and undeserving of such a special opportunity and national platform. I often think of Isaiah 43:19, which reads,

> See, I am doing a new thing!
> Now it springs up; do you not perceive it?
> I am making a way in the wilderness
> and streams in the wasteland.

I love this verse because it is so applicable to my story. The context here is the prophet Isaiah addressing the nation of Israel. Despite being God's chosen people, they were constantly disobedient and strayed away from God in the Old Testament, forgetting all of the ways He had provided for and protected them. In a way, I definitely relate to being disobedient to God at times and not reminding myself of all the ways He has blessed me. The second part of the verse is a reminder of the way that God has promised to provide in our lives. Inevitably, we *will* go through the wilderness and wasteland at times.

When I joined the Bananas, I felt overwhelmingly unprepared and honestly had no idea what I was getting myself into. But God made a way and gave me streams. He surrounded me with teammates and friends of the highest character and allowed me to have interactions with people along the way who make the difficult parts of the job worth it ten times over. While my initial reason for joining the Bananas was to play again, the reason I have continued is because of the motivation I have to share the joy and peace that comes from simply stepping into God's calling for my life.

Next, please meet David Lukov, a licensed funeral director, and a former pastor, hospice bereavement coordinator, and college instructor. He currently lives in Mount Vernon, Washington, and is a member of the Rotary Club of Mount Vernon.

David Lukov—Peacemaking Made Simple

One of the better things I have done in my life is actively engaging in Rotary International. I confess that when I joined Rotary in 1998, I did so because it was the thing to do for a professional. As I became involved with more and more Rotarians, I began to understand that one of the core values of Rotary is peacemaking.

Rotary has promoted peacemaking since its inception. One of its members in the early 1930s created the Four-Way Test of the things we think, say or do:

First, is it the truth?

Second, is it fair to all concerned?

Third, will it build goodwill and better friendship?

Fourth, will it be beneficial to all concerned?

The Four-Way Test encourages people to speak and act with truth, compassion, and a caring spirit. In Rotary gatherings—whether a club, a fellowship, an assembly, or a convention—the Four-Way Test is the benchmark used to promote constructive conversations and positive actions. Through its international ties, Rotary continues to practice peacemaking. Rotary International has clubs in 175 nations and territories throughout the world. Even though we speak different languages, have different traditions, and come from different cultures with their own practices, Rotary has built bridges across these differences to help promote peace among people.

In October 2024, I had the privilege to travel with a group of Rotarians from Washington State and British Columbia to meet with Rotarians in Hungary. While we had differences in language and culture, I was impressed with the opportunities we had to do good with one another. We had the privilege of visiting a Ukrainian refugee school in Budapest promoted by Rotarians in Hungary. Most of these children (from preschool to eleventh grade) had to flee their war-torn homeland, with one of their family members left behind to either work or serve in the military. I recently learned that Rotary Clubs from Japan provided a grant to purchase computer resources for students and teachers. Our group traveled to another community where we toured a school for autistic children and a school for mentally challenged children and adults. Who helped institute these schools? Rotarians from Hungary. I was impressed with how these Rotarians, along with other Rotarians in Hungary, were helping bring peace by meeting the educational and healthcare needs of people from their region.

By being a part of a Rotary Club, we are always challenged to better connect with the needs of our community members. Whether it is education, health care, environmental issues, or food insecurity, Rotarian volunteers work to address these needs. Rotary was not founded as a religious or political organization, and we are discouraged from discussing these issues. What I have discovered is that steering clear from religion and politics means that I find commonalities with people who want to serve others, which helps in peacemaking. Politics and religion often bring division, and instead we are able to unite by focusing on the good in others.

From my years involved with Rotary, I have gained a lot of peacemaking skills. Some of the things I have learned are:

- How to build bridges, not walls.
- We can all find common ground despite our differences.
- Doing service work and getting our hands dirty can help bring peace and hope.
- The importance of biting my tongue and thinking before I speak.
- In a world full of loud and violent voices, it is reassuring that peacemaking is possible.

POINTS TO PONDER

Think. Write. Talk. Action. *(Because practice makes us our best.)*

EXERCISE 9: Reclaim Your Passion Path

OBJECTIVE: To help you reconnect with a passion you've dismissed, buried, or been talked out of and to reignite it through peaceful, aligned action.

INSTRUCTIONS: Take a quiet moment to reflect and write honestly. This is your safe space to name and nurture what lights you up.

1. What is something you've always wanted to do, be, or create—but talked yourself out of?

   (It could be big or small, loud or quiet—no judgment here.)

   Write it out:

   _____

   _____

   _____

   _____

   _____

   _____

2. What stopped you?

   (Check all that apply or add your own.)

   ☐ Fear of failure
   ☐ Lack of time
   ☐ Doubt from others
   ☐ Money concerns
   ☐ Self-criticism
   ☐ I felt I wasn't qualified
   ☐ Other: _____

3. What would it feel like to say yes to this passion now?

Describe what emotions, images, or energy come to mind.

_____

_____

_____

4. What's one small, doable action you can take this week to move closer to your passion?

(No pressure to leap; just one brave step.)

_____

_____

_____

5. Write a short affirmation or mantra that brings your passion and peace together.

(Tip: Begin with "I allow . . ." or "I choose . . .")

_____

_____

_____

● **Bonus Prompt:**

Who might benefit if you fully lived this passion?

_____

_____

_____

_____

_____

EXERCISE 10: The Peaceful Passion Inventory

OBJECTIVE: To help you align your inner fire with your calm and assess how passion is currently showing up—or hiding—in your daily life.

INSTRUCTIONS: Take stock of your passion through peaceful self-awareness. Fill in the blanks honestly and gently.

1. I feel most alive and purposeful when I'm . . .

_____

_____

_____

2. The three things that matter most to me are

_____

_____

_____

3. When I think about my work or personal life right now, I would describe my passion level as

- [ ] A roaring fire
- [ ] A flickering flame
- [ ] Glowing embers
- [ ] Burned out
- [ ] Waiting to be lit

4. One thing I need to protect my passion more peacefully is

- [ ] Better boundaries
- [ ] More time for myself
- [ ] Less comparison
- [ ] A supportive community
- [ ] Permission to go for it
- [ ] Other: _____

5. My passion supports peace in the world by . . .

(Complete this sentence)

"When I live my passion, I . . ."

_____

_____

_____

● Heart-to-Heart with Yourself:

What's one belief about passion you're ready to dismiss?

_____

_____

_____

_____

_____

What's one belief you're ready to embrace?

_____

_____

_____

_____

_____

CHAPTER 6
PURPOSE

In the sixth principle of peace, Purpose, we challenge ourselves to courageously commit to being a more compassionate person. Each day, every day, we have moments of all levels of discomfort. If we take each of these moments as an opportunity to be present in a tender, vulnerable love with ourselves and another, we can individually make a difference and collectively change the world. When peace becomes our purpose, it means our values and actions are aligned, we create, and we inspire. Align your values and make sure you are remaining true to who you are. Create a plan for how you will take your skills, gifts, and talents and contribute to the world. Inspire! Share your passion for peace with others.

While compassion is the heartbeat of peace, passion is the compass of purpose, which means that purpose is your passion directed into peace-focused action. How can we identify purpose? It's when we actively take steps to implement change in ourselves that will benefit others. Your passion is your motivator, and your purpose is the outcome of directing your energy toward peace. According to the great philosopher Friederich Nietzche, "He who has a why to live can bear almost any how."

The big misunderstanding about purpose is thinking you only have one big purpose in life. We've learned over the years that our purpose has evolved, and yours can and will as well. We've learned that purpose is not static. For us, now at ages fifty-five and sixty-five, our perspective on purpose has expanded. We never would have been able to write this book and understand peace had we not challenged our beliefs and purpose about who we are and what we are meant to do. Even in discussing this book, both of us gulped at the feeling that this was too big of a topic and we were not qualified to write about it, yet we both felt called. The calling was so strong that it rose above doubt, and we committed to learn everything we could about our peaceful purpose. We've both felt we were put on the planet since a young age to foster peace. We feel that our sense of purpose evolved with time.

Reflecting on this, we paused and asked each other, "What would you say your purpose was twenty years ago?" Here are our responses:

Elizabeth: I'd say it was my four young sons. Having quit my job to stay at home with the boys, I had glimmers of my professional self but felt purpose was way more about our sons. Professionally, I was dedicated to showcasing and promoting other people's work about personal and professional growth and development on Best Ever You.

Dr. Katie: Similarly, my family has been and will always be my greatest purpose, and raising my daughter to discover her potential and purpose was my focus. Professionally, at that time, children and palliative care were my focus. Now I realize that loss, change, growth, and grief are the foundations of what I learned from my earlier purpose that now has contributed to how I recognize peace.

We didn't find our purpose. We lived our way into it in different moments, in different ways, and at different times. Purpose didn't arrive. It revealed itself whispering in the cracks between who we thought we had to be and who we actually were, and we listened. Purpose doesn't always feel purposeful. Sometimes it feels like chaos. Sometimes it feels like starting over. But we're here to tell you that if you stay long enough in the questions, purpose will show up in your presence.

PEACE POINT 40: Expand Your Definition of Purpose

Your purpose here is to make a difference every day by lifting up yourself and others and making the world better. Many of us think our purpose is what we feel called to do or perhaps some natural gift we have. Many of us grow up believing that our purpose in life is tied to what we're good at, whether it's a job, a talent, or a passion. But purpose, especially when it's connected to peace, is much more layered. We believe purpose reveals itself in three forms: chosen purpose, external purpose, and spiritual purpose.

Chosen purpose is the purpose we define for ourselves. It's the conscious direction we take in our lives based on what matters to us—our values, interests, and dreams. This kind of purpose is fluid and can shift as we grow. It's the version of purpose we choose to wake up to and live each day.

External purpose refers to the roles and expectations shaped by culture, society, and circumstance. These are the roles we step into—parent, caregiver, teacher, leader, healer. Sometimes we choose them with intention and embrace them fully. Other times, they are inherited or quietly expected. External purpose can guide how we contribute to others, but without awareness, it can pull us away from our true selves.

Spiritual purpose is the deepest layer. It's the purpose that transcends titles, tasks, and time. It's not about doing. It's about being. This purpose is rooted in your soul's reason for being here. It may not always be definable in words, but it often shows up as a quiet knowing, a pull toward compassion, and a longing to live in alignment with love and peace. When we integrate these three types of purpose, we begin to live in harmony with ourselves and the world around us.

PEACE POINT 41: Understand Big "P" and Little "p"

When we talk about purpose, it's important to recognize that not all purpose looks the same—and not all of it is meant to. We define two distinct yet interconnected levels of purpose: big "P" Purpose and little "p" purpose.

Little "p" Purpose

This is your *practical purpose*. It's your skill set, your interests, your strengths—the *I'm good at this, so I'll turn it into a career path*. Maybe you're gifted in numbers, writing, teaching, or organizing. Maybe you're naturally good with children or animals or technology. This type of purpose is often what shows up on your résumé or in your daily job. It's the role you step into and the tasks you perform: Your chosen profession, talent, or hobby turned into action. But while little "p" purpose can bring satisfaction and structure, it doesn't always touch the soul. It can evolve, shift, or even lose meaning over time, especially if it becomes disconnected from a deeper sense of fulfillment.

Big "P" Purpose

Big "P" Purpose is what we call *peaceful purpose*. It's the universal purpose that lives within all of us. It's not just what you do—it's how and why you do it. It's your soul's intention to lift others up, bring healing, spread compassion, and leave the world a little better than you found it.

This kind of purpose is not tied to a job title, a specific talent, or an achievement. It's not about what's on your business card; it's about how you show up for others. It's about the love, care, and intention behind your actions. This purpose is rooted in peace—inner peace, shared peace, global peace.

An important aspect of your big "P" Purpose is that it comes from the inside out. Your motivation is from within you, and your experience of success lies within you. It's not dependent on external rewards or accolades. It's you feeling good about your contribution toward the betterment of others that gives you the greatest satisfaction. That is how your big "P"

Purpose shows up and how you know it is soulfully driven. You may have been born with a gift—like singing. That gift, when shared with the intention to uplift others, becomes a big "P" Purpose. A singer might sing just to perform (little "p") or might sing from the soul to connect, comfort, and inspire (big "P"). That's the difference. Big "P" Purpose is heart forward, peace driven, and other oriented.

Both big "P" and little "p" are unearthed, bit by bit, through experience, reflection, and sometimes even hardship. And just when you think you've got it all figured out, life has a way of shaking things up, forcing you to reassess and refine what purpose really means to you.

How They Work Together:

Sometimes, our little "p" and Big "P" align perfectly—and that's a beautiful thing. Maybe your profession is also your platform for healing or peace. A musician doesn't play just to entertain but to lift spirits. A doctor diagnoses conditions and also brings comfort. A chef cooks and they nourishes souls. When little "p" serves the big "P," purpose becomes powerful. It's the difference between vocation and a job.

But even if they don't fully align yet, that's okay. Purpose evolves. Peace grows with practice. The important thing is to stay in touch with your internal compass and ask, *How can I use what I do to uplift? How can I allow my work, my words, and my way of living to be in service to peace?*

PEACE POINT 42: Build Peaceprints

Just like a blueprint designs a structure, your peaceprints are the unique impression your purpose leaves on the world. It's not just what you do once, but how you live, love, lead, and respond throughout your life whenever something asks more of you. It might be how you are remembered. What do you want your legacy to be?

Peaceprints are purpose in motion, the intentional steps you take that quietly impact others, support healing, and ripple out into the universe.

Build peaceprints. They are your legacy—not of perfection, but of meaningful presence.

PEACE POINT 43: Don't Overcomplicate It

People don't generally have their lives all planned out according to some great purpose. We're writing books well after the ages of fifty and sixty about what we've discovered along the way. We didn't sit at age seventeen and think, *My purpose here on this earth is to write a book about peace.*

Purpose evolves over time and shifts with our experiences. Many of us are meandering, still trying to figure it all out. Sometimes even one quick glance at someone who *seems* to have their purpose perfectly in order makes us feel behind, lost, or like we're missing something. We each carry multiple purposes, roles, gifts, and talents. Your purpose in any given moment might simply be to lend a hand, share a kind word, or show up for someone who needs you.

We overcomplicate the word *purpose,* imagining it as some grand, pre-written master plan. But peace teaches us to simplify, to remember that purpose is present, not just future. Maybe your purpose today isn't to win a Nobel Prize—it's to encounter another human being with compassion and to uplift them in their own journey.

If you're wondering what the point of all this is—if you're wrestling with the big questions or feeling unfulfilled, or are short on cash or disconnected in your work or relationships—start smaller. Bring it back to peace. Show kindness. Offer grace. Extend understanding. Our purpose, at its core, is to leave the world and the people in it better than we found them.

PEACE POINT 44: Let Your Purpose Evolve and Breathe

Our purpose can fall into question. Things happen. Life shifts. And just like that, purposeful peace can feel shaken or even stripped away.

And then comes *that* question: "What should I do with my life?"

It's a powerful one—and when you're already navigating change, the question can feel overwhelming, especially when you look around and think everyone else has their life completely together. (Spoiler: They don't.)

Considering what you want to do with the rest of your life shows up most clearly at big milestone moments—graduations, job transitions, retirement, relationship changes—events where it *looks* like everyone else has a perfect plan while you're panicking.

From a youthful point of view, this pressure can feel paralyzing. Not everyone has an obvious dream job, a college acceptance letter, or a five-year plan tied up in a neat little bow. Sometimes you're in your late teens, early or late twenties, or even mid-fifties or sixties, and still figuring out what makes your heart beat faster. That doesn't mean you're behind—it means you're human. Purpose isn't always loud or linear. Sometimes it's quiet and waiting for you to slow down enough to notice it, even though it might always change.

Even in middle age, people reassess. Careers that once brought pride may now bring stress. The house that once felt like home might now feel like a cage. We see people changing careers, downsizing, or moving to a quieter town not because they failed, but because they're listening to a stirring that tells them it's time for change. They want more peace or meaning. It's not about escaping life. It's about returning to it in a newly aligned way.

There's no single age or stage where we figure out our purpose. Some discover it early. Some stumble into it. Others redefine it repeatedly. What matters is not when you find your purpose, but how you live while you're looking for it. Are you kind to yourself in the process? Are you curious? Are you listening?

In real life, comparison is a fundamental thief of peace and joy. Especially in today's highlight-reel culture, it's easy to feel like you're the only one still searching. But behind every polished social media post or confident job title is a person who has questioned their path often.

You're not lost—you're unfolding.

You're not late. You're living.

And you don't need to have it all figured out to begin practicing peace and purpose today.

PEACE POINT 45: Acknowledge the Stirring

As we discussed earlier, there is a name for the period of pause when you choose to explore change. That in-between time is called "liminal space." Liminal space refers to the transitional state that exists between what was and what is yet to come. It is often a time of ambiguity, uncertainty, and potential. In psychology and spiritual traditions, it's seen as a sacred pause—a threshold where transformation becomes possible. This space is not just a gap; it is fertile ground for redefinition, re-creation, healing, and insight.

People often encounter liminal space during life transitions: after a loss, before a new beginning, or amid an identity shift. This space can feel disorienting because the old structures have dissolved, but the new ones haven't yet formed. Yet, in this suspended moment, deep growth and awareness can arise.

PEACE POINT 46: Follow Your Authenticity and Don't Give Up on You

It's hard to live in a world that doesn't accept who you are.

Living with purpose isn't always smooth sailing. In fact, one of the greatest tests of purpose is how you hold onto it when the world tries to shake you.

Maybe you've had moments when others have doubted you. Maybe you've doubted yourself. We've all had those experiences, pursuing something purposefully, only to be met with criticism, skepticism, or outright dismissal. And in those moments, it's easy to question everything: *Am I really meant to do this? Is this even possible?*

If something is placed in your heart—if it keeps calling you back, even when it's hard—it's there for a reason. Purpose doesn't disappear just because the road is difficult. In fact, challenges are often the very things that shape and strengthen our purpose.

One of the greatest acts of peace is living your purpose without constantly seeking permission or validation. If you wait for the world to unanimously approve of your path, you'll be waiting forever. When you embrace your purpose fully, you step into a kind of peace that no outside opinion can shake. It's a peace that says, *I know who I am. I know why I'm here. And I will not apologize for it.*

It means writing your book even if no one understands why. It means starting that business, launching the nonprofit, or pursuing the creative passion that lights you up, even when others raise an eyebrow. It means standing firm in the belief that you are here for a reason, even if that reason doesn't fit into someone else's expectations. Keep showing up. Keep being *you*!

PEACE POINT 47: Follow the Energy

Pay attention to what lights you up. What are the things you could talk about for hours? What activities make time disappear? Purpose often hides in the things that bring us deep joy and fulfillment. Notice where your energy naturally rises. What conversations leave you feeling inspired? Peace and purpose often reveal themselves in the spaces where your heart feels most alive. Instead of forcing a path, allow yourself to be guided by the things that bring you joy, fulfillment, and a deep sense of connection. The more you align with what energizes you, the more effortlessly peace will flow into your life.

PEACE POINT 48: Release the Need for Perfection

Many people hesitate to step into their purpose because they don't feel ready or good enough. Start where you are and let growth happen along the way. One of the biggest roadblocks to living in alignment with your purpose is the belief that you must have everything figured out before you begin. You might be telling yourself, *I'll start when I'm ready,* or *I need to be better before I can make a difference.* But peace isn't found in waiting for perfection—it's discovered in the willingness to start, exactly as and where you are.

The truth is that purpose isn't about flawless execution. It's about showing up, learning, growing, and evolving along the way. Every person who has ever made an impact began somewhere, likely filled with doubts and uncertainties. But they moved forward anyway.

Give yourself permission to take imperfect action. Release the need to be fully prepared before you step into your calling. Trust that each step, even the missteps, will teach you something valuable. Peace comes when you stop striving for an unattainable ideal and instead embrace the beauty of becoming.

PEACE POINT 49: Ask, "Who Needs Me?"

A sense of peaceful purpose is often found in service. Instead of just questioning what you want to do, ask, "Who needs what I have to offer?" When your purpose connects to serving others, it becomes even more powerful.

We are inspired by the story of Nelson Mandela, who understood that pain becomes suffering when we endure it alone. Even from a jail cell, he recognized the human need for connection and community, engaging and encircling his followers to promote unifying peace. Mandela embodied "purpose power"—transforming personal pain into purpose-driven compassion.

Mandela wrote, "Our human compassion binds us the one to the other—not in pity or patronizingly, but as human beings who have learnt how to turn our common suffering into hope for the future."

This quote illustrates his understanding that collective compassionate acts bring about powerful, transformative, and lasting social change. In our individual lives, this lesson of directing our "purpose power"—individually and collectively by seeking out community—is vital to understanding how transformative change occurs.

Live with purpose. Be unapologetic about it. And trust that the peace you seek is already within you, waiting for you to step fully into who you were meant to be.

●●●

Our Pathways to Peace with Elizabeth and Dr. Katie

Elizabeth—Chocolate Chip Cookies

When I was a kid, I thought purpose would come neatly wrapped with a bow—something so clear that the path would simply unfold before me. In high school, I would see people who were good at this or that, such as singing or acting or sports. I was a gymnast, which was not offered as a school sport, so I felt left out at times.

For me, it's been a winding, sometimes turbulent quest. I was born with an undeniable gift of being a gymnast, and I thought that was my purpose. At times, I also wished I had been born with other talents, such as singing or acting, instead of gymnastics, somehow thinking other gifts were more valuable than my own. At school, I used my gymnastics skills to become a cheerleader in junior high and high school. But later, I realized my purpose was not just one thing. Purpose isn't always obvious, and it rarely arrives with a road map.

Over the years, I've learned that purpose is something you create, nurture, and refine. When I was younger, I fully understood the relentless work behind greatness. I never assumed people just woke up one day and were handed their calling, like a script. But I learned that greatness has nothing to do with purpose and that purpose often begins in quieter places. For me, it began in the kitchen with chocolate chip cookies. Let me explain.

In 1997 and again in 1999, as I wrote about earlier, I nearly lost my life to severe allergic reactions to food. Those moments were wake-up calls. Surviving wasn't just luck, it was a reminder that life is fragile, time is precious, and I could no longer take any of it for granted. I knew I had to live with intention and purpose.

My purpose started to take shape through advocacy and awareness. I was featured in the bestselling book *One of the Gang*. I began baking thousands of nut-free chocolate chip cookies—not just for friends and family, but for weddings, Little League teams, story times, schools, fundraisers, writing organizations, and even the late Robin Williams. Over the years, I've baked and donated thousands and thousands of cookies.

Funny thing is—people kept trying to pay me. They wanted to buy the recipe, order cookies, or hire me to cater. And I could have said yes, but I didn't. I realized something important: I would do this whether I got paid or not. That's how I knew this was passion. This was peace. This was purpose.

Following that purpose led me to some unforgettable moments—like this one:

Dear Ms. Hamilton-Guarino,

I am a patient at Dana-Farber, and I have Stage 4 colon cancer. I have been receiving chemo for almost two years now. As you must know from leaving some cookies on the 10th floor, chemo is very hard. I also have two lovely daughters (ages 8 and 10) who have been by my side throughout this rough journey. I brought two of your cookies home to my girls, who both said they were the best cookies in the world. I want to thank you for your kindness. These little things make the road easier. My very warmest wishes to you. Thank you for your help and thoughtfulness.

That note changed my life.

I kept it by my computer. It sat there quietly when I started Best Ever You. It reminded me that the things we do from love and alignment create the most lasting impact—not just for others, but for ourselves. It is still there today.

Cookies taught me what success really means: showing up, giving from the heart, and using whatever gifts we have to lift others. That's peace in action. That's purpose.

If you're still searching for your purpose, I want you to know this:

You are not behind. You are not lost.

You are exactly where you need to be.

Purpose isn't something you chase. It's something you uncover, piece by piece. It lives in the things that bring you joy, the people you love, the work that lights you up. Most of all, purpose lives in the peace that comes when you stop trying to be someone else and start fully embracing who you already are.

My purpose didn't arrive with a lightning bolt. It came in quiet moments—baking cookies with my sons, having late-night conversations with friends, and writing words from my heart to help someone I might never meet.

I've come to understand:

Purpose isn't always one thing.

It's not a single title, mission, or role.

It's a collection of moments, of choices, of love shared in ordinary ways.

True peace comes from living in alignment with your purpose.

It's not about proving anything.

It's about waking up each day and knowing that your life matters.

And sometimes, it starts with something as small—and as sacred—as a cookie.

Dr. Katie—Uplifting Others

I am an uplifter! Kindness and compassion are my core values.

At the end of each day, I ask myself, *Have I uplifted others?* To me, this means being present to the miracle of life—staying aware and awake to recognize opportunities that generate love and joy.

One concrete way I share my peaceful spirit is expressing myself with bright, invigorating colors. If you're familiar with the Rorschach test—those inkblot images used in psychological testing—one key theme they measure is color response. I personally scored off the charts in that category. Everything I do is colorful! I wear engaging scarves with matching shoes and turquoise bling that evoke joyful expression. My house has been called the "Crayola house" because when you enter, you're greeted by a collection of artwork that celebrates the natural world and the magnificence of nature's uplifting hues.

When I host a meal, I embrace Martha Stewart–level attention to detail—fresh autumn leaves with their eye-catching vibrant reds and golds and cheerful orange pumpkins at Thanksgiving, pine cones adorned with bold ribbons at Christmas, and for everyday, matching linens and accessories to say that every visitor matters. I want my family and friends to feel nurtured and special. "Colorful Katie" is what I bring to every situation, even grief-related ones.

I recently met with a group of teachers after one of their colleagues died suddenly. My intent was to bring them together with an experience to provide them space to grieve and uplift their spirits by remembering her and how she lived. I placed a vase and a colorful array of flowers at the front of the room. One by one, each teacher placed a flower in the vase and paused to share a special moment or story. The act of collectively creating something that symbolizes the essence of the person lost brought comfort. What was expected to be draining and overwhelmingly difficult became a joining of hearts as the group remembered someone whose love of children and tender heart inspired them to be better teachers. Each person left with a renewed sense of purpose to make a difference in a child's life.

By using color in creative rituals, I aim to help groups transform their pain into higher meaning and purpose. Over my thirty-plus years of ritualizing loss, I've created memory wreaths with residents in skilled nursing facilities, quilts with circles of friends, photo collages with families, videos with bereaved teens, and many, many flower arrangements.

Living a peaceful, purposeful life for anyone can be as simple as smiling at a stranger or as complex as showing up at a protest with a sign advocating for greater compassion. For me, one simple approach is bringing joy through color. My colorful gestures are my small way of practicing daily compassion.

I once was told by an AIDS patient that my jewelry made his day, and children used to tell me that my clothing made them smile. These comments throughout my life make me, Colorful Katie, sleep better knowing I generated peace that day.

Purpose is not always born from ease. Often, it arises in the fire of challenge, loss, and deep reckoning. In this section, we share two stories that reflect the unshakable spirit of peaceful perseverance in the face of life-altering diagnoses, grief, and uncertainty. These are not just stories of hardship, they are stories of fierce love, radical resilience, and the unbreakable will to create meaning from pain. Shani Taha and Catherine Parrillo remind us that purpose isn't something we wait to find—it's something we choose, even when life gives us every reason to quit. Let their stories be your compass. Let them inspire your own path forward.

Stories from the Heart

Shani Taha—Finding Peace and Never Giving Up

I moved to Casa Grande, Arizona, in 2019 after forty years in Washington State. The Pacific Northwest had become too expensive, and while had I rented several homes on the reservation in La Conner, I was anxious to settle. Casa Grande was charming, about a forty-five-minute drive south of Phoenix with its own special blend of architecture and spirit. More importantly, family was nearby. Things were looking up until I received a call from medical folks in Washington. They informed me that I had a brain tumor. They recommended that I seek medical attention and have another MRI. Whoopee!

Thankfully, another friend referred me to a neurologist in Seattle. I had a conference call with the doctor, and I said to her, "If I'm going to be a fruitcake, let me know." She laughed and said, "No, Shani . . . try a crepe Suzette!"

Apparently, the tumor was on the edges of my brain, on the membrane, and would not penetrate the brain. Surgery could be done with three to four days of recovery. I wasn't relaxed, but this news left me feeling more at ease. Still, I didn't know what this tumor could do to my brain and my ability to function. Would I be able to recognize people, family, friends, associates? Would I forget events and activities? If so, I could not conceive of a life like that.

Given my lack of information and the medical risks associated with my condition, I decided to move to Michigan to be closer to my daughter and her family. They could provide support when needed. I packed up. My daughter secured a rental in Grosse Pointe Woods, just outside Detroit. My neighbor there advised me to sign up with the University of Michigan Heath Care system. He was a cancer survivor after having both lungs successfully transplanted. I respected his advice and honored his recovery, so I took his suggestion and signed up there.

Along with medical care, the support of my daughter, her family and friends, and my neighbors helped keep my stress level down as much as possible. I would not have been able to keep up with even the routine things in life without them.

My purpose was to secure a plan for the treatment and removal of my tumor. I received conflicting and confusing answers. One brain doc said the tumor was too small for surgery and that I had some early indications of dementia. Another brain doctor who worked with radiation said he also could not remove the tumor because it was too small. A third brain surgeon diagnosed no cancer. I became friends with the brain doc who worked exclusively with seniors. She authorized a number of tests because my tumor had not grown in four years. She told me to stop drinking wine and required an exercise routine. The protocol was rigorous and demanding but, worse yet, didn't lead to any resolution. I had what was to be my final meeting with this brain doc. A visiting doctor with whom she consulted about my case was also in attendance. Neither doctor appreciated nor asked for my input. They deduced:

- I had lost my executive functions.
- I should not live alone.
- I should not drive.
- I should not drink alcohol (wine).

I did not respond. These recommendations would put me in an asylum! I have spent the past forty years managing money and managing people. I was able and successful with particular attention to creating opportunities for women and women of color. I developed strategies for implementing 911 service in King County, hired the first women as line workers and execs at City Light, and brought energy conservation to Sweden and Italy.

When the meeting was over, I shook hands and left their office. I no longer considered the doctor my friend.

On the way home, I said to myself, *This diagnosis is bullshit!* I called my children and said, "I'm moving back to Seattle." They were a little startled, but after I shared what happened at my doctor's office, they understood. I told my daughter I would need her help to donate stuff to Goodwill. I decided I wanted to take the train back to Seattle and leave Chicago.

My eldest son jumped in and said, "I've got plenty of room in Covington [Washington]; stay with me." I agreed. It was a done deal. The train ride was a three-day affair. It left on Sunday and arrived on Tuesday. When I woke up Tuesday morning we were cruising through the Cascades, surrounded by breathtaking scenery. I remembered that we'd skied and camped and hiked in the Cascades. I even coached a small group of Black downhill racers and took them to events in Oregon, Washington, and Colorado. The terrain and greenery here were part of my soul. I knew I had made a smart decision to return home. Covington was a lovely small town, and my son was right. He had lots of room.

My other son temporarily joined us when he retired from the Air Force. This was paradise for me. I did a conference call with my children and told them that when I died, I wanted my ashes spread in the Cascades. All the men in our family had their ashes spread at sea, but I wanted mine in the Cascades. I warned them, however, don't come after me too soon. I have twenty more years to live and enjoy! I found peace!

Catherine Parrillo—The Spot

February 2018. As the dermatologist pointed to my husband's face, she said, "I don't like how that spot looks." Frank and I both looked quizzically in the mirror she held and replied, "What spot?" It was tinier than a pencil point: the spot that brought "melanoma" into our vocabulary.

Within the week, Frank had an appointment with the oncologist, who removed and biopsied the spot. Then came the plastic surgeon, who literally removed half of his cheek to ensure there was no scar. This spot was in situ, meaning it was on the surface, and the only follow-up was a skin check every three months. Survival rate: 95 percent. Nothing to worry about.

Fast-forward to 2020, the middle of COVID. Again, the doctor sent Frank to the oncologist for a second spot—this time on his arm. They told us it wasn't metastatic. It was a stand-alone Stage 2A. There was no lymph involvement. Just skin checks every three months. Frank was diligent.

Prior to our move to Florida in October 2021, he had a full-body check that came back all clear. Six months later, he found a new dermatologist who did his six-month follow-up, and that was clear as well.

In August 2022, we took our daughter to college for her last semester. The day we were leaving, Frank woke up with a case of what we assumed was vertigo. He took some Dramamine and drove us home. A few weeks later, as we were heading into Walmart, he got out of the truck, unsteady and dizzy. If I didn't know him, I would have thought he was completely inebriated. He swore he was fine. I tried to get him to the doctor, but he wouldn't hear of it.

At our daughter Alexandra's graduation in early December 2022, he nearly fell over when the ceremony ended. "Don't tell anyone. I'm fine." I made him go to our primary doctor that following Monday. The doctor told him it was likely low blood pressure. I wasn't convinced but couldn't get an appointment with a neurologist until April 2023.

Then the day came when I knew our life together would change forever.

On that day, my instincts were telling me something was wrong. We were enjoying a show at the theater and during the show I was distracted, not watching the play. Instead, I found myself researching "emergency rooms near me." When we got home, he vomited. I finally yelled at him, "Get in the darn car. We are going to the hospital." This time, he didn't argue. Within an hour, the CT scan showed four brain tumors. Metastatic melanoma. I called them the Four Stooges.

We were sent by ambulance to a local medical center for neurology. We met a neurosurgeon who immediately made us feel like we were in good hands. Shemp, the largest tumor, was removed the next day—the first of four craniotomies Frank would endure over the next ten months.

It was then that I had my first run-in with the corporatization of medicine. Frank was referred to an oncologist and radiation oncologist, and after twenty-three hours, no one had come to see us. Word to everyone: Don't get sick during the December holidays.

That was when my "Jersey" came out. I was close to rolling him out in his gown and driving to New Jersey. But that mishap and those miscommunications led us to an amazing radiation oncologist: Dr. Shiv Desai.

Because of my research, I knew what the survival rate was for Frank's disease but he was blissfully unaware he was going to die from this. And honestly, I believe that kept him alive and fighting for the next thirteen months.

Dr. Desai, a specialist near us, performed stereotactic radiation on the other three tumors. He was amazing. I don't think Frank could have received better treatment anywhere. The doctor answered all of our questions. He offered us options. He offered us hope.

I felt like some members of my husband's medical team weren't looking at my strong husband as an individual but more like a statistic. My quest for learning "everything melanoma" began. I searched. I researched. I asked questions. But nothing made sense.

In February 2023, he had another craniotomy. More immunotherapy. In May, my birthday gift was him in near liver failure due to therapy toxicity. It was discovered that Frank had an NRAS gene mutation, rarer and more deadly.

By now, I was relentless in my search for answers. In August, Frank had another craniotomy with the doctor, followed almost immediately by another in September at Mayo. That one scared me.

Then insurance didn't want to cover more stereotactic radiation, but the neurologist was relentless in getting it approved. However, by then, I could see the toll it was taking on my once-strong, vibrant, funny husband.

Finally, in November, I came across a clinical trial that checked every box. Dr. Bentley Doonan was studying a new medication combination for metastatic melanoma to the brain with Frank's specific mutation. Off I went to get Frank on this trial. Immediately, I felt a bit of hope, but it was marred by his daily decline. I feared that I had found it too late.

Thanksgiving came. Then Christmas. Then New Year's. We welcomed 2024. I celebrated, knowing it was likely our last.

On January 3, Frank asked for a burrito from Chipotle. I got it and brought it home. He couldn't see it on the plate. Then he couldn't lift his arm. I thought it was a stroke. We rushed to the ER. By the time we got there, he couldn't walk. This was it. I knew it.

We had talked after his last craniotomy and agreed he was not having any more surgeries. When the ER doctor said it was possible to correct a brain bleed, he said, "Okay. I'm not ready to go yet."

It broke me. I knew. He wasn't listening to me.

The neurosurgeon came the next morning. He explained that the tumors were growing faster than the surgeries, immunotherapy, and radiation could kill them. "You fought a good fight, Frank. I wish we could do more." He cried with us.

Frank's response: "Well, that was fast." He honestly hadn't thought he was going to die.

He was sent home with hospice care on January 5.

Still, Frank was full of joy. Friends and family came to spend time with him. We laughed. We drank coffee and ate chocolate donuts. He was *himself again*—up until the night of January 9. He had a rough night. All I wanted was to keep him comfortable and pain-free. He was coughing and couldn't breathe. He looked terrified.

Once he calmed down, he looked at me and whispered, "I love you, Catherine." Those were the last words he ever uttered. I had to ask my brother-in-law if he heard it too—just to be sure I wasn't imagining it.

The morning of January 10, the nurse came to care for him. He smiled that beautiful smile in gratitude. I walked her to the door and asked, "How long?"

She estimated twelve to twenty-four hours. In the ten minutes we were chatting, my friend, who had been sitting with him, came running out. "I didn't hear him exhale." We rushed to his bed. My love, my best friend, my home—was at peace. My daughter and I snuggled up with him and cried. Friends and family came to see him. The dogs said goodbye too. When the flurry of goodbyes ended, I locked the door. I honored the man he was. Frank never left the house without being dressed and put together.

I spread lotion on his body. Brushed his teeth. Combed his hair. Changed his clothes. Sprayed him with his favorite cologne. Then I helped the funeral home take him to the hearse.

I didn't want to leave him.

Immediately after, I gave the orders to get the medical stuff out. I started organizing the trip back to New Jersey. Planning the funeral. Doing the things that needed to be done. And done it was. A week later, we were in New Jersey. It was the most beautiful tribute to such a kind and simple man. So many people came—for him, for us, our daughter. My heart still could burst thinking about all the love he was shown.

Then came my next plan. In lieu of flowers, we asked for donations for Dr. Doonan's melanoma research. We raised over $3,000. His death would not be in vain. There *has* to be purpose in it. There needs to be change.

While I'm grateful for finding the trial, I feel a sense of purpose to help others understand and seek out better post care for early-stage melanoma. To me, standard of care is not a one-size-fits-all solution. I wish I had known that melanoma spreads to the brain via nerve cells, fat cells—not just lymph. I would have asked for a brain scan earlier.

I wish brain scans were a mandatory part of early follow-up care after an initial diagnosis. Had we done them earlier, maybe we could have caught it. Maybe better treatments would have been available. I know nothing I find now will bring Frank back—but if we can save another, it will be worth it.

Alexandra and I are planning to spread melanoma awareness. We worked with our little New Jersey town to create a memorial 5K wellness walk for melanoma research. In Frank's name, we walked. We educated. We advocated. We stand for better care, earlier screenings, more transparency, and personalized treatment. We speak so that others can have better experiences and outcomes.

I made a promise to Frank that last day in the hospital: We would be okay. We would be sad—but we would be okay.

Grief is hard. It is unpredictable. But we have to go through it. And if my grief allows me to honor him, his memory, and create change—it is worth the pain and sadness I feel so deeply every day. Frank's legacy is not just in the memories we carry but in the momentum we create. His story calls for more than remembrance; it calls for change.

Frank deserves to be more than his death. We remember the man behind it all, not the diagnosis, not the data point, not the patient ID, but the kind, joyful, strong soul who loved donuts, made us laugh, and gave us everything he had until his final breath.

More than the little spot that altered our hopes for the future.

His life is to be remembered and celebrated.

POINTS TO PONDER

Think. Write. Talk. Action. *(Because practice makes us our best.)*

EXERCISE 11: Aligning Purpose with Peace

When our purpose feels unclear, it's often because we've become disconnected from the qualities that keep us grounded in peace. These ten areas serve as gentle mirrors, helping you see where your purpose is asking for more awareness, healing, or expression.

Each question is an opportunity to reconnect with the peaceful essence that wants to guide your purpose forward.

Ten Pathways to Purpose and Peace

1. EMPATHY

How can I expand my ability to truly understand others and still honor my own experience?_____

_____

2. FORGIVENESS

Where am I holding on to resentment that may be blocking the flow of peace and purpose in my life?_____

_____

3. HUMILITY

In what ways can I let go of the need to be right so that I can stay open to growth and learning?_____

_____

4. KINDNESS

What small, intentional act of kindness could I offer today that reflects the purpose I want to live by?_____

_____

5. RESPECT

How can I show up with deeper respect for others' paths—and my own—even when they differ?_____

_____

6. DIGNITY

Do my words and actions allow others (and myself) to feel seen, heard, and valued?_____

_____

7. GRATITUDE

Where can I express more appreciation for what already is, instead of focusing on what's missing?_____

_____

8. SELF-COMPASSION

How can I extend to myself the same patience and care I offer others while pursuing my purpose?_____

_____

9. COMPASSION

Who in my world might need a reminder that they matter, and how can I offer that today?_____

_____

10. TRUST

Where am I being asked to trust the unfolding of my path, even when I can't see the outcome?_____

_____

EXERCISE 12: Developing Purpose and Your Impact

PURPOSE: To help you recognize the natural rhythms of your inner peace and identify where your purpose is trying to emerge.

INSTRUCTIONS: Take a moment to breathe and center yourself. Then reflect on the following prompts and fill in the blanks with what comes to mind—no judgment, just awareness.

You feel most alive when you are _____

_____.

You feel most drained when you are _____

_____.

When you were a child, you used to lose track of time doing _____

_____.

One cause, issue, or community you deeply care about is _____

_____.

The last time you felt deeply peaceful was when _____

_____.

A compliment you receive often is _____

_____.

If you had to teach a lesson to the world based on your life so far, it would be

_____.

You feel pulled toward _____, even though it scares you.

Your inner voice is gently asking you to _____

_____.

If you could take one peaceful action today that moves you closer to purpose, you would _____

_____.

JOURNAL PROMPT: Look back over your answers and notice the themes. Where do peace, joy, and energy intersect? What wants to emerge from you? Write for ten minutes without stopping on the topic "My peaceful purpose is revealing itself through . . ."

_____

_____

_____

_____

_____

● Heart-to-Heart with Yourself

If someone gave you all the resources you would need to improve someone else's life, where would you use them?_____

_____

What are your unique skills (what you learned how to do), gifts (what you are naturally able to do), and talents (what you excel at)?_____

_____

How can you direct your energies toward this particular cause or issue using your skills, gifts, talents, and resources?_____

_____

What are three things that bring you the most joy and fulfillment?

_____

_____

_____

If you didn't have to worry about money or opinions, what would you do with your time?_____

_____

When have you felt the most in flow, completely immersed in something meaningful?_____

_____

What message, ideas, or passion keeps coming back to you, no matter how much you try to ignore it?_____

_____

How can you use your gifts, skills, or passions to create a positive impact in the world?_____

_____

CHAPTER 7
POSITIVITY

In the seventh principle of peace, Positivity, we root ourselves in a growth mindset that sees the possibility for life's events as opportunities to learn something that will make us better. Learning to appreciate more and discover reasons for gratitude in the midst of even the most challenging experiences is the focus of this chapter. This principle isn't about blind optimism or forcing happiness in every moment; it's about maintaining a mindset that affirms, validates, and embraces the power of peaceful living. It means recognizing that even in difficult moments, there are opportunities for learning, healing, and growth. When we embrace positivity as part of our identity, we approach the world with openness, resilience, and an unwavering belief in the possibility of peace.

People confuse happiness with positivity. Peaceful positivity is a mindset that acknowledges difficulties while staying open to hope, resilience, and the potential for transformation. Sometimes positivity is a peaceful pause to recognize a moment of peace.

Thinking we were blissfully happy at the time, we began writing this chapter while we were both on vacation. Elizabeth was thinking it was the rainbows-and-puppy-dogs section of the book! She genuinely thought this was going to be a *rah-rah* cheerleader section to help you be happier in your life.

To give you some insight into what we mean, here is our dialogue.

Dr. Katie: As someone who has worked with people struggling with real-life situations for over forty years, my perspective on positivity is very different. I believe that happiness is fleeting, and positivity is choice. We can choose a positive perspective in any situation, but in order for us to experience true positivity, it must be grounded in reality. Ignoring what is hard gives us a false sense of happiness.

Elizabeth: Hang on, Dr. Katie, I have a question and comment. Culturally, we're being fed a diet of happiness. We see it everywhere in courses, books, memes, and so forth. Both of us generally choose a positive attitude. So are these resources supposed to guide us all to lasting happiness?

Dr. Katie: They're great! Except they don't last. They are wonderful in the moment and give us a boost and yet when tough things happen, we need a practical approach that helps us flex our resilient spiritual muscles and beliefs that can support us.

Elizabeth: I love our conversations. I think we need both. I know I sure do. Let me give you an example. Can you help our readers better understand some of the practices our family put in place when my dad was in ICU with his strokes and survived? He wanted to do everything in his power to survive. He didn't want to be left alone, and he wanted our positive energy around him. So we covered walls of his room with photos, played movies, were positive, and kept him positive and in survival mode rather than giving up.

Dr. Katie: Of course, that is wonderful. Following the lead of someone who is hurting is essential, and so it is also important to recognize that not everyone in every situation needs a positive statement. For example, my father was dying in a palliative care unit surrounded by our family in quiet grief. A perky nurse bounded into the room, failed to read the room, and started making positive comments. She even asked my father how he was today with a tone of voice that would challenge any cheerleader at a football game. My father's response was, "Jesus Christ, I am dying. How the hell do you think I am doing?" This is what I mean when I say we need both; it is up to the person who is challenged in any situation to dictate how much positivity they want.

People have moments of hope where positivity can be received and it lifts them up, but it needs to be okay for them not to be able to receive it as well. We are complex with our moods and our experiences.

PEACE POINT 50: Don't Stick Your Head in the Sand
Don't be the lid on a conversation that needs to breathe.
Read the room.

One critical opposite of genuine positivity is not negativity but **positive toxicity.**

Positive toxicity occurs when positivity is used as a social expectation rather than a supportive presence. It is the subtle pressure to "stay upbeat," "keep things light," or "look on the bright side" in moments that require honesty, listening, and emotional space. Unlike healthy optimism, positive toxicity prioritizes comfort over truth and appearance over alignment.

Positive toxicity often sounds cheerful, but it lands as dismissive. It shows up when someone chirps, "Look on the bright side," while another person is falling apart. It denies lived experience through forced reassurance and premature encouragement. The intention may be kind, but the impact is invalidating.

Some people describe this behavior as being "tone deaf," but positive toxicity goes deeper than tone. It reflects a discomfort with emotional complexity and a desire to bypass pain rather than sit with it. When positivity becomes compulsory, it stops being supportive and starts becoming harmful.

This is closely related to what many clinicians refer to as **toxic positivity,** a term used to describe the broader cultural pattern of emotional invalidation through forced optimism. Licensed therapist Whitney Goodman defines toxic positivity as *"the overgeneralization of a happy, optimistic state that results in the denial, minimization, and invalidation of the authentic human emotional experience."*

Where *toxic positivity* describes the cultural pattern, **positive toxicity** names the lived, relational moment when positivity becomes misaligned with reality. Peace does not ask us to bypass discomfort. It asks us to stay present with what is real—without rushing, fixing, or covering it up with cheerfulness.

Alignment requires honesty.

Peace requires presence.

And sometimes the most supportive response is not positivity, but permission to be authentic.

We favor balance and realism. Authenticity allows for positivity and pain to coexist. Neither are completely right nor wrong. We define positive toxicity as when positivity is used as a shield or even a weapon—for example, when someone asserts their version of "rightness" in a way that harms or invalidates others. It's when someone knowingly speaks about a situation that causes great suffering for another person with a positive spin. A cringeworthy example is someone taking a smiling selfie in the midst of a devastating situation and posting it on Facebook. That is tone deaf and causes many people pain.

True peaceful positivity doesn't demand agreement. It doesn't impose. It invites. It listens. It holds space for both grief and gratitude, for rage and relief. It allows all of it—without judgment and without shame.

Positive toxicity robs us of our voice, and we want to instead emphasize, "I see you. I hear you. I am with you. I love you."

Another example occurred one day when Dr. Katie was sitting by the pool, enjoying her calm. Then someone walked by wearing a T-shirt with an offensive slogan. It was bold. Jarring. Suddenly, the peace around the place dissolved. Sure, she could choose not to give that moment power—but she still had to ask: Why would someone deliberately provoke others in a space meant for rest?

Nearby, a loud conversation broke out—opposing views, passionate voices, regurgitating prepackaged opinions. And she thought: *This is it. This is what positive toxicity can look like.* It's not disagreement itself, but the absence of listening. It was all noise. No depth. No space.

That same shallowness is what we sometimes hear in the phrase "No worries." It sounds friendly, but it can feel like a way to dismiss rather than engage. That's the danger of positivity without depth, which silences instead of supports.

PEACE POINT 51: Hold Space

Sometimes even the word *positivity* makes people cringe. For each of us at different times, the word is delightful and paves a path to gratitude and light, which can and has brought us through a variety of various situations and circumstances. For others, it brings to mind phrases like, "Don't worry, be happy," which, if interpreted or timed wrong, may feel dismissive when we're facing real-life pain. There is a complexity to human experience that no quote or platitude on Earth can properly address.

Each of these Peace Points invites us to cultivate a life in which positivity isn't just a feeling. It's a practice rooted in authenticity, awareness, and grace.

PEACE POINT 52: Read the Room

We found ourselves asking, why is positivity so hard and the source of so much discomfort? We decided to explore this chapter from the perspective that we don't want you to fall into the happiness trap.

Life isn't meant to be a nonstop joyride. It's meant to be *lived,* with effort, growth, and grace. We cringe when we hear people say they just want to be happy all the time. What a setup! If that were life's purpose, there'd be no calories. We mean, really: Life would have no alarm clocks, and every line at the DMV would come with free coffee and doughnuts! Fortunately, life doesn't cater to extreme comfort; it calls us to evolve, exert effort, and discover meaning.

Our cringing has a lot to do with the fact that lack of happiness is probably one of the psychological concepts that sets people up the most to feel inadequate. "Why am I not happy?" is a phrase we hear all too often, leaving the person asking the question even more confused.

Happy is one of the most misunderstood words in the field of psychology. Why? Because what most people mean by happiness is actually more likely related to peace of mind. Peace involves a steady choice to seek something positive in every situation. It's a mindset, a framework from which to make choices and decisions. It's a lifestyle, a general sense of well-being. In other words, it's how you *want* to live.

We are all in different places and have different emotions and circumstances in all moments. To honor and respect that, we want to explore what we call "peaceful positivity," which is the practice of gently finding moments of light.

It's about being fully present with what is real for you and choosing peace when and where you can. After all, who is anyone to tell you how much happiness and positivity to bring into your life at any given time? Bring in as much as you need, when you need it. You get to define that. When positivity becomes part of your identity, you move through life with grace, courage, and an unwavering belief in the possibility of peace.

In contrast, happiness is a state; it's fleeting, temporary, and based on external circumstances. Peaceful positivity is the thought process that motivates us to experience moments of happiness. To seek happiness in all things at all times is to miss the most important step—a peaceful mindset.

No matter what the circumstances are in our lives, a peaceful, positive mindset leads to more frequent moments of happiness. That's the confusion; peace comes first. . . .

At the beginning of this chapter, we told you we started to write this chapter while on vacation. We finished back home and, *boom*, reality set in.

It felt like a happiness zapper. We both said to each other multiple times, "I want to go back on vacation!"

We're not alone in this. Why do people do this? We have such a skewed vision of happiness. On both ends of the vacations, we experienced relief from our real life as though those moments were happier or more joyful or more peaceful. The reason is that we both caught ourselves measuring our happiness with external influences.

This was our a-ha moment for this chapter. Actually, there were a few challenges when we returned home. Dr. Katie came home in a state of jet lag to hear the piercing noise of a smoke detector that required climbing up a six-foot ladder in the living room at 2:00 AM. Elizabeth returned home to an unexpected septic tank disaster. Nothing screams, "Welcome home!" more than real-life problems, knowing there's no peaceful external setting for escape. This was a wake-up call for both of us. We learned that we have to find authentic positivity that has nothing to do with anything other than our own ability to draw from ourselves, from our own perspectives about how to handle tough situations. An honest, peaceful, positive response is not simple; however, it can be learned.

PEACE POINT 53: Put Away the Platitudes

One of our greatest challenges is helping people understand that when someone is hurting, platitudes do not help—especially, "It will be okay." When someone experiences a significant loss, it will never be "okay," but how you cope with it and integrate it into your life makes you feel better. Sometimes a loss is just too horrific to ever be okay. It's an important distinction that causes people great distress. We have witnessed many people expressing platitudes to make someone feel better when in reality it's about making themselves feel better.

Resist the temptation to fill an uncomfortable situation with placating words and instead simply say the most peaceful statement: "I am so sorry, and I am here for you." That is what those who are hurting need to hear most.

PEACE POINT 54: Feel the Feels

We don't want you to set yourself up to think that if you choose happiness all will be well. We have a myriad of emotions for a reason. There is no such thing as a negative emotion, only a discomfort we feel when we experience some of them. We want you to experience all of them when they come; it's like the rainbow of being human. After the emotion comes a message, a lesson, an opportunity. Life isn't meant to be all positive. The potential for growth can sometimes include anger, sadness, and discontent. These all signal to us that something needs our attention. As a recovering Pollyanna, Dr. Katie can attest that life is much richer when we live it colorfully, experiencing all of it. That's what we learned about Elizabeth's rainbows.

Peaceful positivity is facing *all* the colors of emotion.

There are times and situations when the majority of people gathering are celebrating while other individuals, because of their hidden pain, are not experiencing happiness. It becomes a dilemma for people who are silently having a different experience.

Are baby showers supposed to be happy occasions? Mother's Day? Father's Day? Yes, but not for everyone. In fact, there are elements of joy for most, but for some, like Dr. Katie who struggled with pregnancy losses, there is sadness. Does that mean she should ignore both emotions? No, it means the positive, peaceful approach is to show up and engage in the activities until it becomes painful and then make a quiet exit.

For Elizabeth, it means doing painstaking planning when she goes anywhere that food is involved to ensure she doesn't come in contact with anything that will affect her serious food allergies.

Planning for challenges is the mindset behind peaceful positivity—and provides the best opportunity to remain peaceful and grounded.

PEACE POINT 55: Adapt Your Mindset

Feeling deeply is the beginning of peace; thinking differently is how we sustain it. Once you've honored your emotions, the invitation is to bring that same honesty and openness to your thoughts. This is where peaceful positivity turns practical, by learning to adapt your mindset in real-world situations, even when the "vacation calm" fades.

For example, when you go on vacation, don't set yourself up by believing that your issues won't be there when you return. Find ways to relax when you are away, so that you can face the challenges when you return. People often try to re-create the vacation experience when they come home, but that is not possible! What we can do is adopt a different mindset to help us cope with our everyday lives. We want you to stop putting yourself down when your real life doesn't feel the same as vacation. You can escape for a period of time, but it's how you live when you return that has the greatest impact on your overall life.

There's a reason people say, "This is my happy place" or "I need my nature fix." You can recapture those vacation moments by spending time in a garden or walking in a park or even something as simple as listening to soothing water sounds—whatever calms you and allows you to access your positive and hopeful attitude. Studies show that spending time in nature helps us reset and bring in peace. Peace can feel easier in certain places. We aren't denying that our circumstance impacts how easily we can access natural beauty but think bigger. We can all look up and see that same expansive sky! The truth is, we are all connected by the earth and sky, so let's remember this when we begin to think about discovering for ourselves how to find peace in nature. For most of us, it's only a footstep or a glance away.

PEACE POINT 56: See Possibilities

Our approach to positivity is not fluffy optimism that denies hardship. We know how difficult life can be. We're not asking anyone to pretend things are fine when they're not.

Do us a favor and replace the thought *I am positive* with *I see possibilities*. It's a subtle but important shift. It acknowledges that positivity isn't about being relentlessly cheerful 24/7 but about recognizing potential, even in challenging circumstances. Staying upbeat and optimistic sometimes isn't effortless, to say the least. Many of us need to seek out deliberate activities, surround ourselves with uplifting people, or hold onto brief but meaningful moments of joy.

So, before we go any further, we want to say to those of you who are barely making it through each day just trying to get by: *We see you.* We understand that some days, positivity feels like an impossible ask. We're not here to pile on pressure or tell you to simply "think happy thoughts." Instead, we invite you to consider a different perspective—one that allows for both struggle and hope and honors everything in between.

Let's explore what positivity can look like in a way that fits your reality. It's not about denying hardship; it's about finding a way forward, one possibility at a time.

Positivity may feel like it is relative to your circumstance, and sometimes it just might be. There are times—sometimes moments, days, or if you are lucky, months—when life seems even-keeled and being positive is simpler, but for most of you, that's not real life. We are a no-fluff zone, so we want to encourage you to be real about positivity in recognizing it and looking for and creating a mindset that tries to find something positive when you can. It's looking for the crack where the light creeps through.

PEACE POINT 57: Anchor in Gratitude

Gratitude has the power to ground us, especially when life feels uncertain, overwhelming, or even heartbreaking. It doesn't mean ignoring pain or pretending that difficult situations don't exist. Instead, true gratitude is about acknowledging what is real while choosing to find moments of light within the darkness. Flip, shift, reframe, re-create, and rethink it to make gratitude a regular practice. When life feels heavy, finding something to be grateful for can shift your perspective and soften the edges of hardship. Gratitude reminds us that even in the midst of uncertainty, there is always something worth holding onto. It's not about minimizing the difficulty of what you're experiencing but recognizing that gratitude and grief can coexist and that both can be honored without canceling the other out.

Gratitude doesn't ask us to deny our pain. Instead, it invites us to expand our perspective—to notice the moments of grace, the hands that help, and the lessons that emerge when we least expect them. By practicing gratitude in difficult times, you allow yourself to stay rooted in hope and possibility, which can create a pathway to healing and inner peace. Learn to recognize that even in the midst of difficulty, there is always something—no matter how small—to be grateful for.

Use our "Gratitude Flip" to create a powerful practice of shifting your mindset from *I have to* to *I can* or *I get to*. It's not about minimizing hardship. It's about reframing your perspective to see everyday tasks and challenges as opportunities, not burdens.

Here's how it works. When you catch yourself thinking,

- I have to go to work.
- I have to take care of this.
- I have to deal with this situation.

Pause and ask yourself,

What if I see this as something I can do or I get to do?

The simple act of changing "I have to" into "I get to" or "I can do" shifts your energy and opens the door to gratitude.

- "I get to go to work," where I have the opportunity to contribute, learn, and grow.
- "I can take care of this," which means I am capable, strong, and trusted to handle life's challenges.
- "I get to experience this moment," which means I am alive, present, and connected.

Again, having gratitude doesn't erase the challenge, but it reframes your experience, helping you approach life with a sense of appreciation, empowerment, and possibility.

You teach yourself to cultivate peaceful positivity by seeing life through a lens of gratitude that transforms even the most ordinary moments into opportunities for growth and joy.

Pause and ask yourself,

"What happens when I reframe this?"

"What if I see this as something I can do?"

By practicing gratitude consistently, you teach yourself to cultivate peaceful positivity and see life through a lens of gratitude that transforms even the most ordinary moments into opportunities for growth and joy.

PEACE POINT 58: Find Grounded Happiness, Joy, and Peace

We often associate happiness, joy, and peace with external experiences, vacations, sunsets, and moments of stillness. But true peace isn't something we need to *chase*; it's something we can *cultivate*. It's an inner state that can be nurtured by intentionally creating micromoments of joy wherever we are.

Imagine this: You're standing barefoot on warm, sun-kissed sand, the rhythmic crash of waves echoing in the distance. A gentle breeze carries the salty scent of the ocean, and the sun paints the sky in soft hues of gold and blue. For just a moment, everything feels still, calm, and infinite—like the sea stretching endlessly before you.

Now, wouldn't it be amazing if we could carry that same sense of peace into our daily lives no matter where we are? Here's the secret: You don't have to be standing on a beach to feel the calm of the ocean. Your brain can't differentiate between imagining a peaceful place and being there. You can experience the same sensations living in the middle of Manhattan as on the beaches of Cape Cod. Allow yourself to imagine what it would be like to be standing wherever your ideal peaceful spot is. Where do you feel that same sensation? Go there in your mind and feel what happens. Your heart rate will steady, your pulse will go down, and your body will experience a gentle state of calm. Your brain will bring you there.

Peace, joy, and happiness live in ordinary moments too. They're in the quiet sip of morning coffee, the warmth of a loved one's embrace, or the rhythm of raking the pile of fall leaves in your front yard. The trick is learning to notice these moments, to pause, breathe, and soak them in—just like you would be standing on that beach. Think about a place or moment where you've felt deep peace and joy. What emotions or sensations did you experience? Next, think about how you can re-create that feeling in small ways throughout your daily life.

Give yourself permission to pause even in the busiest moments. Take thirty seconds to breathe deeply, close your eyes, and ask yourself, *Where can I find a moment of peace right now?*

● ● ●

Our Pathways to Peace with Elizabeth and Dr. Katie

Elizabeth—Maintaining Peaceful Positivity with Life-Threatening Food Allergies

I've learned that every nanosecond of your life matters and not to waste them. We aren't entitled to time.

I've learned this from having life-threatening food allergies since 1997 and nearly losing my life on several occasions due to anaphylaxis. When I have a reaction, it's not about struggling to breathe—my blood pressure drops rapidly, creating an immediate medical crisis. There is no warning, no slow buildup. It happens in an instant, requiring swift emergency intervention.

Living with severe food allergies means constantly navigating a world that doesn't always understand the seriousness of the condition. Every meal, every social event, and even something as simple as grocery shopping requires vigilance. Food isn't just nourishment; it can be a threat. I didn't grow up with these allergies. They developed in my mid-twenties, and the shift was life-changing. I went from eating without a second thought to having to question and analyze everything I put into my body.

The reality of this condition hit hardest when I was six months pregnant with our son, Cam, and suffered a severe anaphylactic reaction that required resuscitation. That moment changed everything for me. I realized how fragile life is and how quickly it can be taken away. From that day forward, I knew my life would require an extra layer of caution, preparation, and advocacy—not just for myself but for others facing similar challenges.

One of the most difficult aspects of living with food allergies is the unpredictability. No matter how careful I am, there have been terrifying close calls—times when a mislabeled ingredient or cross-contact at a restaurant turned an ordinary moment into a medical emergency. I've spent nights in the ER as doctors worked to stabilize my blood pressure and prevent the worst-case scenario. These experiences never get easier, but they have made me resilient and deeply aware of how precious each moment is.

Social situations can be challenging. Well-meaning friends and family don't always understand the severity of my allergies. I've lost count of how many times I've heard, "Are you sure you can't have this?" or "Just a little won't hurt you." The truth is that even microscopic amounts of an allergen can be deadly. Eating at restaurants is always a calculated risk, involving detailed conversations, checking ingredient lists, and sometimes walking away if I don't feel safe. It's exhausting to always be on high alert, but it's necessary.

Traveling adds another layer of complexity. While others enjoy the spontaneity of trying new foods, I have to meticulously plan ahead—researching restaurants, packing safe snacks, and sometimes bringing my own meals. Even air travel requires careful preparation, as airborne allergens can pose a risk. But despite these challenges, I refuse to let my allergies keep me from experiencing life. I've learned how to balance caution with adventure, making adjustments that allow me to participate fully while staying safe.

Beyond the physical dangers, the emotional toll of food allergies is significant. There's an underlying anxiety that never fully goes away. Every bite of food is a decision, a risk assessment. The fear of a reaction lingers, even in spaces that should feel safe. It takes immense mental strength to navigate this reality every day.

Yet through it all, I have found gratitude. My experiences have taught me to appreciate the little things—the safe meals prepared with care, the people who take the time to understand, the moments when I can simply exist without worry. I have deep appreciation for those who take food allergies seriously, for restaurants that go the extra mile, and for the growing awareness that is making the world a little safer.

Through my work, I've been able to turn my struggles into something meaningful. I founded Food Allergy Zone to raise awareness and provide resources for others living with severe allergies. I coauthored, with Sally Huss, the bestselling children's book *A Lesson for Every Child: Learning About Food Allergies* to help educate kids, parents, and teachers. I also serve as a spokesperson for FAACT (Food Allergy and Anaphylaxis Connection Team) and the MedicAlert Foundation, advocating for education, safety, and support for those with life-threatening allergies.

Having a positive impact brings me peace. Knowing that my experiences and advocacy can help others stay alive and thrive makes every challenge I've faced feel purposeful. I choose to focus on what I can control—spreading awareness, supporting others, and making the world a safer place for those with food allergies. And that, to me, is one of the best ways to spend the time we're given.

Dr. Katie—Positivity and Loss

One of the times in my life when my peaceful positivity was greatly challenged occurred when I joined a club I never wanted to join—the divorced club. I found myself leaving a comfortable, cozy home to live in a square box, a seasonal rental midwinter beach cottage. It was probably no more than ten-by-ten feet that literally fit me, a cot, and space for a table and chair. I wrote my doctoral thesis on that table looking through a twelve-inch-by-twelve-inch window. With the companionship of my two cats and my resolve to discover something positive about myself and my new situation, that little square space became the shelter for a very significant sojourn. Living simply taught me to simply live peacefully, and when I emerged from my four months of writing and quiet walks and, most important, times of self-reflection, I discovered that peaceful positivity can be found in the smallest of ways and the tiniest places.

Others don't always recognize that what we view as an opportunity can be something positive. They may not share the same growth mindset as us. This was the case for me when my parents first visited me at this little healing place. My mother cried (and she rarely cried). She expressed her disappointment that I was living in such a place. She didn't yet understand that it was here that I felt closer to myself; to be alone with so little except my furry family meant that I could get to know myself, to grieve and gain wisdom from my pain. Later, after that winter, when I returned to living in a spacious apartment reborn and with a new attitude about living, she told me she had great admiration for my courage to live there. People may not share your perspective, but what is most important is that you are clear about your positive intention. That is one of the many lessons I learned there.

That winter season in my ten-by-ten box led to a new chapter in my life. Dr. Katie was born there. Long walks navigating the snow and ice brought me to an expansive view of water and sky that reminded me of life's endless possibilities. During those peaceful walks and writing in my journal, I took the time to allow my loss from the divorce to inform me about what mattered. I discovered my positive new direction and transformed the lessons that I learned from loss into a career. Loss, change, and growth were the themes of my doctoral dissertation and my life, and I needed to find a way to bring my new wisdom to others. Dr. Katie, the author, counselor, Master Grief Coach, and change consultant emerged in that tiny peaceful space when the power of peaceful positivity became clear.

For many people experiencing a transition like divorce, they find themselves asking how and why they got there and what they can learn to prevent themselves from getting into a similar situation. That requires taking a positive approach to what hurts—not with the intention of ignoring the pain but rather letting it teach you something. My time alone, with only my furry family and a confined space in nature, left me free to hear my own longings and gain a better understanding of what my peaceful life would be like. Asking myself tough questions allowed me to discover what prepared me for my next phase of life, my new season with my now-husband, John. If I hadn't taken that time to identify what I needed to live with peaceful positivity, so many things would have been different. I gratefully approached this opportunity and learned so much!

Here were some of my gratitude gifts: I woke up every morning to the sound of the wind and the waves crashing against the icy shore. I loved the sound, and each morning when I walked headfirst into that energy force of wind against my face, it reminded me of the power that I too possessed. No longer did I allow myself to feel helpless and powerless; rather, the power of the sounds of nature empowered me.

The importance of feeling nurtured was brought home to me by the gentle touch of my cats snuggling up beside me to stay warm when the heater stopped working. I took extra special care of myself, paying special attention to having the right clothing. I loved the feel of my boots with my warm wooly socks keeping my feet warm when

I braved the icy walkway to the frozen beach. The list of my learnings is long, but the reality is that with very little I found more peace than I had living in the comfort of a large, expansive home. Why? I chose to experience this place with peaceful positivity, and for me it became a refuge and a place and time in my life when my circumstances led me to an opportunity I never would have imagined for myself.

I left there in spring. I was renewed, eager, and ready to garner my spiritual muscles and focus on meeting my needs and ensuring that my future surroundings would maintain that sense of peace. My cat is curled up on my lap as I write this. No matter where I have been, that same simple sensibility and the value of personal power, self-nurturance, and care are still vital aspects of my peaceful positivity.

True positivity doesn't bypass pain—it meets it with courage, wisdom, and compassion. In this chapter, we are honored to share two deeply moving and honest reflections from contributors who embody the transformative power of choosing peace and purpose through adversity. Actor, author, and musician Michael McGlone offers a poetic meditation on finding peace through presence, surrender, and perspective, even in life's darkest moments. Ameenah McCann-Woods shares her powerful journey of parenting and advocacy after her son's autism diagnosis, reminding us that positivity often looks like patience, resilience, and unconditional love. Both stories illuminate how positivity, when practiced with integrity, becomes a radical and restorative force for peace.

Stories from the Heart

Michael McGlone—Peace

I wish you peace. By that, I mean I wish you a positive approach to whatever situation you find yourself in, whether it's a challenge, a feeling, a thought, or a relationship. The best we can do is engage each circumstance with the most positive outlook possible. This isn't always easy, but it's always worth it. Holding onto negative energy or opinions only leads to stagnation and defeat. Peace begins when we accept what's happening, both inside and around us.

To have peace is to engage everything—even negative feelings—with openness and compassion. Negativity itself is simply waiting to be accepted and understood. If you meet it with curiosity instead of resistance, negativity becomes a teacher. Often, our persistent negative emotions are signals pointing to something unresolved within us. The way forward is through positivity and acceptance, not denial.

A positive perspective allows us to see more completely, because it's rooted in acceptance, which fosters peace. Negative energy is rooted in resistance, which breeds conflict. Fear, anger, resentment—these all narrow our view and separate us from truth. When we approach life positively, we see more clearly and love more fully. Love expands understanding, while negativity contracts it—building walls to protect us from pain, but in truth only making the pain greater. Only by choosing to feel, to be vulnerable, and to face discomfort with faith and positivity can we find freedom.

Years ago, I was greatly challenged—financially, professionally, and personally. A woman I dearly loved had left my life, and I was in debt, without income or work. It appeared to me that anything, everything that I wanted had been universally ordered to remain out of my grasp and that all my efforts to bring them to me were to fail.

The vulnerability of this time and the temptation to see my circumstances as negative were abundant. Finally, unable to keep the struggle to myself any longer, I called my mother and found myself openly crying, and then said, "Mom, I don't know what to do." I was ashamed to say it but had to say it.

I do not believe our hearts break, I believe they only break open. And that is what happened to me that day. In surrender, I found strength. I gave thanks for my mother, for the Lord, *and* for the struggle and humility that deepened my relationship with both.

Challenges did not cease overnight, but my resistance did. I humbly, with the Lord's support, accepted them all, positively knowing I was loved and accounted for and the best I could do was remain positive.

Some months later, a young man asked me for my advice, and I told him my story and said, "Even what I feared most, 'not knowing what to do,' was an illusion. The Lord showed me what to do: admit I didn't know."

Now in daily prayer and thanks I acknowledge the blessing of that time and all the blessings throughout my life, one of which surely was *The Brothers McMullen.* This was the film that started my career, and one we have just made a sequel to, to be called *The Family McMullen,* which is a perfect reminder of the wonderful adage, "The light always returns.... It is simply a matter of the time it takes to do so."

So, when darkness comes, remain positive. Negative energy will close your eyes, positivity opens them. Explore what's happening within you. Ask yourself, *Am I living in acceptance or resistance?* If it is acceptance, you will know peace.

And I wish you that, now and always.

Ameenah McCann-Woods—Leaning into Positivity with Autism Awareness and Unconditional Love

Our journey with Lorenzo Jr. (LJ) began the day he was born, July 11, 2015. I had him one day before my thirty-sixth birthday.

I had waited with intention before becoming a mother: I wanted to enjoy my youth, complete my education, and build a solid career. Most of all, I consciously wanted to find the right partner with whom I could build a healthy family. While I had a loving mother, I also witnessed unhealthy relationships growing up—experiences that left me with anxiety and a clear sense of what I didn't want.

My husband and I met in 2005 and were married in 2012. We had a lot of growing to do together, but by the time we married, I was ready. I stopped using birth control. Around the same time, I was diagnosed with uterine fibroids, which made conceiving more difficult. Still, in October 2014, we learned we were pregnant. We were ecstatic—and nervous. My husband had been laid off a few months earlier, and financial uncertainty shadowed our joy. But we moved forward with love and gratitude.

When LJ was one and a half, I sensed something different about him. He hit the typical milestones—walking, running, saying "Mama," "Dada," and "bye-bye." But his speech stopped progressing. Instead of words, he led us by the hand to what he needed. His frustration was growing, and so was mine. I didn't know how to help him.

I searched online for information. Most sources said he should be speaking at least fifty words. What did this mean? I worried about all the possible scenarios: Autism? ADHD? Some kind of developmental delay? Yet LJ was joyful and curious—full of life. His doctors and even family members couldn't see what I saw. Many told me, "He's a boy—boys take longer," or "Give him time." But I couldn't shake the feeling.

As a Black mother, I was also wary of how little Black boys are often unfairly labeled or misunderstood. There was fear that seeking help might lead to judgment or harm.

But I also knew I couldn't let fear override my intuition. We delayed preschool and social outings. Isolation set in.

In early 2019, we finally enrolled LJ in speech therapy. We didn't have a car, so we spent money weekly on Lyft rides to get him there. Slowly, he began speaking more—sometimes in a sweet, singsong voice; sometimes just one word at a time. But they were his words. His confidence began to grow. He played more. Smiled more. He realized that even a single word could open up his world.

Six months into therapy, his therapist recommended further evaluation. That fall, we had him assessed in preschool and again later. In February 2020, LJ was diagnosed with autism.

I wasn't scared. I already knew.

My husband, Lorenzo Sr., struggled more with acceptance at first. As we walked out of the evaluation center, I said to him, "Nothing about our son has changed. Now we just have more information. And information is power."

That was the beginning of our peace.

We quickly enrolled LJ in early intervention services. He went to school for half the day and continued speech therapy once a week. By then, my husband had come around too. He saw what I saw: Our son was still amazing, still intelligent, still independent. The diagnosis didn't define him—it gave us a way to support him.

Then COVID hit.

Everything shut down—school, therapy, routines. It was heartbreaking. He cried. I cried. He ran and hid. I chased and consoled. The virtual format didn't work for him. The faces he trusted were now behind screens. He didn't want anything to do with it.

So I leaned into him.

We walked—sometimes for hours. We played scavenger hunts and did science experiments in the yard. I bought books, flashcards, and workbooks. Our home was covered in sticky notes to help him learn vocabulary and reading. I even bought a book on how to do speech therapy at home.

It was exhausting. And it was beautiful.

I'm a working mom, usually racing the clock. Before the pandemic, I often felt like I was squeezing motherhood in between tasks. But during that pause, I became a full-time mother in every way. I saw who LJ truly was. He is literally my twin—he looks like me, moves like me, feels like me. I learned his likes, dislikes, and quirks. I saw his joy, his challenges, his spirit.

And I saw my own strength in showing up, over and over.

Autism has changed our family—for the better. We have a newfound respect for patience, timing, and emotional autonomy. We've dismantled generational norms. In our house, LJ's voice matters. His emotions matter. He understands he is different, and we make sure he knows that "different" is not less.

His peace is knowing he can be fully himself. Ours is watching him grow in that truth.

LJ is now nine years old. Since 2020, he's gone from nonverbal to beautifully verbal. He excels in school. He's recognized for citizenship in and outside the classroom. He trains in Hapkido and earned his yellow belt. He's active with a local nonprofit that supports neurodiverse children. Recently, he was honored at the inaugural PHLAbilities awards hosted by the School District of Philadelphia.

But beyond the milestones, LJ is loving, empathetic, funny, independent, and deeply aware. He reminds us of important dates and tiny details we forget, like where we left our keys. He expresses his feelings with clarity and nuance. He knows when he's frustrated, content, excited, or confused. That kind of self-awareness is a superpower.

And every day, he teaches us more about what love looks like in action.

Autism didn't steal anything from us. It gave us a new way to see the world. It taught us to celebrate small wins and lean into the hard days. It taught us that positivity isn't pretending things are easy. It's choosing joy even when they're not.

I am still leaning into him.

He is LJ.

He is autistic.

He is made with love.

And he is deeply, joyfully loved by everyone who knows him.

POINTS TO PONDER

Think. Write. Talk. Action. *(Because practice makes us our best.)*

EXERCISE 13: Practicing Positivity

INSTRUCTIONS: Think of a recent situation where you found it difficult to stay positive. It could be a challenge, a disagreement, or a moment of self-doubt. Take a deep breath and reframe the situation by focusing on the lessons, growth, or hidden blessings within it.

Describe an event or moment that challenged your peaceful positivity.

_____

_____

_____

_____

_____

Identify the positive aspects or lessons learned. *(What did this situation teach you? How did it strengthen you?)*

_____

_____

_____

Reframe your perspective. *(Rewrite your thoughts about this experience in a way that promotes peace and positivity.)*

_____

_____

_____

EXERCISE 14: Creating a Grounded, Peaceful Mindset

INSTRUCTIONS: Peace begins within. In this exercise, you will define "peaceful positivity" for yourself.

What is peaceful positivity for you? *(Describe the emotions, thoughts, or sensations you associate with peace.)*

_____

_____

_____

_____

_____

List three things that help you feel peaceful and grounded:

_____

_____

_____

Define your idea of toxic positivity. Have you experienced it?

_____

_____

_____

Define your idea of positive toxicity. Have you experienced it?

_____

_____

_____

How can you transform these experiences into examples of peaceful positivity?

_____

_____

_____

CHAPTER 8
PERSEVERANCE

In the eighth principle of peace, Perseverance, we never give up on the hope that our world and the world around us can be peaceful. When it gets really tough, we persevere. Reflecting on our why, our purpose, and our passion gives us the power to persist. Recommitting our energy helps you pivot and carry on by redirecting our attention back to peace and impacting others. Peace and perseverance are partners. Peace is a way of being, and perseverance is how that way of being survives the world. Every time you choose to keep showing up, even gently, even slowly, even with a heavy heart, you are practicing peace. Peace is not a place we land when the storm passes. Peace is how we choose to move through the storm with wisdom, intention, and grace.

Peace is the soul of perseverance. It's the quiet energy that keeps us moving forward with purpose, even when progress feels slow. It's not the chase for success; it's the steady flow that sustains us along the way. We have navigated decades of health challenges, public scrutiny, and the emotional terrain of both raising a family and building a media platform. We can tell you firsthand: Perseverance is not always heroic.

Both of us were type AAA+ driven in all aspects of our lives. We were having another one of our chats for this chapter about how hard we had both worked in our lives to get to the point of bringing this book to life. We've both had our share of rejections along the way. There were multiple off-ramps, twists and turns, and definitely a broken road. Life is not predictable, and we have learned that perseverance does not mean success.

We have redefined success many times through the years. In fact, we both feel like the older we get, the less we care about the small things that at one time felt so important. We both find ourselves looking back a bit, not with regret, but with greater wisdom, hoping that we inspire people much younger than us to catch on faster than we did.

This is the heart of peaceful perseverance: It's not about forcing the outcome; it's about staying available to what's possible while embodying grace.

PEACE POINT 59: Reframe Perseverance

We live in a world where burnout and resilience are often confused with exhaustion. What if we reframed perseverance not as a blind march forward but as an elegant alignment between our inner peace and our external purpose?

Peaceful perseverance is not about hustling through hardship or suppressing emotion. It is about choosing to remain anchored in your essence, committed to your values, and energetically congruent even when the outcome is uncertain.

When you see your life as rich with meaning, even when messy, you unlock a deeper dimension of peace that reveals the choice to persevere. You stop reacting and start evolving. That is a sacred shift. You're not just pushing through, today you're *building something*. Your perseverance is shaping the emotional DNA of everyone around you.

What legacy are you building?

What are you modeling in the moments when no one is watching?

If your children, your community, and your colleagues could see your inner world, would they see love in motion?

Let that guide you. Let that ground you. Let that carry you. You don't have to be perfect to keep going. You don't have to be fearless to be faithful to your path. You don't have to wait until you're "ready"—you just have to begin.

One of the greatest myths about perseverance is that it ends with a mountaintop moment. That there's a moment of arrival after which all struggle dissolves.

But the truth is this: The mountaintop isn't really the top or the end. It's integration.

You don't persevere to achieve peace.

You persevere because peace is your guiding energy.

You keep going, not because you're chasing something, but because something within you refuses to give up on becoming. That's the kind of perseverance that redefines what it means to live a peaceful life.

PEACE POINT 60: Know When to Rest

The decision to rest is a form of perseverance. Yes, that is correct, rest.

Pausing isn't quitting, it's strategic.

Stillness isn't stagnation, it's sacred.

Real peace requires us to know when to stop. People don't abandon themselves because they stop, shift, or pivot.

In Elizabeth's own life—as a mother of four sons, a CEO, an author, a coach, and someone navigating life-threatening allergies—there are days when the highest act of perseverance is simply choosing presence over performance.

For Dr. Katie, navigating a full-time therapy practice, writing a book, and maintaining a personal life requires time spent playing, enjoying life, and working . . . in that order. In sixty-five years around the sun, she has learned how to prioritize that time to rest and restore, and to make space for enjoyment with family and friends.

PEACE POINT 61: Never Give Up on Your Peace

We often hear the phrase "Never give up," but it's usually directed outward—toward achievements, goals, or challenges—rather than inward, toward ourselves. We want to challenge you to think differently. Perseverance can sometimes be quiet. It shows up in the steady drip of a morning routine that grounds you, even when no one is watching. It's the decision to open your heart again after disappointment, or to send the email, write the page, make the call, knowing the result might be silence. It's turning toward the mirror and saying, "I believe in you," even when the world has given you reasons to doubt.

Perseverance is often described as pushing forward despite adversity, but that definition is incomplete. True perseverance is not just the continuing effort; it is the mindfulness or elevation of consciousness (subconscious) in the presence of difficulty. It is the deliberate decision to root into peace while everything around you invites chaos, collapse, or resignation.

For example, we dissuade others from using the words *try* or *trying*. The reason we suggest you replace those words in most circumstances is that we want your language to be empowering. The brain sends a different signal when we speak with messaging that says we've already done something. It registers the same chemistry that signals we have completed it. Our response, then, is positive. In other words, the brain can't differentiate between doing and envisioning. So instead of *try* or *trying,* use *I am* in the present tense, such as "I am _____."

This is the unseen labor of peaceful perseverance. It's also how we access our resilience.

Perseverance isn't just about grit. It's about pattern recognition.

It's asking.

What gets you up when you're down?

What keeps calling you forward, even when it's hard?

What are the themes that return to you in times of doubt?

Right now, as we are writing this, two wonderful women in Dr. Katie's life are battling cancer. Dr. Katie is inspired by their courage and their approach, living each day with a resolve to experience moments of joy. This reminds her of the preciousness of time, and she understands firsthand the need to support others when they need to persevere through those battles. We prioritize time spent with loved ones now more than ever because of our realization that when life happens, we need the reserve to be able to rise up and lift up others. Perseverance sometimes means being there for another—even if it means working differently, more consciously aware of your need to rest and recharge.

PEACE POINT 62: Protect and Direct Your Energy

Your energy is your most sacred currency. Peaceful energy is when we choose to move through life with wisdom, intention, and grace. Peace isn't just about slowing down or staying calm. It's about conscious, energetic stewardship. When you learn to manage and direct your energy with purpose, you stop leaking power into people, patterns, and environments that drain you. You recognize that your presence is potent, and where you place your energy, you place your life. This isn't about doing more. Rather, it's about doing the right things with deeper focus and intention. When you direct your energy toward healing, creativity, rest, and aligned action, peace becomes the natural byproduct. Mastering your energy means becoming both the source and the channel for your own peace and that of others. It's where sovereignty meets serenity.

PEACE POINT 63: Persevere Together in Shared Peace

Peaceful perseverance doesn't always begin alone. Sometimes it's born in community, in a circle of people holding the line for one another when everything feels like it could fall apart. It's easy to think of perseverance as an individual effort. More often than not, the kind of peace that truly endures is sustained together.

One of the most powerful examples we've witnessed during a time of extraordinary loss and uncertainty was the COVID pandemic. Many think COVID just went away and that all is well again. However, we're still seeing the fracture and side effects from that time. As we were writing this book,

Dr. Katie had recently done a seminar with burned-out healthcare workers. These frontline workers and first responders collectively rose up against unmanageable situations and are just now experiencing and processing what they endured.

It was not grand. It was not loud. It was peace in motion—through hands, presence, and follow-through. We are reminded that peaceful perseverance isn't always about how strong you are. It's about how willing you are to show up and work together while holding one another as you gather your strength again and again.

This kind of collective perseverance is quiet. It lives in casseroles and check-ins. It lives in group texts that say, "No update, just thinking of you." It lives in vigils and community forums, offices, and classrooms wherever someone shows up and keeps teaching, even after the headlines fade. It lives in the daily, mutual commitment to *not give up on one another*.

Whether you're leading a team, supporting a loved one through illness, standing with your community after tragedy, or simply trying to create a ripple of kindness in a divided world, your perseverance matters. Together we protect peace. Together we practice peace.

Peaceful perseverance is not about doing it all. It's about holding space for one another to keep going. And sometimes, showing up for someone else becomes the very thing that keeps you going too.

Here is a great example from our friend and colleague Grace Fraga. Grace describes how she found her voice in the silence of a dictatorship.

> I never wanted to talk about this. Not publicly, not privately. I buried it so deep inside me that for years, I convinced myself it was just a part of history, something I had left behind when I packed my bags and moved to the US. But the truth is, history doesn't stay in the past when it lives inside you.
>
> I grew up in Argentina under a military dictatorship from 1976 to 1983. Seven years that felt like a lifetime. Seven years of fear, censorship, and disappearances—where speaking your mind could mean you'd never be heard from again.

I was just a kid when the military took control, and suddenly, the world I knew became something out of a nightmare. Picture this: You're young, and you realize that just saying the wrong thing—asking the wrong question—could make you, or someone you love, vanish. The fear wasn't just in my head. It was in the air we breathed, in the hushed whispers of adults, in the empty chairs at school where friends once sat.

They were called Los Desaparecidos—The Disappeared Ones. Tens of thousands of people—students, journalists, teachers, artists, everyday citizens—labeled as "communists" by the regime, taken in the dead of night. If you had even a hint of leftist ideas, if you spoke out against the government, if someone even suspected you were a threat, you could be abducted, tortured, and erased. Gone, just like that. No good-byes. No justice. Just whispers and rumors—and then, silence.

My family was lucky. We were safe. No one in my immediate family disappeared. But that didn't mean we weren't afraid.

My parents spoke in whispers. Not because they wanted to—but because they had to. Conversations were carefully curated, even at home. And in public? You said nothing. You agreed with whatever the government wanted you to believe. You watched your words as if your life depended on it—because it did.

I remember my cousin, eleven years older than me, coming home one day, pale as a ghost. She had been in college when the military rounded up students they suspected of being "rebels." She wasn't a communist; she wasn't part of any underground movements, she just believed in human rights. But during those years, even believing in fairness was dangerous.

She made it home that day. Many others didn't.

We didn't know what happened to the people who disappeared until later. But rumors spread. We heard about the concentration camps. Yes, concentration camps—hidden in plain sight. People were tortured, brutalized, and murdered.

Pregnant women gave birth in captivity, only to have their babies stolen and placed into military families, raised by the very people responsible for their parents' deaths. Even today, there are adults in Argentina searching for the truth about who they really are.

And yet, as a child, you don't fully understand the weight of the horror. You just know something is terribly wrong.

Censorship was everywhere. Books were banned. Music was restricted. Newspapers printed only what the government wanted you to read. The military even burned books they deemed "dangerous." They weren't just controlling our actions—they were controlling our thoughts.

Even art wasn't safe.

I learned to adapt. I learned to stay quiet. I learned to observe, to say what people wanted to hear, to avoid confrontation at all costs. But inside? I was screaming.

I wanted to speak. I wanted to be heard. But I was terrified.

So how do you find peace when the world around you is crumbling? When fear is your constant companion?

For me, it was humor.

Laughter became my lifeline. It was how my family coped. It was how I coped. I found small joys in the chaos, moments of light in the darkness. Even when the world was telling me to be silent, I found a way to express myself—through jokes, through stories, through laughter.

And I dreamed.

I dreamed of a place where I could be free. Where I could speak without fear. Where I could be loud, opinionated, and unfiltered.

That place was the United States.

When democracy was restored in Argentina in 1983, we celebrated like never before. Families took to the streets, waving Argentine flags, honking car horns, singing in the streets. We had hope again. But for me, the scars of silence were too deep. I couldn't stay. I had seen how easily freedom could be taken away, and I wanted to go somewhere I knew I could keep it.

So, I left.

I left for a country where I could say what I wanted, where I could build a life without fear of disappearing. And, in the most ironic twist of all, I chose to do stand-up comedy, a career that demanded I speak my mind, that I take up space, that I be unapologetically myself.

Comedy was my rebellion. It was how I took back my voice.

Today, when I look back at those years, I understand why I buried this story for so long. It's painful. It's terrifying. But it's also a part of me.

It taught me resilience.

It taught me that fear can silence you but only if you let it.

It taught me that even in the darkest times, truth finds a way.

And most importantly, it taught me that laughter is an act of defiance.

When life threw more bricks at me—losing my mother, my marriage ending, my cancer diagnosis—I knew how to survive. Because I had already done it before.

I had already learned how to find light in the darkness.

I had already learned that no matter how much fear tries to silence you, there is always a way to speak.

And now? Now I tell my story.

Now I help others find their voice.

Because silence may have been my childhood reality, but my voice?

That's my legacy.

PEACE POINT 64: Trust the Carry—The Spiritual Strength to Continue

Some call it grace. Others call it divine timing, universal energy, soul presence, God, source, Spirit. You don't have to name it to feel it. But it comes. And if you're quiet enough, you'll know. You'll feel the shift from effort to allowing. From force to flow. From survival to surrender.

Spiritual perseverance isn't about giving up; it's about giving over.

Not to defeat. But to alignment.

Not to collapse. But to connection.

Not to fear. But to faith.

There comes a point when perseverance isn't something you *do* anymore, it's something you *let* happen. It's no longer about strategy, muscle, or mindset. It's about soul.

Spiritual perseverance is what carries us when the body is weary, the mind is clouded, and the heart is heavy. It is the quiet force that doesn't scream, but whispers, *"I've got you."* It's the breath that arrives when you've forgotten how to inhale. It's the invisible net of love that catches you when you've fallen so far, you've stopped trying to climb.

There is a moment, maybe more than one, in every life when you cannot take one more step by will alone. You've planned. You've tried. You've pushed. And still, the terrain is too rough. That's when a different kind of perseverance emerges—not powered by you, but through you.

We've both been in moments when there was nothing left to "do." The plan failed. The path disappeared. The grief overwhelmed. And still . . . we found ourselves carried forward. Not by achievement, not by control—but by *presence*. That is the miracle of spiritual perseverance: It doesn't erase the pain. It wraps it in meaning. It transforms isolation into belonging. It opens a channel to something larger than the wound.

Peaceful perseverance, at its core, is an act of spiritual trust.

●●●

Our Pathways to Peace with Elizabeth and Dr. Katie

Elizabeth—Joy in the After

Over my fifty-five-plus years, I've experienced more than my share of things not going as planned. There have been countless seasons where it felt like I was pushing through relentless storms just to survive—let alone practice what we call peaceful positivity from Chapter 7.

Some moments left me breathless, asking, how am I going to get through this?

Sometimes I found answers. Sometimes I just kept going.

But here I am. Still moving forward. Still believing in peace. Still choosing hope—even on the days it whispers instead of roars.

I'd say April 12, 1997, when I was in labor with our son Quinn, was the scariest moment of my life. He was stuck. His heart rate was dropping. I was exhausted. A nurse refused to give me an epidural. Quinn had shoulder dystocia, meaning his shoulder was stuck. When he was finally born, he was blue and silent, with an Apgar score of 4 out of 10, in the range for needing medical attention.

Everything in the room froze. And then—he cried. That tiny sound was everything. His first breath felt like *my* first breath all over again.

But I was wrecked. I was in a failing marriage, completely depleted—emotionally, physically, spiritually. I carried the weight of years of exhaustion and emotional pain. I had two beautiful boys I adored, but my soul felt hollow. I tried to hold everything together: corporate job, long commutes, work travel, motherhood. But eventually, what collapsed wasn't the career or the logistics—it was me.

My immune system shut down. I developed multiple life-threatening food allergies and on April 10, 1998, had a near-fatal allergic reaction to almonds. Soon after, my first marriage ended.

In 1997 and 1998, we gave everything we had to our boys. They were loved and cared for. But as a couple, we couldn't keep it together. Everything unraveled. And then somehow, everything realigned.

That unraveling led me to the love of my life. I remarried on May 15, 1999—three months pregnant with our son Cameron.

Then, on June 5, 1999, came the second-scariest day of my life. I was six months pregnant and took a bite of a homemade chocolate chip cookie my mom had made.

Within seconds, I went into full-blown anaphylaxis. I didn't know I had developed a severe allergy to walnuts.

Cam and I were rushed by ambulance to the hospital in Burnsville, Minnesota. I was revived. We stayed in the hospital for two weeks. Every doctor called us "extremely lucky."

What followed was something I didn't yet have a name for: PTSD. All I knew was that I didn't feel right. Years later, I would finally name it. But at the time, I just tried to keep going.

And here's where I want to say something really important. I didn't always feel joy. For a long time, I didn't even know if it was possible. I just kept doing the next right thing, sometimes for myself, often for others.

But now, decades later, I look back and I see what was growing beneath the rubble: true joy. I'm talking about the kind of joy that's rooted. Earned. Scarred, but shining. The kind that shows up in the stillness. The kind that sits next to pain and says, "I know."

It's the joy I feel when I hear Quinn's voice when we hear him talk about the weather. It's in watching Cam pitch—alive, vibrant, after everything.

It's in loving my husband, Peter, who helped rebuild the pieces of my life with kindness and patience.

It's in Quaid's laughter and academic excellence. It's in Connor's steadiness and incredibly kind personality.

It's in chocolate chip cookies I now make with awareness and care. It's in my kitchen, my writing, my breathing. Joy returned slowly, like dawn after an endless night. It came in forgiveness. In healing. In the decision to love myself enough to try again. True joy isn't the absence of hardship. It's the meaning we create in spite of it. It's what happens when you survive, then look around and realize—*you're still here*. You made it.

Joy is in the after.

And I wouldn't trade that kind of joy for anything.

Dr. Katie—I Will Be a Mom! Finding Peace Through Perseverance

I turned sixty-five years young this year. Why do I say it this way? Because the older I get, the younger I feel as I realize there is more, and more I want to know and understand. In some ways, I feel like I am just getting started.

As I reflect on the words *peace* and *perseverance,* my thoughts move to my late forties, when I literally battled my body and members of the medical profession to become a mother. I remember my first D&C after my first of several pregnancy losses. I entered the building like most expectant mothers, expecting the ultrasound to show a beautiful fetus, whom I had already named Precious. Instead, the technician gasped and ran out of the room to get the physician. When they returned, I heard the words that were to be repeated to me several times as I endured this loss: "Your fetus is no longer viable." After these stinging words in each instance, I was ushered to an out-of-the-way room where the sound of life being literally sucked out of me remains in my head. In each of these moments as the loss ensued, there grew within me a passionate, persistent resolve to become a mother.

It was a time when I felt at war with my body. I didn't know at the time that I had twenty years of endometriosis growing rampant, which had gone up my spine. Barely able to walk from constant pain, I made my way to a surgeon and had a hysterectomy. Three surgeries later and the hormonal hell that followed left me with a love-hate relationship with my body. So, what did I do?

I trained for a marathon. Yes, at age fifty, after multiple invading assaults on my body, I picked myself up, found a trainer, and completed a full marathon. How? The event was to benefit those amazing kids and families receiving palliative care who had served as my inspiration, and I literally ran with a shirt my niece had made with their names and carrying the rattle of the most recent child lost. My pain became my purpose.

I persevered through those miles, remembering every moment of struggle, every minute of physical pain, and in many ways each mile represented an opportunity to put the past behind me and claim a new life. As I finished the race, there was a little girl who ran in front of me—she was Chinese with a pigtail sticking straight up on her head, and she gleefully ran right in front of me.

A very wise woman once told me that while I figured out how to become a mother, I could nurture other people's children, and for a while, I did just that. Redirecting my pain into a higher purpose by helping mothers with children who were leaving this world too soon, children's hospice became my world.

These moms and their persistent love under the most heart-wrenching of circumstances became my pathway to peace. I made peace with having to wait until it became clear that my journey to motherhood would be revealed. We couldn't afford IVF, surrogacy wasn't really available, and one physician who said, "Just have more sex, eventually one will take," particularly leaves me wanting to punch a wall. There was no peace in those options.

When peace came to me, it was in the form of a mother and daughter—the daughter was Chinese, adopted by her mother as an infant. I had never heard of this at the time, but the indescribable energy that surged through me when I met this wonderful duo definitely got my attention. By the end of our visit, they had explained to me the Chinese belief about the "red thread." If someone is destined to meet you, then people and circumstances will bring them. I asked myself: *Is this a red-thread moment?*

Yes, and there were several more, when in that week alone I met three more children adopted from China. On Easter Sunday, the year our daughter was born, we found peace in making the decision to adopt. We found our peaceful way by persevering through the ups and downs, the uncertainties, the insecurities, the overwhelming self-doubt that comes from enduring a life-altering challenge. It took two and a half years of waiting for the person who was coming to appear, and when she did, I cried for days. Just seeing her photo, sent to me from the adoption agency, unleashed years of pain and disappointment, and my body flooded with overwhelming relief and joy in the form of tears.

Peace showed up in a sixteen-month-old bundle of love with a pigtail sticking straight up and a smile that still lights up a room twenty years later. And her destiny was further revealed when her birthday was the same as a bracelet I had worn since my twenty-first birthday, a gift from my parents with my own birthday inverted. Our dear girl was born on 6/7 and I on 7/6. A coincidence? No, we believe she was meant to be ours, and together we were meant to be a family.

We persevered because we listened to the peaceful message of the red thread. It was with that peaceful resolve that we endured the wait.

What have I learned about peace from persevering through the pain of pregnancy loss? Children aren't always born in our bellies; sometimes they are born in our hearts. Sometimes in life the pathway to peace is unclear, but believing and remaining hopeful and being willing to wait for your red thread to bring whomever you need to face your challenge can lead you to a peaceful resolution.

We have also been the red thread, introducing other families to adoption. I encourage you, regarding whatever challenges you, to remain open and wait for your peaceful resolution.

Even as I write this, the tears still flow from the body memories. The trauma keeps being released as I go through life; the loss revisits and the grief shows up. Perseverance and rediscovering peace are in the understanding that even when in the most unimaginable physical and emotional pain, the resolve to wait for the peaceful resolution is present. Peace will come, and I know this now.

Perseverance meant finding a new way.

It was just about that time that I met a wonderful woman named Elizabeth Hamilton-Guarino, who became a beacon in my quest to make a difference in the world. Our conversations when we met and spent many hours in her heated pool led us to write *Percolate*, and through the Best Ever You Network, we both began the process of passing on our peace.

Life took us in different directions, but the red thread brought us back together now to write this book and rekindle our shared passion for peace. And we are both grateful that after all of our struggles and challenges, we have this opportunity to bring what we have learned to make the world more peaceful, one story and one reader at a time.

Peace is often mistaken for ease—but these stories remind us that peace is not the absence of struggle; it is what emerges when we choose courage again and again. In this chapter, Rebeccah Silence and John B. Grimes invite us into their deeply personal journeys of perseverance. Rebeccah shares the raw truth of facing cancer while pregnant and reimagining her identity beyond survival. John recounts life after a sudden illness—learning to live with invisible challenges and embracing tools that helped him reclaim his dignity and freedom. These stories don't gloss over pain; they show us how peace is forged in fire, choice by choice, when we dare to keep going, even when life reshapes us.

Stories from the Heart

Rebeccah Silence—Unbreakable Peace:
How I Endured, Healed, and Found Freedom

Getting diagnosed with cancer while pregnant isn't for the faint of heart. Neither is surviving your biggest fears. I had battled self-hatred for as long as I could remember.

I was in a hell of my own making, and I didn't believe I was worthy of taking up space in my own precious life. Then cancer forced me to listen to the truth that, deep down, I was. There had to be a better way to live beyond overachieving my way into worthiness, peace, or mattering. You see, I didn't believe I mattered just because I breathe, or just because I'm human. I thought I had to do, to be needed, to give people a reason to want me in their lives. What I did know was I could handle fear and darkness, but I wouldn't admit that I was also addicted to both, along with trying to prove myself. I didn't know I was worthy of taking up space in my own precious life until cancer forced me to listen to the truth that, deep down, I already knew. I didn't know that taking care of myself was a nonnegotiable option if I really wanted to make a difference—until, on a random Tuesday, I was blindsided with a diagnosis of malignant melanoma while seven months pregnant.

Prior to the diagnosis that changed everything, I identified as an endurance athlete. I'd run a few marathons in my twenties. Before that, in high school, I swam distance. That training shaped me into someone who took life in bite-size chunks. Just get to the next water station. Just get to the next lap. Just get to the next mile, one heavy foot in front of the other. It's how I survived my abusive childhood and then later my own domestic violent marriage. It's how I survived bankruptcy and divorce. It's how I rebuilt my life with sole custody of a two-year-old whom I had no idea how I was going to provide for or take care of. That was how I navigated my life, day by day, for decades before I got sick—or should I say, before I knew I was sick.

By the time I was diagnosed with cancer, I thought I had my life completely under control. My past was behind me, for good. I had won. Not my abusers. Not my pain. Not suicidal ideation that tempted me, pretending to be the most wonderful relief and path to taking back control. Enduring had been my way, and it had brought me far. On paper, I had it all. I was running a thriving business. I served my community powerfully. I was married again, this time to the love of my life. The life my husband and I built together made my head spin and my soul dizzy daily, but in the most refreshing, delightful way. And now we had a baby, our little love child, on the way.

But my dream of a bright future for the rest of my life seemed impossible when I was given a mere 5 percent chance to live. And even if I survived, I was told I'd be on disability for the rest of my life. Twenty-two surgeries. Cancer in my lymph nodes. Chemo. A baby I couldn't hold on my own for the first year of her life. An older child who said, "Great. I don't have a dad, and now you're going to die." It felt so unfair. It felt so cruel. But then I realized something that changed my life forever: The person I thought I needed to be was a lie. The sexy wife. The doting mother. The business owner with sold-out retreats and a continual six-month waitlist while making multiple six figures. The overachiever. The high performer.

None of that was who I really was. And, frighteningly, I realized that if none of that was who I was, then I had no idea who I should be or what I had to offer. The woman navigating cancer and leading the mission called "her life" had to be the healed version of myself that I loved and trusted. But I didn't love or trust myself yet. Talk about an "Oh, shit" moment. Thankfully, by the grace of God, I had already done the work to emotionally heal through childhood and early adult traumas, but if I'm honest, the path to knowing who I really was lay ahead of me and felt more impossible to discover than the cancer and my odds to live ever could.

This is how cancer gave me everything I wanted and didn't know I needed. It brought me home, to me and to God. I felt like I was dying—and I might have been—but I decided to live like I was going to survive. I decided this wasn't the end of my story. It's easy to be your best and emotionally clear when you are living your dream-come-true life. But what about now? I had a big decision to make. Was cancer going to win—or was I? Was I going to decide to learn how to love and trust myself—or not? I decided that discovering who I really was, was a pursuit worth my all. And cancer? It was going to be the most profound seminar I had ever attended. I had a lot of self-analysis to do, but I was up for the challenge of my life.

I'll admit that this was far from easy. Every day, I wanted to die just as much as I wanted to live. But I refused to let sadness, fear, or a cancer diagnosis win. I knew the pain was temporary. And I knew my soul was eternal. I knew this was bigger than me. I knew I might die. But I also had a direct download from God letting me know I had the power to live like I was going to survive. And while I had identified as an endurance athlete, which was helpful during this season, I refused to identify myself solely with cancer. It wasn't more powerful than me. Nothing outside us is more powerful than we are. Ever. Not ever.

So I screamed when I needed to scream. I laughed as much as I could when it felt genuine. I cried tears of "Why is this happening to me?," grieving tears, and tears of joy. I shook through the fear. It was intense. It was visceral. Some days, I could hardly breathe because the fear was so palpable I felt like it was choking me to death. But I took in the air I could and kept breathing while dreaming of a future where I was healthy again and a version of myself I hadn't met yet. And I made it a law that my body was just preparing room for my soul's expansion. Ironically, the fight of my life required me to relax powerfully into the truth of who I already was and into the loving arms of God. I asked for guidance and let go of the need to figure out anything. I kept my heart open. I kept my mind open. I kept my emotions clear. And from there, I could hear my own voice and God's voice, which was a powerful place to keep my focus.

Cancer taught me how to take up all the space in my one precious life. It taught me resilience that proves, as long as I'm still here, that I am on a divine assignment, serving every life I touch. After cancer, my life became a life that fit me. There was no more fitting in required—ever again, maybe the greatest gift I've ever been given. Today, I take cancer with me not as my identity but as a reminder—focusing on what keeps me emotionally well and free while paying attention to any emotional cancer I am tolerating or putting up with unnecessarily. This has become my everyday life. Letting go of what is no longer needed and what I am committed to making room for, the instant I recognize both.

Our lives are precious. You are precious. And your life is meant to be glorious. But more than anything else, I want us all to realize that we don't need a crisis to live our lives our own way. Breakdown to breakthrough is not a requirement. You can choose starting right now to make your life yours. You can choose to tend to your own soul. You can choose to honor your body because it holds you through it all. What I learned from cancer was how to let me become me, and that needing to be needed to feel valuable is not the way. I learned the art of mastering receiving so that I could give even more. I let myself admit I am love and I am loved and I have always been more than enough. The peace from this knowledge allows me to live fully, embracing that I signed up for the full human experience. What a gift.

John B. Grimes—Finding Peace Through Discomfort

In February 1998, I was a typical nineteen-year-old college student: ten feet tall, bulletproof, and confident I had life all figured out—my days revolved around intramural sports, classes on campus, and weekends that blurred into one another. Life felt predict-able, vibrant, and mine to shape. But all that changed overnight.

What began as a seemingly common bout of flu quickly spiraled into a fight for survival against bacterial meningitis—a disease I had never heard of but would come to know all too well. This rare but devastating infection inflames the membranes sur-rounding the brain and spinal cord and is often mistaken for less serious illnesses in its early stages. In less than twenty-four hours, it can escalate, leading to severe complica-tions or take the life of an otherwise healthy person. For me, bacterial meningitis struck with vicious brutality and left me in a coma for eight days—unconsciously fighting for my life. Against the odds, I made it—but survival came with a heavy price as I woke to a reality forever altered by the lasting effects of the disease.

Meningitis left its mark in ways that were entirely invisible. Among the most pro-found were permanent neurological and physical challenges, as well as overwhelming emotional hurdles. I was left legally blind, with total blindness in one eye and severe impairment in the other. My body and nervous system, once reliable and automatic, now struggled with even the most basic functions everyone takes for granted: swallowing, sitting up, and speaking, to name a few. Each day presented new battles, from relearning how to form words to grappling with the disheartening truth that critical parts of my body, like my eyes and bladder, no longer worked as they once had. What appeared to others as a miraculous recovery masked the invisible struggles that had become my new reality.

As I worked to rebuild my life, I wrestled with the stark contrast between who I had been before meningitis and the person I was becoming. Once independent and brimming with youthful certainty, I now relied on others for tasks as simple as managing basic bodily functions. This seismic shift in my identity was disorienting, but it also forced me to confront uncomfortable truths about resilience, self-acceptance, and the strength to adapt. My story is not just one of survival; it's about finding the courage to live fully and confidently, even in the shadow of what meningitis took from me.

I faced new, unexpected challenges, including one I didn't even have the vocabulary for: a neurogenic bladder. Fancy words for something that was anything but glamorous. In the hospital, I was introduced to an intermittent catheter, a device that would manage my bladder function. At first, I thought it was just a temporary inconvenience. Nurses handled everything for me, so I didn't dwell on it. Like everything else—swallowing, walking, talking—I believed my body would recover. It had to. I was nineteen, after all. Bladder issues were for old people, not college students.

But as the weeks turned into months, reality started to set in. Not all of my body was bouncing back in the way I'd assumed. The device wasn't a temporary fix—it was becoming a permanent part of my life. And I refused to accept it. I was determined to get back to "normal." I discovered, through sheer determination and stubbornness, that I could actually force my bladder empty with the right mix of abdominal muscle power and body contortion. It certainly wasn't pretty or practical, but it made me feel more like my old self. The problem? This DIY method was painful, exhausting, required me to sit down, and—if I was being honest—an exercise in futility. I was straining my body to do something it clearly wasn't designed to do. The only one I was fooling was myself. There was nothing normal about this.

Worse, skipping the catheter meant I would just hold it—way beyond my bladder's natural capacity. The pressure quickly became uncomfortable and made me susceptible to accidents. And let me tell you, there is nothing remotely "normal" about being a young adult who can't trust their bladder. We're talking about moments of sheer panic and embarrassment, the kind that makes you rethink every decision leading up to that point. It's hard to feel ten feet tall when you're wondering if someone has noticed your strategically tied jacket around your waist.

Let's just say it's not a confidence booster.

Even as I struggled with the practicality of using a catheter, the emotional weight of it was heavier. How would I fit in socially? I didn't know anyone else who relied on one, much less someone my age. It felt like I'd been handed a problem meant for someone decades older—a problem I wasn't ready for and didn't know how to navigate. The shame I felt every time I used it was suffocating. I hid it from everyone, including myself. I fought against the idea that this was my reality because admitting it meant surrendering to a future I didn't want.

Eventually, though, reality caught up with me. I couldn't keep forcing my body to do something it wasn't capable of, and I couldn't keep living in denial. I had a choice: I could keep fighting against certainty, or I could make peace with it.

A combination of stubbornness, optimism, and youthful naivety made the obvious choice to embrace the catheter impossible. Then it dawned on me that I was focused on the wrong normal. I was striving to fit in with what others thought of me, not what made me feel normal— literally, on the inside. I ultimately realized that normal means not always having a full bladder and being uncomfortable. I would never get to peace until I embraced the solution and healed my own ego.

That peace didn't come overnight. It took time to build, arriving gradually as I started to explore my options, not just the outdated solutions I'd been handed in the hospital, but the modern, more discreet options available. Believe it or not, technology had positively disrupted the bladder management world too, and advancements had come a long way. Turns out, dignity and convenience had finally gone high-tech. There were portable, easy-to-use tools that didn't scream "medical device." Who knew?

The more I learned, the more empowered I felt. Slowly, I began to see this new tool not as a burden but as a gateway to regaining control over my life. There's nothing quite like the freedom of knowing you can leave the house without worrying about an accident. That sense of normalcy I'd been chasing? It was waiting for me on the other side of acceptance.

Acceptance was a profound relief, but it also came with a dose of regret. Looking back, I realized how much time I'd wasted resisting what was inevitable. I'd missed out on so much peace by clinging to the idea of who I was before meningitis. I wish I could go back and tell my younger self that acceptance isn't a surrender; it's a reclamation of your life.

Today, I don't just accept this part of my life. I embrace it. It allows me to live fully, to go places, to be present in the moments that matter. Quiet confidence has replaced the shame that once consumed me. My condition hasn't changed, but my perspective has.

Peace, I've learned, isn't about fixing everything. Sometimes it's about letting go of the fight and learning to live in the moment. And if I've learned anything from this journey, it's this: Peace isn't something you find. It's something you create by making room for what is, instead of clinging to what was.

POINTS TO PONDER

Think. Write. Talk. Action. *(Because practice makes us our best.)*

EXERCISE 15: Perseverance in Practice

FILL-IN-THE-BLANK:

A moment I almost gave up but didn't was _____

_____.

When things get difficult, the value I return to is _____

_____.

The part of myself I'm proud of for continuing is _____

_____.

The people who quietly support my perseverance are _____

_____.

The emotion I most associate with perseverance is _____

_____.

I feel most at peace when I choose to keep going by_____

_____.

The way I encourage myself to persist is by saying_____

_____.

One practice that helps me reconnect with my purpose is_____

_____.

I want my legacy of perseverance to be _____

_____.

I am building peace through perseverance by_____

_____.

JOURNAL PROMPT: Look back at your answers. What patterns or truths emerge? Which answers surprised you? Choose three answers to expand on in your journal. Ask yourself: What keeps calling me forward? Where have I demonstrated quiet strength? What does my perseverance say about who I am becoming?

_____

_____

_____

_____

EXERCISE 16: The Peaceful Reframe

FILL-IN-THE-BLANK:

When I hear the word *perseverance,* I think of _____

_____.

A limiting belief I used to have about perseverance is _____

_____.

I now understand that perseverance also means _____

_____.

I am allowed to pause when _____

_____.

Rest supports my perseverance by _____

_____.

A peaceful decision I made during a hard time was _____

_____.

When I align my energy with peace, I feel _____

_____.

A time I honored my values while persevering was _____

_____.

Peaceful perseverance looks like me when _____

_____.

I am learning to trust myself most when _____

_____.

JOURNAL PROMPT: Using your answers, write a new definition of perseverance that includes rest, peace, and personal alignment. Then ask: How can I make space for that version of perseverance in my daily life? What actions or thoughts would I need to shift to embody it fully?

_____

_____

_____

_____

PART 3

HARMONY

CHAPTER 9
PARTNERSHIP

In the ninth principle of peace, Partnership, we learn that creating our best lives and a more peaceful world begins with alignment—first within ourselves, and then with others. When we are living in integrity with who we truly are, we stop abandoning ourselves for approval, roles, or expectations. We become our own most trustworthy partner. From that grounded place, we naturally attract relationships that reflect our values and support our peaceful purpose.

Partnership, at its core, is not about losing yourself in service to others. It is about standing firmly in who you are, knowing you are already enough, and choosing connection that honors that truth. Through aligned partnership, with ourselves and with one another, we create a ripple effect of peace that expands possibility, deepens belonging, and quietly transforms the world. Peace partnerships don't just change lives; they expand global consciousness.

We need one another. Someone out there needs you in some way every day. We begin each day asking this question: "Who needs us?" We spend moments thinking about what we can offer someone else. What we've learned is that energy and action toward meeting a collective need is more powerful than meeting just our own needs. It is the collective "we." When we understand that shift, "we" over "me" becomes a fundamental practice of peaceful living.

Life graces us in the most unexpected ways. We've each had moments when someone has arrived in our lives and we've said to ourselves, *Where have you been?* or *I'm meant to meet this person.* When this happens, it's as though they were dropped into our lives for a reason.

In fact, we met that way! Serendipitously, at 4 AM, when Dr. Katie was going through a transition period professionally, she picked up a copy of *Best Ever You Magazine* at a twenty-four-hour gym. Instinctively Dr. Katie was drawn to it because of the self-help subject matter. Then, learning that Elizabeth was local, she reached out with a friendly phone call, and the rest is history. Upon receiving the phone call, Elizabeth had that feeling of thankfulness, and it became immediately clear that we had much in common and so much to learn. We also shared interests and passion in service to others, which is a rare combination. We both needed this kind of partnership.

The ripple effect of that one moment when Dr. Katie listened to her inner messenger has changed lives all around the world.

PEACE POINT 65: Reach Out

We are two women who tend to trust easily, and because of that quality, unfortunately we've got some scars. We've both lived through partnerships that made us better and partnerships that made us question ourselves entirely. We've stood in rooms where we felt seen, safe, and supported. We've also sat at tables where our intuition was screaming, *This isn't it!*

Partnership is one of the most sacred human experiences. Whether it's romantic, professional, familial, or creative, it holds the potential to be a mirror, a messenger, or a magnifier—sometimes all three. Riane Eisler, a well-respected scholar who has written extensively about partnership models in contrast to domination models—applied to relationships, work, society, and even economics—said, "Partnership is not about creating sameness but about creating a context where differences can flourish and contribute to a greater whole."

Here's what we've learned: Peace doesn't automatically arrive just because you're doing something together. Peace must be built, protected, and nurtured over time. And some of the most damaging relationships don't seem chaotic from the outside, but inside, they drain you, dim you, and disconnect you from yourself and others.

PEACE POINT 66: Know the Energetic Truths

We've identified five dynamics that consistently show up in peaceful versus unpeaceful partnerships. These are not just personality differences; they're energetic truths. If you're wondering why a relationship feels expansive or exhausting, peaceful or destabilizing, these might be your keys.

1. Energetic Integrity

- **Peaceful Partnership:** When both people manage their energy with self-awareness, emotional maturity, and respect for their shared emotional space.
- **Unpeaceful Partnership:** When one person regularly drains the other through unspoken expectations, passive-aggressiveness, or emotional volatility.

2. Honesty and Transparency

- **Peaceful Partnership:** Rooted in honest, sometimes uncomfortable conversations. You can express your needs, speak the truth, and stay rather than pretend, suppress, or walk on eggshells.
- **Unpeaceful Partnership:** When one or both people avoid conflict to keep the illusion of peace.

3. Shared Values

- **Peaceful Partnership:** Built on values like compassion, respect, and growth—even if the goals differ. Shared vision comes from a shared why, not just a shared what.

- **Unpeaceful Partnership:** When two people pursue similar goals (success, parenting, legacy) but from radically misaligned values, creating conflict in execution, tone, or energy.

4. Reciprocal Versus Transactional
- **Peaceful Partnership:** Both people give freely and receive with grace. Help is offered without the need for constant reward. Reciprocity is not about equal effort.
- **Unpeaceful Partnership:** Giving is conditional. Receiving is weaponized. One or both people operate in a "What have you done for me lately?" mindset.

5. Expansiveness and Growth
- **Peaceful Partnership:** You both grow. You both evolve. You both expand and are celebrated for it. You rise in tandem, not in competition. It's about mutual nurturing and lifting each other up.
- **Unpeaceful Partnership:** One person's growth threatens the other. Jealousy, insecurity, or control creep in. You begin to shrink yourself to "keep the peace." True peace partners don't just support your growth; they *invite* it.

PEACE POINT 67: Envision Your Ideal Peace Partners

Who are your peace partners? We all need them. They are the ones who support us in applying the principles outlined in this book. They hold you accountable and lift you to a higher standard because they see your potential. They challenge you and lift you up closer to your stated goals and desires. They mirror the best of you!

We've all heard the vision of Martin Luther King Jr.'s dream. We espouse, as he said, that creating peaceful partnerships is like a beloved community.

> Our goal is to create a beloved community, and this will require a qualitative change in our souls as well as a quantitative change in our lives.
> —Martin Luther King Jr., "Nonviolence: The Only Road to Freedom," May 4, 1966

The concept of the beloved community for King was a vision of a society based on justice, equal opportunity, love of all human beings, and the presence of true peace and reconciliation.

Before you can choose your peace partners, you must first define the values you hold to be sacred. This isn't just a list of words that sound good on paper. It's about understanding the nonnegotiable energies that you need in order to feel safe, seen, and supported. Peace values are soul-level truths that reflect how you live, lead, and love.

Ask yourself,

What are the principles I would defend in the face of adversity?

What would I stand up for, even if I stood alone?

Then ask,

Am I currently living in alignment with these values, or am I compromising them to keep the peace?

True peace comes from having the courage to live in truth. Peace partnerships are only possible when values are clear, consistent, and courageously honored. Once you know your values, you'll naturally attract others who reflect and respect them. Peace begins within, and clarity is its beacon, sending light out to those who share your vision.

They are the ones who show up with soul and often believe in you more than you believe in yourself. Peace partners are not just cheerleaders. They are the ones who stand with you in silence and sing with you in celebration. Whether romantic, platonic, familial, or professional, these people don't just support your goals. They support your *growth*. They make us better and tell us the truth. They are honest and may even constantly challenge us to be better. They are collaborative, cooperative, and compassionate in addition to being mission driven.

PEACE POINT 68: Identify Your Top Five Values

How do we find those people, and how can we trust that they are our tribe, those we want to call our peace partners? It begins with one word:

values. Those who are your partners in peace share your values. They promote, preserve, and prioritize what you consider to be most important.

- Who are you when no one is watching?
- What principles guide your decisions?
- What do you protect?
- What would you never compromise?
- Who in your life protects those same things?

When your relationships are rooted in shared values, trust becomes effortless, and alignment becomes magnetic. Peace partnerships aren't forced; they *flow.* They feel like breath. Like ease. Like home. These relationships create sacred reciprocity—where love, truth, and power are exchanged.

Ask yourself, *What matters most to me, and what would I passionately advocate for?* Now ask yourself, *Who in my life shares that passion for those five values?* Hopefully you have a long list! We want you to include romantic partners, spouses, friends, and business colleagues as well. Are you living a life with people who believe in your top-five values?

PEACE POINT 69: Establish Collective Values

You too can create a new direction for any aspect of your life.

As parents, we have constantly revisited this question: What do we want our families to learn and value? As parents, like you, we struggle with impressing on our kids that their value is from the inside out and being good people is our priority for them. As spouses, we found on the second time around people who make us better. Peter and John are definitely our peace partners, as are our children. And that requires constant clarity of what matters most.

As professionals, we frequently work with others as presenters for workplace leadership events. We often see simple values missing in organizations. As work colleagues, together and separately, we bump up against people who think differently, and each of us has been burned by someone who took advantage of us. In hindsight, we didn't recognize the red flags that would have warned us to wait for the person who fits with our values.

Warren Buffett, considered to be one of the most successful humans on this planet, recommends that it's in the waiting that we discover our team. Buffett says that his favorite word is *no* because he waits for someone who shares his values before he will work with them. He waits for the right fit and doesn't waste his time fitting square pegs into round holes. He would likely agree that he finds his peace partners.

For example, we waited for the right partner to write *The Peace Guidebook*. This is a work rooted in deep emotional truth, spiritual clarity, and compassionate leadership, and we share a powerful alignment in values, including these key principles:

Compassionate Presence

Over countless hours on Zoom, on the phone, and in person, we practice peace by showing up with empathy, patience, and understanding. Whether it's guiding each other through grief or change, we sit with each other in the hardest moments without needing to fix anything. We hold unconditional space for healing. We are each other's safe place to land, and we extend that presence to the world.

Aligned Integrity

There is a deep commitment between us personally and professionally to walk our talk. We live the practices we teach. There's no performative peace here, only embodied peace. We lead with truth and model what it means to be in ethical, soul-level alignment.

Shared Purpose

We both believe that the world can be more peaceful, and we've committed our lives to helping people discover that peace within themselves and extend it outward. Our shared purpose is to create a meaningful, lasting impact. We aren't just writing a book. We're building a movement.

Mutual Uplifting

We amplify each other's voices. We celebrate each other's strengths. There's no ego, no competition, only shared celebration and sacred reciprocity. This is one of the rarest energies in a partnership and clearly thrives in ours. We rise together and help others rise too.

Sacred Responsibility

We both carry our work as a calling, not a task. There's a sacredness to what we do. We know that our words, choices, and energy percolate outward. That awareness fuels our responsibility to write, teach, coach, and lead with clarity, love, and peace. We take our work seriously because we take humanity seriously.

PEACE POINT 70: Reimagine Collaboration as Ceremony

Peaceful collaboration isn't just about projects or productivity; it's about shared purpose. When you approach partnership as ceremony, you bring reverence into the way you co-create with others. Imagine beginning a meeting with a breath, or starting a shared project with a question like "What is the highest intention for this work together?"

This transforms ordinary interactions into sacred ones. When partnership is ceremonial, ego steps aside and vision steps forward. Partnership invites trust, depth, and creativity to emerge.

Ask yourself,

What would happen if I treated each collaboration as a spiritual agreement?

Who do I need to be to show up with integrity to the spiritual agreement?

When partnership is sacred, the work becomes meaningful, and peace is built into the process, not just the result.

PEACE POINT 71: Lead Peacefully, Even When You Stand Alone

Not every peace partner walks with you forever. Some enter for a season, a lesson, or a chapter of evolution. When their time is done, peaceful leadership means you let go with love, not bitterness. To lead with peace is to release the need to be understood. It's the ability to stay rooted in your vision even when others fall away. It's about *energetic self-leadership*, the ability to create alignment inside yourself so clearly that others naturally fall into resonance or release.

Ask yourself,

Am I trying to hold on to relationships that have effectively expired?

Am I forcing harmony at the expense of my truth?

Leadership in peace is not loud. It's firm. It's clear. And most of all, it's honest. Peace partners align with your future, not your fear.

●●●

Our Pathways to Peace with Elizabeth and Dr. Katie

Elizabeth—The Best Partnership You'll Ever Have

I've always had this love-hate partnership with myself.

If I was skinny enough, young enough, blonde enough, made enough money, had the right clothes, the perfect kitchen, the flawless smile—I was proud of myself. I was "on track." I felt good in my own skin. But if I wasn't? If the scale tipped the wrong way, if my roots showed or my jeans didn't fit, if the email inbox overflowed or the dreams I had felt out of reach—I wasn't just disappointed. I was brutal. I became the kind of partner I wouldn't tolerate from anyone else.

My internal dialogue turned harsh. I judged myself by impossible standards and measured my worth against a to-do list no human could complete. I forgot I was a whole person. I treated myself like a project to be managed, not a person to be loved.

Over the years, especially through personal and professional growth, I started to understand something essential: The most important partnership I'll ever have isn't with a company or a friend or even a coauthor or life partner; it's with myself.

And that realization didn't arrive with fanfare or ease. It came through tears, grief, disappointment, and repair. It came after moments of collapse and in moments of grace. It came when I started listening to the voice inside me that wasn't trying to be perfect but simply trying to be at peace.

That inner voice? She's not always easy to hear. Sometimes she's drowned out by the old narratives, the ones that whisper, "Not enough," or shout, "Try harder." But when

I slow down enough to hear her, she tells the truth. She says, "You don't need to prove anything. You just need to be here, now. You just need to be kind to yourself."

In many ways, building a partnership with yourself is like tending to a fragile but wildly intelligent garden. Some days you're full of sunshine and intention and everything blooms effortlessly. Other days, you forget to water, or a storm hits, and something wilts. The true partnership isn't about the perfect bloom. It's about being willing to tend to yourself anyway.

That's what I've come to know. I used to think self-love would arrive when I had all the answers, when I achieved all the goals. But I've learned it's something you practice when you're in the thick of *not* knowing. It's choosing to treat yourself with care, not criticism, especially on the days when you feel least deserving.

And truthfully? It's not always graceful. I still fall into comparison. I still have moments when I roll my eyes at myself. But now, instead of abandoning myself when I falter, I pause. I take a breath. I try again. And that is partnering with yourself.

For a long time, I believed I had to be everything to everyone. I believed rest had to be earned. I believed I couldn't celebrate until I had "arrived." But the truth is, you're always arriving. Every single day, you are waking up and choosing yourself again. Or not. And in that choice, a relationship is built.

This self-partnership doesn't mean isolation. It's not about turning away from others, it's about learning how to be with yourself so fully that your relationships with others are healthier, softer, and more honest.

This is the heart of what I teach through The Best Ever You Network. It's not about pretending to be the best. It's about practicing what brings out the best in you and passing that on to others. It's about being gentle with the parts of yourself that are still healing, still learning, still figuring it all out. It's about being curious rather than critical, soft rather than sharp.

There's something sacred in realizing that you are with yourself in every single moment of your life. You are your own constant. Your own inner witness. Your first responder. Your final editor. You are the one who knows your full story.

The questions become: Are you being kind to yourself in the process? Are you honoring your growth? Are you showing up for yourself with the same tenderness you offer others?

I used to wait for external validation to tell me I was okay. Now I know that the validation that matters most comes from within. It comes from trusting my own voice. It comes from showing up, again and again, not with perfection but with presence.

And presence, I've discovered, is everything.

If you take nothing else from this, I hope you take this truth: You are already enough. You are not behind. You are not broken. You are in relationship with a living, breathing, beautiful human being. And that human being is you.

Care for yourself. Laugh with yourself. Forgive yourself. Let yourself. Be yourself.

That's the best partnership you'll ever have.

And it begins with love.

Dr. Katie—An Unexpected Partnership

The phone rang on a gorgeous summer day in Maine. I didn't recognize the number, but I decided to answer. "Hello, I am Doris Buffett, and I just read about your program. I would like to learn more about it." To say I started shaking and sweating and my heart beat as fast as a freight train would be an understatement. I knew she lived in the area, but never did I ever think she would be calling me!

That call led to six months' worth of reports and reviews and discussions about the direction of our nonprofit children's hospice organization and how she could provide support. She was one shrewd business partner and became the epitome of a peace partner. Doris was a straight shooter, and she pulled no punches in pushing me to be my best in business. Like her brother Warren Buffett, she valued the people she worked with and sought out people who were mission- and value-driven. It took six months for her to finally trust my authenticity, but she taught me a very valuable lesson about partnership when she told me rather bluntly that I didn't have the right team. She critiqued my board and staff and basically told me they were not in alignment with my mission and even though she was willing to invest in us, she didn't believe we would succeed because of the people I had selected.

She was right. In 2008, when the financial crisis hit, despite the efforts of several very committed board members and volunteer-led members' efforts, we were forced to close our doors. I had to send $100,000 back to Doris Buffett and her foundation.

Heeding her advice, I found new partners and started over with a new team of mission-driven people who successfully kept the organization going until it was no longer needed.

What did I learn about peace from this partnership? So much! Doris taught me to stand up for my values, to give trust time, to lean on partners so that you know they will be there during hard times, and to weather the unexpected by always having a plan *B*, *C*, and *D*. Clarity of purpose doesn't pay the bills in a crisis. I learned the value of planning and also each of my five *C's*. These are the five primary values Doris taught me that are the foundation of my leadership intelligence model: compassion, clarity, courage, connection, and change. These values guided how Doris conducted her life and business. She was a spitfire and an amazing mentor and truly a peace partner who accomplished so much by helping people before she died. If I can live long enough to have touched even half as many lives as she did, I will have met my goal of creating a more peaceful world.

Peaceful partnerships come in many forms—some stretch across a lifetime while others emerge in a single, powerful moment. In this chapter's Stories from the Heart, Sally Huss and Liz Olberg show us the transformative power of connection. Sally shares a remarkable story of fifty years of marriage built not only on love but on mutual encouragement, creative courage, and unwavering belief in each other. Her story reminds us that true partnership is a sacred collaboration that uplifts both people beyond what either could achieve alone. Liz's story, on the other hand, takes us on a fifty-six-day solo bicycle journey across America, where unexpected allies became temporary peace partners—offering kindness, shelter, and humanity in brief but unforgettable exchanges. Whether built over decades or found in fleeting moments of mutual trust, these stories show that partnership is the heartbeat of peace—and that every act of shared support becomes a thread in the fabric of a more peaceful world.

Stories from the Heart

Sally Huss—Fifty Years and Counting

"Fifty years and counting." Those words became a refrain between my husband, Marv, and me during our golden anniversary year. We married in Aspen, Colorado, where we were hired to build and run a new tennis club. I had just stepped off the women's pro tennis circuit, and Marv had recently finished several Emmy-winning years producing the Hallmark Hall of Fame series. It was the start of a shared adventure that would span five decades.

Before that chapter began, our paths were already filled with determination and creativity. Marv, a gifted athlete, had put himself through Cal Berkeley on athletic scholarships, then served as a Marine pilot in the Sea of Japan. I had been raised to compete, spending my youth on the tennis court and studying fine art at USC. Tennis was my ticket to the world—eventually leading me to coach a celebrity clientele in Malibu and Beverly Hills, where my "Zen tennis" approach drew as much interest as my backhand.

One day, that same world brought me face-to-face with Marv Huss on a Beverly Hills tennis court. I instantly felt something shift—a certainty, a light. Meeting him felt like destiny. It took time for our lives to align, but two years later, on Halloween 1976, we were married. A son soon followed, and we traded the fast track of Aspen for a more grounded California life.

Our lives blended creativity and courage. While Marv shifted into real estate, I began writing and painting messages of happiness. Small art shows became the first Sally Huss Gallery in Laguna Beach, then twenty-five galleries across the United States, Japan, and Switzerland. Marv's business sense and my art made the perfect team. When 9/11 changed the retail landscape, we pivoted again—this time to publishing. We learned everything about digital books and built a new life from a small cabin with no plumbing, full of gratitude and ideas.

From there, our creative partnership flourished. I wrote and illustrated over a hundred children's books—each designed to help kids find self-worth, make kind choices, and face life with courage and joy. Marv edited, encouraged, and cheered every line. Together we created a body of work that continues to brighten hearts.

Looking back, our story isn't just about accomplishments. It's about love and perseverance. We built a life rooted in respect, humor, and faith. Marv, at ninety-two, and I, at eighty-four, have learned that people come together for reasons beyond understanding. Our strengths became each other's gifts, and our love, the foundation for everything that followed.

Today, I no longer count the years. Fifty was a milestone, but what remains is timeless—the laughter, the lessons, and the love that carry on beyond the calendar. I couldn't have been loved more, and neither could Marv. May everyone be blessed with such joy.

Liz Olberg—Finding Peace Through Partnership

I have found my greatest peace through partnership. Peace has swirled through my life as I walk life's path alongside others who share my journey. To actively choose peace is hard work, but I have found that load lightened when I collaborate with fellow travelers. I used to be surprised when I found others who would join in peacemaking with me, but the more I practice it, the more I see that peace flourishes through alliance if we allow ourselves to trust that others will bear the load with us.

This truth about the power of cooperation has been demonstrated in my life over and over. As a teenager growing up in Los Angeles following the Rodney King riots, I participated in the cleanup effort after the destruction left by looters and demonstrators. I was deeply impacted by my neighborhood's emotions running high in the wake of mounting frustrations and palpable injustice. I felt helpless as one person, yet when I joined forces with my neighbors and friends, we were able to demonstrate peacemaking through service, which in turn brought harmony to ourselves and our community.

Later that year, I moved to Spokane, Washington, to begin my college career, just as the Aryan Nation was rising up in nearby Hayden Lake, Idaho. Confused by how our world could be so polarized by hatred and race, I recalled the power of solidarity in serving my neighborhood in California and the tranquility it had brought. Once again, I formed coalitions on my college campus, and together we committed to serving children in Spokane's poorest neighborhood through a weekly dinner. Service through joint venture has remained a consistent expression of peacemaking for me throughout my life.

A peaceful life might be viewed as quiet and still, but mine has been quite the opposite. The more I engage in teamwork with others, the more opportunities I have for peacemaking. Peacemaking has been a contemplative practice in my life, but it is rarely quiet or still. It is quite the contrary: active, busy, and full of passion, tears, and deep, deep joy that comes through meaningful unions with others working toward common goals.

In 2018, in the wake of a divorce, a transition to an empty nest, a move, and a career change all within eighteen months, I decided to take a little bike ride. I have always loved being on my bike. From the time I was a small girl, my bike was a path to freedom and inner peace. I could explore, see the world at my pace, and be outside where I was happiest. As my world crumbled and reformed, I needed solace and time to think. I wanted a big adventure as a way to start my new life out of the ashes.

I had heard of people riding a popular route across the United States called the Northern Tier and had dreamed about making this fascinating trip. I had thought that I might try it when I retired, but in 2016, I found myself single, with summers off and no responsibilities except to return to work in late August. I began to form some plans, but there was a piece missing—I needed a solid reason to keep me from chickening out. I thought of the students in my school and the programs that fed them on weekends. I met with a friend and developed a collaborative plan to use this adventure to benefit United Way's CHOW (Cutting Hunger on Weekends) program. My next chapter would begin, as so many chapters in my life had, with an eye on service, reconciliation, and contemplation.

I began blogging as I prepared for the trip and touched a place in my soul that needed exploring. I grew so much and thought to myself, *There it is, the new growth I was looking for*—but that was just the beginning. What I didn't realize yet was that this journey would teach me that synergistic relationships can take many forms, sometimes appearing in brief but meaningful encounters with strangers who become allies in my pursuit of peace.

I set out for Bar Harbor, Maine, the day school let out for summer. My bike and gear had been shipped to the local bike shop, so I boarded the plane at SeaTac with only a cycling magazine, a few snacks, and a small toiletry pouch. After arriving in Bar Harbor (literally on the other side of the United States) and sleeping a few hours in a quaint motel, I walked to the bike shop to collect my bike and gear. In just a couple of hours, I would begin my pilgrimage.

On my planned fifty-six-day trek, I stopped every two hours to rest, refuel my body, or refill my water bottles. Most of the time, these stops were at gas stations, bars, or ice cream stands. I met hundreds of people curious about where I was headed. When I would say Seattle (no one east of the Cascade Mountains knows where Anacortes is), people would often look at me like I was crazy. I was struck during each hour of that trip by the goodness of people and the pride they carried for their hometowns. Being solo and self-supported, there were only a couple of occasions when I felt fear. Mostly, I felt compassion and care flowing from unexpected alliances. As I talked with people about CHOW, I encouraged them to get involved in feeding hungry kids in their own hometowns and making a difference for people in need in their communities—to form their own peace networks.

Each night as a solo woman traveler, I was acutely aware of my vulnerability. However, I discovered unexpected mutual aid in campgrounds, RV parks, city parks, and private residences. These temporary but genuine bonds provided me with hot showers, home-cooked meals, and much-needed conversation after days of being alone.

- Near the beginning of my trip, in New Hampshire, I was caught in a rainstorm. I stopped at a local bike shop to get advice on where to stay for the night. The owner of the shop became an impromptu collaborator in my journey, taking me to his home, cooking me a meal, and giving me a cozy spot to sleep—a brief but powerful alliance that restored my sense of peace.

- In Indiana, a lovely older gentleman formed a fellowship with cyclists passing through his town. He met me at a park, opened the community center where I could take a shower and wash my clothes, and provided me with a cot to sleep on in an air-conditioned space—a welcome relief after riding in ninety- degree temperatures all day. This was communion in its purest form: expecting nothing in return but offering what was needed most in the moment, creating an oasis of tranquility.

- In Iowa, I stopped at a local pub where I met a woman who was waiting for her daughter to finish swim lessons. Later that night, she created a safety consortium, stopping by the city park where I was camping, bringing her daughter and her friend, the police chief, to check on me and bring me ice cream. The police chief extended this protective partnership further by telling me she would have her patrols check on me throughout the night—strangers becoming accomplices in ensuring my well-being and peace of mind.

- In Montana, I was welcomed onto a ranch to rest for two days. This lovely family formed a nurturing association with me, touring me around their community, feeding me amazing meals, and spending time just resting on the porch while I let my body recover for the last stretch of my ride. Almost home, I had a mechanical issue with my bike rack. A man in Republic, Washington, established a problem-solving pact with me, fixing my rack and loading my bike in his truck to take me back to the highway so I could pedal on my way to a hotel where my brother had arranged a room for me—another link in the chain of peaceful collaboration.

Peace begins with oneself but flourishes through collective effort. I could share stories from each day about the harmonious connections formed with kind people across the United States. My journey restored my faith in my belief that more often than not, people will unite for good if given the chance. This willingness to form bonds with strangers is the beginning of peacemaking. This kind of peacemaking is only possible with vulnerability from both parties. In that mutual vulnerability, true alliance creates peace and strength.

When we forge partnerships, we create pockets of peace that then blend into one another. I dream that these blended partnerships of peace become an unstoppable flood of harmony that dominates our culture and washes over the seemingly vast landscape of fear and conflict. Seeds of peace begin with the curiosity to know another person instead of making assumptions, with conversation instead of accusations, and with a general spirit of openness to cooperation. When we make small moves toward connection, we can see glimpses of what our communities can become. In joining hands, not in isolation, we find peace. A small gesture, even something as simple as offering a high five, can start the cascade of solidarity that builds toward lasting peace and reconciliation in our divided world.

POINTS TO PONDER

Think. Write. Talk. Action. *(Because practice makes us our best.)*

EXERCISE 17: Defining Peace-Aligned Partnerships

Fill in the blanks below to gain insight into who truly supports your mission and aligns with your peace values.

A person who consistently shows up for me, even when things are hard, is

_____.

When I think about what I value most in a partnership, the first word that comes to mind is _____.

Someone in my life who challenges me to grow without compromising my integrity is _____.

One past partnership that drained my energy was _____,
because _____.

A trait I now know is essential in a peace partner is _____

_____.

I feel most aligned in my work and relationships when _____

_____.

I know someone is a good fit for my team or vision when they _____

_____.

A red flag I will never ignore again in a partnership is _____

_____.

One value I will no longer compromise in my work or relationships is

_____.

The feeling I want to experience more in all my partnerships is _____

_____.

JOURNAL PROMPT:

Reflect on a time when you ignored your intuition about a person or partnership. What was the cost of that decision—mentally, emotionally, financially? What would it have looked like to trust yourself and say no sooner? What would it look like now to hold your partnerships to a higher standard of peace, trust, and alignment?

_____

_____

_____

_____

EXERCISE 18: Learning from Misalignment and Starting Over

This exercise invites you to name what no longer serves you and instead name what allows you to serve others. Here we clarify how to build stronger, more values-based partnerships moving forward.

The last time I had to walk away from a partnership was _____, because _____
_____.

When I reflect on my part in a failed partnership, I now realize I _____
_____.

I tend to ignore red flags when _____
_____.

I feel most unsupported when _____
_____.

One difficult lesson I learned from a former partnership is _____
_____.

I now give trust _____ [immediately, slowly, not at all],
and here's why: _____

_____.

In the past, I chose people based on _____,

but now I choose based on _____

_____.

A successful peace partnership I've experienced is _____,

because _____.

I define a peace partner as someone who _____

_____.

I am currently dissolving partnerships that are _____,

_____, and _____

_____.

JOURNAL PROMPT: Imagine your life, work, or purpose being surrounded only by peace partners. These are the people who challenge, support, and elevate you. What becomes possible when you no longer compromise your values to keep the peace, but instead create peace through aligned, conscious collaboration? Write your new standard for partnership as a personal manifesto.

_____

_____

_____

_____

_____

CHAPTER 10
PEACE

In the tenth principle of peace—Peace itself—we recognize that we are part of a greater whole. Our oneness is not something we have to create; it is something we remember. Our oneness is our strength. Peace is not only possible—it is the natural state of a humanity that lives in alignment with itself and with one another.

Peace is a living, breathing presence. It begins within us and ripples outward, restoring wholeness in quiet, meaningful ways. It is not the absence of struggle, but the presence of awareness, compassion, and conscious choice.

Peace is created moment by moment, breath by breath, conversation by conversation—each time we choose understanding over separation, responsibility over reactivity, and unity over fear. Peace begins within each of us . . . and because we are connected, our collective process of seeking peace never ends.

PEACE POINT 72: Turn Grief and Loss into Peaceful Purpose

When our early losses go unacknowledged, they can settle deep within us as invisible wounds. Over time, those wounds can harden into grievances—quiet resentments that cloud our hearts, shape our choices, and disturb our peace.

We believe in the 3 *Gs:* grief, grievance, and grace.

- **Grief** is the natural response to loss—the ache that reminds us how deeply we've loved, hoped, or cared.
- **Grievance** is grief that has nowhere to go. When pain isn't expressed or witnessed, it turns inward or outward, creating separation, blame, or bitterness.
- **Grace** is what transforms both into growth. It allows us to recognize our connection to one another and our responsibility to heal our own wounds. Grace restores peace where pain once lived, inviting compassion, forgiveness, and understanding.

When we name our losses and allow ourselves to grieve, healing becomes possible. We free ourselves from carrying pain as proof of reason for resentment, and instead, transform it into understanding, empathy, and wisdom. In tending to our own grief, we prevent it from becoming the grievance that divides us from ourselves and from one another.

Imagine every child, including children born into a war-torn land being taught how to manage grief. Instead of learning to hate or inheriting not only the sorrow of their own losses but the unresolved grief of generations before them, they were taught to forgive.

Unless we guide our child in the direction of peace, grief can harden into grievance. We, as adults, have a responsibility to give our children the greatest opportunities for living peacefully. Feelings of hatred, resentment, and entitlement perpetuate the very suffering they were born into. It's our sacred responsibility and duty as adults to lead our children with grace.

Imagine if every child were taught to allow grace, to see the light and worth inside everyone, even those they have been taught to fear and understand, and grief becomes their teacher—to name, feel, and transform those inherited wounds. Then the cycle of trauma could give way to compassion, and the legacy of loss could become the foundation for peace.

One of the greatest disruptors of peace is unresolved grief. When loss goes unrecognized or unhealed, it can shake us to our core—influencing our reactions, our relationships, and our ability to communicate with compassion.

Grief has the power to close our hearts or open them. Without awareness and support, pain can turn inward, creating barriers between us and the peace we seek. But when we honor our grief, give it language, and allow healing to unfold, we transform suffering into strength.

Peaceful purpose grows in the space where acceptance meets action. When we tend to what hurts, we discover what matters. When we heal what was broken, we uncover deeper belonging.

Turning grief into peaceful purpose does not mean forgetting what was lost—it means allowing love to continue. It means letting your heart's hardest moments guide you toward a life of empathy, meaning, and peace.

As Robin Roberts—the former athlete and beloved TV anchor—often reminds us, "Make your mess your mission." When she was battling cancer, those words weren't just inspiring. . . . They were a lifeline, transforming pain into purpose and turning survival into a calling to uplift others.

Grief and loss, when channeled with compassion, become peaceful purpose.

Consider Candy Lightner, who transformed her daughter's tragic death into the founding of MADD (Mothers Against Drunk Driving), and Samantha Smith, the young peace activist whose letter to the Soviet Union became a symbol of hope in a time of fear.

These are legacies of love.

Grief is not the enemy we've made it out to be. It's not a thief in the night or a shadow to be outrun. Grief is a companion—uninvited, yes, but deeply loyal. It arrives when love has nowhere to go, when something or someone dear has been torn from our grasp. It doesn't knock. It just appears, settles in beside us, and stays for a time until it revisits. Learning to accept grief as lifelong mentor allows us to learn from loss and transform it into purpose.

Grief isn't here to destroy us. It's here to walk with us. To witness what we've lost. To say, "This mattered."

Over time, grief can change its shape. It shows us what we love and what we still carry.

Grief becomes a mirror, reflecting our capacity to love and to change. It teaches us that sorrow is not a sign of weakness, but of depth. It does not demand we move on—but asks instead that we move with it, at our own pace, honoring the weight we bear.

Loss breaks us open, but grief, over time, can re-create us into a wiser, stronger version of ourselves. Not as we were before, but as something braver, more compassionate, more alive.

Because when grief is our companion, so too is love. Still here. Still felt. Still shaping who we are.

What pain have you endured? What love can you pass on?

Grief can feel like the end—but it can also mark the beginning of something deeply meaningful. If you're in that space, try this:

● Heart-to-Heart with Yourself

- What loss changed me forever?
- What lesson or insight came from that pain?
- Is there a cause, story, or person I feel called to honor?
- What one small action can I take in their name?
- Who else needs to know they're not alone?

You don't have to start a movement. Sometimes the most powerful peace work begins with a note, a garden, a gesture, a poem, a program, a quiet offering of your heart.

Your pain is valid.

Your story matters.

And your love can live on—

as purpose.

PEACE POINT 73: Imagine Your Vision of a Peaceful World

Let this be your moment—an anchoring presence you can return to anytime, anywhere.

Begin now.

- Sit quietly. Let the world soften around you.
- Place one hand gently over your heart, the other over your belly.
- Inhale slowly and deeply, feeling your breath fill the space beneath your hands.
- On your inhale, say silently: **I am peaceful.**
- Exhale gently. Let the breath carry your peace into the world.

Repeat three times.

Now ask yourself, not as a task, but as an invitation:

- Where will I carry peace next?
- Who in my life is quietly waiting for a moment of calm, of presence, of kindness?
- What can I create, change, or soften with the peace I now hold?

Stay here for a moment longer. Let your breath steady.

Let your thoughts settle.

Let the whisper of peace become your rhythm.

You are no longer just a reader.

You are a peacekeeper. A guide. A light.

And the world needs you.

PEACE POINT 74: Find Your Place in a Peaceful World

In this final chapter, we Percolate Peace. We expand our understanding of both inner and outer peace and commit to embodying it in every facet of life. We intentionally lift others to see their worth. We align with the idea that peace is both personal and global. When we cultivate a deeper sense of inner peace, engage in compassionate communication, and participate in collaborative, peace-driven action, we set in motion a powerful force of change. We unite. We empower. We transform.

From the beginning of civilization, we've moved steadily toward greater connection. What began with handshakes and shared stories around fires has become a global dialogue spanning continents, cultures, and consciousness. In every corner of history, peace has made itself known, sometimes softly and sometimes unmistakably. Peace reminds us that, at our core, we are not separate. We are one human family reaching for the same essential truth: to live in harmony, dignity, and hope.

From the earliest trade routes in 3000 BCE to the first printing press in 1440, the telegraph in 1844, and the creation of the Internet in 1983, humanity has invented its way toward connection. With every leap in communication, we've become more exposed to one another's joys, griefs, and needs. We've become more aware. More available. More responsible.

The twenty-first century has accelerated this connectedness at a profound rate. Social media has redefined our capacity for empathy and outreach. In mere seconds, a video from a village in Kenya can stir hearts in Toronto, Tokyo, and São Paulo. A call for help in Gaza, Ukraine, or Sudan can echo in every ear that chooses to listen. Activism is no longer reserved for the few; it belongs to the many. When voices rise in harmony across borders, peace no longer feels like a dream. It becomes an act of daily, deliberate connection.

Our digital networks have brought a level of transparency we've never seen before. We now witness, in real time, the pain of injustice—and the courage of those who rise against it. We are beginning to understand that peace is not just the absence of war but the presence of equity, inclusion, and truth.

As we evolve, so does our awareness. Science reveals we are biologically wired for compassion; mirror neurons in our brains respond empathetically to the emotions of others. Quantum physics shows that everything is energetically connected, suggesting that intention itself has power. In other words, what we believe and how we behave matters—not just to us, but to the entire human ecosystem.

When we say, "We are all connected," we are not speaking in metaphor, we are speaking in truth. Peace is no longer the responsibility of governments alone. It lives in everyday human choices, multiplied across billions of lives.

Peace shows up in how we treat one another, how we listen, how we respond, and how we care, whether or not we hold a vote, a platform, or a public voice. It lives in our values in motion, in the quiet decisions we make when no one is watching.

When we live in alignment with kindness, when we choose to elevate rather than divide, when we build bridges in the spaces available to us instead of burning them, we are practicing peace.

The idea that peace is probable isn't naïve—it's visionary. Probable because we are more informed than ever. Probable because the next generation is rising with a deep hunger for justice, truth, and sustainability. Probable because technology is a tool we can use to heal, to organize, and to unite. Probable because we are remembering what we've always known: We belong to one another.

Peace is a choice we make over and over again. Not just when it's easy—but when it's hard.

Let us move forward knowing that we are linked across oceans, generations, and time zones. Let us recognize that the ripple of one peaceful action, online or offline, can become a wave of transformation.

We are not just witnesses to a new world. We are co-creators of it.

PEACE POINT 75: Percolate Peace

Are you Percolating Peace? Percolating Peace isn't a one-time decision. Peace is a daily intention.

Ask yourself,

What motivates me?

When I wake up each day, what are my first thoughts?

We know it's a lot to think about in the morning, but remind yourself you are valuable and carry that with you throughout the day.

The truth is that you matter. Your voice matters. Your energy, your choices, and your very presence are powerful tools of peace. Too often, self-doubt interrupts our ability to show up fully. It disturbs our inner calm. But peace isn't about perfection. It's about alignment. When we are grounded in self-acceptance and courageous authenticity, we naturally radiate calm and offer others permission to do the same.

Dan Millman's *Way of the Peaceful Warrior* reminds us that peace is not passive. It is bold. It is fierce. It requires the strength of a warrior and the softness of an open heart. When we choose peace from within, we shape our actions with compassion, presence, and fierce purpose. That's what it means to Percolate Peace.

Ask yourself: *If I had the energy, time, or tools—what small or large act would I take today to bring more peace into the world?*

PEACE POINT 76: Take Action for the Greater Good of Humanity

As we've said, we are empaths and changemakers. In our youth, we felt "different," observing chaos while clinging to calm. As adults, we witness a world steeped in disconnection—gun violence, war, division, despair—and we feel it in our bones.

But instead of becoming numb, we step forward. We hug our families tighter. We write. We speak. We offer this book to the world, not from a pedestal, but from the front lines of human experience.

We do not dismiss conflict. We understand that friction can lead to growth. But when disruption becomes a permanent state—when people remain angry, isolated, and lost—that's where we must intervene. That's where peace work begins.

Answer the Call

Now, it's your turn.

You don't need to be famous or influential or make a big effort to make an impact. You just need willingness to start.

Ask yourself,

- What breaks my heart and what can I do about it?
- Who in my life needs peace right now and how can I bring it?
- What small action can I take today that serves someone else?

Start where you are. Speak kindness. Interrupt cruelty. Share your story. Volunteer your time. Help a neighbor. Raise your voice when it matters most—and quiet your voice when someone else needs to be heard.

You are part of a global family of peacebuilders. This book is your beginning, not your end.

We're inviting you to be one of the million moments of peace. Let your life be an answer to that call.

PEACE POINT 77: Make Peace a Normal Conversation

Peace is not fluff. Peace is strength. And it must become part of our daily dialogue.

Ask yourself,

- Am I a peace ambassador?
- Am I teaching calmness, compassion, and acceptance through my actions—or am I contributing to division?

Please rise with us with your love and presence to normalize peace in conversations, online and in person, in classrooms, in boardrooms, and beyond. This is a movement. You are the messenger.

Start by practicing these five conversation shifts:

1. **Replace blame with curiosity.** Instead of "How could you think that?," try "Help me understand what led you to that belief."
2. **Use pauses to de-escalate.** Silence can be more powerful than a sharp retort.
3. **Acknowledge common ground.** Even one shared value can create connection.
4. **Name the emotion.** "It sounds like this really hurt you." Peace grows from being seen and heard.
5. **End with intention.** Try saying, "I hope we both walk away feeling more open than when we started."

Let peace become your *language*, not just your intention. Speak it often. Model it consistently. Invite it in, even when it's uncomfortable.

Peace becomes possible when we give it words.

PEACE POINT 78: Imagine a Peaceful World

We each woke up today with a quiet but powerful vision in our hearts: *What if the world had already chosen peace?* What if today was the great peaceful reset, the day humanity woke up differently?

Pause and imagine:

A world where **children are taught that emotional intelligence is valued.** Where their feelings are honored, their voices uplifted, and their natural empathy nourished as deeply as their intellect.

Imagine **schools where mindfulness is integrated into every class.** Where teachers begin the day without the need for control, but instead with fuller compassion. Where no child is left feeling invisible, and every child knows what it feels like to be safe and heard.

Imagine **CEOs opening board meetings with a breath**—inviting clarity before strategy, presence before performance. Imagine workplaces designed around human thriving, not just output. Where burnout isn't a badge of honor, and rest isn't a reward, it's a right.

Picture **politicians pausing to listen,** not to respond and deflect, but to *understand.* Imagine elected leaders whose highest aspiration is to serve, not to win. Imagine disagreement without destruction. Debate without cruelty. Policy shaped by empathy.

Imagine **elders honored for their wisdom,** not sidelined. A culture where aging is sacred, not hidden. Where we ask the generations who came before us how we might live better now—and actually listen.

Imagine **preventative health care rooted in whole-being wellness,** where healing includes mental, spiritual, emotional, physical, and relational care. Where medical visits are infused with dignity. Where grief is supported, not silenced.

Now imagine **art and activism woven together**—murals that speak to justice, poetry that reshapes laws, music that mends divides. Imagine the walls we build replaced by gathering spaces. Imagine neighborhoods stitched together by gardens, libraries, and shared meals.

Imagine **news cycles driven not by fear but by progress and unity.** Imagine headlines that celebrate peacemakers, not just power. Imagine waking up to stories of community kindness, of restored ecosystems, of people helping people—not for clicks, but for care.

Imagine every single person starting their day with one question:
How can I bring peace into the world today?

For millions of people across cultures, faiths, and philosophies— Buddhists, Taoists, pacifists, Mennonites, and those who consider themselves spiritual but not religious—this question is already a daily practice. And still, imagine what could shift if that same intention were shared more consciously, more collectively, and more visibly across the world.

If even one percent of the global population—roughly 80 million people—practiced peace with intention each day, not in theory but in action, we believe it would change the tone, the energy, and the direction of our shared humanity.

Because peace is contagious. Peace builds momentum.

Peace is not passive. It is a form of intelligence. A form of bravery. A form of human evolution.

And it begins with imagining peace fully, vividly, and without apology— and then choosing, together, to build it.

PEACE POINT 79: Practice Cultural Curiosity

Peace begins when we choose wonder over judgment.

Every person carries a culture within them—a story of where they come from, what shaped them, and what home feels like in their heart. When we approach one another with curiosity instead of assumptions, belonging replaces bias and understanding replaces fear.

Ask questions. Learn pronunciations. Try others' food. Honor their traditions. Celebrate their holidays. Listen to their history. Welcome their worldview.

Cultural curiosity is a peaceful act because it acknowledges dignity. It says, *Your story matters to me.* It reminds us that the world is richer—and more peaceful—when every culture is allowed to shine. The most powerful way to create global belonging is not through convincing others to be like us . . . but through the courage to be curious about who they truly are.

PEACE POINT 80: Lead the Children Toward Wholeness

Children learn peace not by what we tell them but by who we are becoming. Every interaction with a young person, whether parenting, teaching, mentoring, or passing one in the grocery store, is a chance to plant a seed of peace.

When we speak with calm instead of criticism, when we model empathy instead of entitlement, when we repair instead of react—we show children how to turn humanity's wounds into humanity's wisdom.

To lead children toward wholeness is to show them

- They belong in every room they enter.
- Their feelings are worthy of understanding.
- Their questions are welcomed curiosities.
- Their differences are threads in our shared tapestry.

Peace is generational. It grows through the hands and hearts of those who inherit the world from us. If we want a more peaceful future, we must be the peace our children can imitate—and trust them to take it even further than we can imagine.

Your Pathway to Peace—A Call to Action to Create 1,000,000 Peaceful Moments

We will never stop worrying about the world.

And that includes you!

Why? Why Us? Why This Book, and Why Now?

We need to believe peace is possible. Peace becomes possible the moment we remember our oneness and choose to act as one humanity.

The world we are living in can feel like a beautiful tapestry coming undone. A tapestry woven from every culture, every community, every story—and now some of those stitches feel like they're being pulled apart.

Peace, once something we assumed we were slowly building together, can feel fragile. Our sense of connection, the truth that we belong to one another, feels threatened.

Every one of us contributes a thread to the fabric of humanity. We are meant to be intertwined, strengthened by what each of us brings. When one thread frays, the whole tapestry feels it.

But here is the hope:

If it can unravel, it can also be rewoven.

We wrote this book because peace isn't just a dream for the world. It's a daily practice for each of us. And when enough people choose peace in the way they show up, speak up, and love . . . humanity holds together.

We are here to restitch what matters.

To remind one another that we are connected.

To choose peace—in big ways, small ways, and everyday ways.

Because when we believe peace is possible, we bring it back into the world.

We, Elizabeth and Dr. Katie, were each raised to embrace the idea that all souls matter. We just don't understand in our hearts why others think differently. From writing this book, however, we have come to understand it in our heads. We think what prevents us from peace is forgetting we are all connected, and collective compassion—directing unconditional love to everyone—is the most important way to promote peace.

We each learned this from different experiences, but we came together with the resolve to share this message:

We are one world. Each of us, and our loved ones, can rise up and claim a life of peace that extends into every encounter. We commit to learning and practicing the tools in this book each day, knowing that peace is a living practice, not a perfect destination.

We talk with our children about empathy and responsibility. We ask them what matters, who needs help, how they can show up better. We remind them that peace is not passive. It's how we listen, how we lead, how we live. Every moment offers a choice: to act from fear or to rise in love. To withhold or to extend. To isolate or to connect.

These are the quiet revolutions that build a peaceful world.

Are you paying attention?

Our Pathways to Peace with Elizabeth and Dr. Katie

Elizabeth—Worrying About the World

I'm never going to stop worrying about the world and everyone in it. I've known this about myself since I was in preschool. Even then, I could feel the tension in a room when others couldn't. I noticed when people weren't kind. I paid attention to disagreements big and small. And in the quiet corners of my heart, I'd ask myself the same question over and over: Why can't everyone just get along?

It was a question I whispered as a child. It's one I still carry with me as an adult.

As I grew older and was taught history in school, I remember feeling confused, even heartbroken, that someone had to write a speech or form a movement to declare the value of human rights. I remember learning about Dr. Martin Luther King Jr. and feeling the ache of injustice in my chest. Why did someone have to fight and die for what should have already been given, something that was written in the founding documents of our nation? Why did someone have to stand on the steps of the Lincoln Memorial and proclaim a dream for equality when dignity and kindness should have been our collective starting point? Shouldn't those truths be embedded in who we are? Shouldn't they just be?

The world felt heavy on my shoulders then. Sometimes it still does. I don't say that with despair. I say that with purpose. Because I believe deeply that sensitivity is a strength. I believe compassion is a form of leadership. And I know without a doubt that the world needs more of both.

I have always felt a profound ache for people in pain, even strangers. Maybe especially strangers. I've never been able to turn away. Whether someone is grieving, struggling, angry, misunderstood, or afraid, I feel it. In every cell of my body. And while it might sound overwhelming to live that way, it's also what makes me who I am. It's what drives my work. It's what led me to create The Best Ever You Network, to write, to teach, to serve, and to dedicate my life to being a peaceful presence.

Today, we are more globally connected than ever. What happens in one corner of the world is felt in another. We can see one another, hear one another, reach one another in real time. And while this connectedness can sometimes amplify the noise, it also opens extraordinary pathways to peace.

I recently read a story about Sarah Inama, a middle school teacher in Idaho, who was reprimanded for a classroom poster that read, "Everyone Is Welcome Here." Below the words were ten raised hands in varying skin tones. The school district had issue with the hands, not the words, they proclaimed, because they said it violated district policy that all classroom materials needed to be "content neutral." She was forced to remove the sign by the principal. When her students questioned why she did this, she had no good answer for them. She then defied the district and put the poster back up. Eventually, she resigned rather than face disciplinary action. By then, her story of standing up for her students—all of her students—had spread internationally.

This woman's courage and resolve to do what is right stopped me in my tracks. In a time when division is loud and compassion is too often quiet, Sarah's sign wasn't just paper and ink. It was a declaration. It was a stand for humanity. It was peace in action. One teacher. One classroom. One message that echoes far beyond school walls. She reminded me, and all of us, that sometimes the most powerful change comes in the smallest, bravest acts.

For me, peace has always been connected to a deep and sometimes overwhelming sensitivity. I am extraordinarily attuned to the injustices of the world: to intolerance, to cruelty, to anything that undermines another person's dignity or humanity. Pandemics, violence, inequality, and the collective grief they bring—these aren't just headlines to me. They land in my heart and stay there. I feel the disruption of peace long before I have the words to explain it.

I've come to understand that I am not alone in this sensitivity. Many of us walk through the world with open hearts, absorbing not only the beauty but also the burdens of others. We feel for strangers. We grieve for communities we've never visited. We ache for peace because we know what it's like to carry chaos.

When the world feels shaky politically, environmentally, emotionally, I feel it at the deepest level. I worry for the children, the elderly, the caregivers, the teachers, the animals. I think about those without a voice or platform. I think about the people quietly struggling, unseen and unsupported. And that's what keeps me up at night, but it's also what keeps me going.

In my life, peace has become more than a value. It's a mission. It's a way of being. It's the lens through which I view everything: how I make decisions, how I speak, how I lead, and how I love. I don't always get it right, but I try. And I believe that trying matters. I've seen firsthand how peace transforms. I've seen someone who is angry soften because they were heard. I've watched grief become a purpose. I've watched a moment of presence shift an entire conversation.

Sometimes peace looks like writing a book. Sometimes it looks like being quiet when someone else needs to speak. Sometimes it's walking away. Sometimes it's staying even when it's hard. Peace isn't passive. It's not always soft. Often, it requires fierce boundaries, intentional energy, and the courage to confront what's unjust. But peace is always worth it.

Dr. Katie—Beyond Labels: Making Peace Our Heartbeat

Seeing the beauty in diversity and the power of compassion was instilled in me from a young age. I remember my dad reminding us that "the person next door had less than us and our job is to lift them up." My parents enrolled me in a different school to ensure I would learn the value of diversity. My friends in junior high school were from India and South Africa. I was a cheerleader, along with other Christian friends, for the synagogue's basketball team. My parents advocated for me to take a missionary trip to Juarez, Mexico, when I was sixteen. The list is long in the ways I learned that a human being's value lies in their *being*, not in their *doing*. Labels were never important to me. Labels are external and never offer a complete picture of a person. It's no wonder I went on to become a child psychotherapist—to help children see their value from the inside out.

Today, I find myself perplexed and bewildered by a world where labels divide and conquer, isolate and destroy the capacity of a well-woven tapestry to provide comfort and joy and connection with people throughout the world. Labels that provide cultural, political, religious, or any number of preconceived ideas about someone are the enemy of peace.

Why can't we set aside labels and share our common bond: humanness?

As a psychotherapist, I have been listening to people who hold many different labels describe their fears, their anger, their mistrust, and unfortunately, whomever carries the "right" label to be the target of their blame. "This group did this" and "they are this" and "if only we could get rid of them"—these are the statements I have been trying to help people resolve by discovering a peaceful solution and response. The challenge has been to imagine everyone as a person without labels and view their situation with compassion. This is in the context of having lost jobs, fearing deportation, worrying about their future. It's so much easier to blame someone else for your pain than it is to let go of blame and empower yourself to compassionate action.

What can you learn that can make the world more peaceful?

We've all heard the stereotypical beauty pageant contestant made fun of for asking what their dream would be when they respond, "world peace." What if we took their answer at face value? What if instead of making fun of that idea, we all agreed and envisioned the same dream?

We have given you thoughts, ideas, exercises, and ways to practice, but now it's time to manifest peace. Compassionate, collective, and unconditional acceptance that we are all in this world together and we need one another—that is our fundamental belief.

We care about you and we won't stop worrying about the world because we care.

We remember being taught in Sunday school that if we didn't learn a life lesson, it would keep presenting itself until we finally understood it. We think it's time we learned compassion. Our mission is that this lesson be learned by everyone and for peace to become our natural inclination. We won't stop believing that it's possible. Peace needs to be our heartbeat.

Peace isn't just something we hope for in the world. It's something we must actively build, beginning within ourselves and extending outward through the choices we make, the people we care for, and the actions we take. In this final chapter on peace, we share the deeply personal stories of two very different but equally powerful journeys. Danielle M. Reiff shows us how peace begins in the sacred space between parent and child—through love that is learned, fought for, and ultimately lived in practice. Her courageous story of healing generational trauma reminds us that peace is the presence of compassion, even in our hardest moments.

Zach and Chase Hartman, teenage cofounders of Eco Brothers, embody peace in motion—through community service, environmental advocacy, and a commitment to youth leadership that spans continents. Their story proves that peace isn't passive or quiet; it's a vibrant, purpose-driven force built through generosity, creativity, and meaningful connection.

These stories are not just inspiring, they're instructive. They teach us that peace is found in the messy middle, in the doing and becoming, and in the brave decision to love anyway. Whether in a child's quiet return to trust or in a global ripple of service-led impact, peace is something we each have the power to create.

Stories from the Heart

Danielle M. Reiff—Love Is Greater Than Peace,
for Peace Is Founded upon Love

He was my first and only child. Before the hospital let me take him home after he was born, they made me spend two hours in a session about purple rage. "Don't shake your baby," they said, "no matter how angry you get. That could kill him." But they didn't say a word about how to love him. Maybe they assumed I already knew. Maybe they assumed everyone knows that. But I didn't, not really.

As an American diplomat, I had been posted in Bogotá, Colombia, when I was medically evacuated to Washington, DC, to give birth. Six months later, I transferred—stroller, portable crib, and all—to the Republic of Georgia in the former Soviet Union. By the time he turned one, my son had lived in three countries and racked up more airline miles than most Americans do in a lifetime.

I did my best to love him. I read and sang to him endlessly. He didn't watch a screen or eat processed sugar—even for his birthday and Halloween—until he started preschool. I taught him to observe nature carefully, to relish the moments when we encountered a colorful blossom or a unique bird.

But when our home life became unbearable, I did the unthinkable. Desperate for my own respite, I left my son alone with his father for a year while I took an unaccompanied assignment in South Sudan. I told myself he was too young to remember a prolonged separation, but that wasn't true.

When we reunited in Sri Lanka afterward, my son and I were both extraordinarily angry. I was working sixty-hour weeks, fighting for women's political leadership and democratic renewal on that gorgeous island, while exhausted and overwhelmed at home. My son was rebelling, desperate for my time and attention. But I didn't have enough time, and I didn't have enough energy. I was crying and yelling more than I care to admit. I just needed him to behave and give me space. But he couldn't do that anymore than I could muster the energy to play. I didn't know then that I had PTSD from an outbreak of war in South Sudan or that my son struggles to adapt to new routines. I just knew that we were both suffering—and we were at an impasse.

I had been a peacebuilder in my soul for as long as I could remember. I later pursued a career in peacebuilding, where I contributed to peace processes and historic democratic transitions around the world. When I realized the irony that I did not have peace in my own life, we left our diplomatic assignment in Sri Lanka early to seek help.

Within months of moving home to the United States, a miracle happened, disguised as tragedy. I was working when I received an unexpected call from school. My six-year-old had told his teacher that he wanted to die. "He doesn't think anyone loves him," she said. That day, sitting in the school lobby with my sobbing child in my arms, both of us heartbroken, I knew we needed to do something differently. But what? *Please, God, help us. I don't know what to do. Please show me how to love my son.*

Help came through a children's therapist named Eli. He explained that healing required both of us. "Your son's feelings and behavior can't be separated from the home environment," he said, inviting me to join a parenting group. There, I learned about fifty years of research on cultivating safety for our children through healthy attachment. I learned that children's instinct is to explore the world around them. Over and over again, they move toward something new—a new person, a new skill, a new space, or a new experience—only to return to their safe person when the exploration is over. To enable them to develop, the adults who love them are supposed to accompany them, help them, and delight in them. When the exploration goes awry, we are supposed to comfort them and help them learn to regulate their feelings.

Every week, I was triggered by the training videos of parents soothing their kids. Through my own inner distress and uncontrollable sobbing before or after class, my body remembered that, as a child, I myself had not experienced safety, attention, and a parent's delight. When I was a preteen, my mother told me she couldn't handle being a parent anymore and abandoned me on my father's doorstep. My father yelled at me a lot and made me feel worthless. Throughout middle school, he wouldn't let me leave the house during the summers to play with other kids. I had grown up feeling—and continued to feel—deeply alone and unlovable.

With Eli's help, I began to heal. He taught me mindful breathing, and I learned how to keep my body relaxed and get into a meditative state when my trauma was triggered.

I became adept at letting excruciating emotional energy pass through my body without blocking it, burying it, or numbing it with screens or addictions. It's not wholly unlike breathing deeply through the pain of childbirth.

As I released my pent-up bitterness and sorrow through this practice, slowly but surely, I could feel love rising in my heart and soul. As I learned to regulate my own feelings, I no longer shouted when my son tested my patience. Instead, I listened to understand and held boundaries nonviolently. I became calmer, more attentive, and genuinely safe for my son. Only then did I finally understand what I had been doing wrong. Love isn't proven through sacrifice or control. It's demonstrated through healthy emotional presence.

It took a few years of practicing love like that before my son came to trust me again. First, his skepticism softened. "Do you really love me?" he would ask, as he weighed whether I had become safe and if I truly valued him. Then, one day when I picked him up from school, I told him I loved him and asked if he believed me. I watched as a soft expression came over his face. "Yes, Mama," he said sweetly. Finally, he could feel my love.

Today, he often confides in me and climbs into my lap to snuggle. With our new-found trust, he is finally able to cooperate with me when I need him to. When we disagree, we have learned how to dialogue until we find a way forward that makes sense for both of us. Precious are the days when we banter back and forth, joking and laughing uncontrollably. I had never been able to do that with him. Ultimately, I have broken a toxic cycle that my family has been in for generations.

I have learned that love is transformational. As the Bahá'í teaching says, "Love is greater than peace, for peace is founded upon love." Now I understand. We had to learn to love each other in practice before we could finally live in peace.

Chase and Zach Hartman—Building Peace Through Purpose: A Brotherly Journey of Service and Impact

Peace is often pictured as quiet stillness—a sunset over the water, the gentle rustling of trees, or the calm of a silent moment in thought. But for us, peace looks different. It is not always quiet, and it is rarely still. Peace is something that moves, something that is made. It lives in conversations, in community service, in the joy of giving, and in the ripple effects of kindness passed from one person to the next. Peace is not found in isolation—it is built in the spaces between people working together to make the world a little better.

We are teenagers who cofounded Eco Brothers, a Florida-based nonprofit we started in elementary school to promote literacy, environmental action, and youth leadership. Over the past nine years, we've donated more than 300,000 books, reached over 70,000 students, and raised $200,000 to support our work. We've also kept over 125,000 pounds of reusable goods out of landfills and upcycled nearly 7,000 unwanted stuffed animals into pet toys. But beyond the numbers, our work is rooted in one core belief: Peace is built through service.

Our journey began with small, simple acts. For Zach, it started at just seven years old while taking our household trash out to the curb. Like most kids, Zach grumbled a little at first at having to do this chore, but soon, he started to notice something that didn't sit right with him. Our recycling bin only got picked up once a week, but regular trash went out twice. That meant a whole lot more waste was going to landfills than was being recycled. It got Zach thinking: *Where does all our trash go? And what could we do about it?*

That curiosity sparked the beginning of Zach's Planet, a service project created in 2017 to help the planet and our local community and that later evolved into Eco Brothers. Zach started simply by researching trash and was shocked to learn that more than 300 million books are thrown away every year, just tossed into the garbage. Add to that the thousands of stuffed animals that are discarded because resale shops don't accept them. So Zach started organizing collection drives for books and gently used toys. Over time, what started as a small project grew into something much larger, an ongoing effort. We've shipped thousands of handmade pet toys made from upcycled stuffed animals to animal shelters across the country, spent countless weekends picking up trash in local parks and beaches, and most importantly gave children the chance to own books they otherwise wouldn't have had.

For Chase, peace was always found in connection—whether delivering books to Title I schools, leading his high school student council, or supporting global youth changemakers through microgrants. Every project we've taken on has been driven by one goal: building peace through purposeful action while inspiring others to understand the problem and work toward the solution. Chase's community service efforts began with a simple book collecting project in the fifth grade as part of his school's chapter of the National Elementary Honor Society. One book drive made him question why kids in his area didn't own books, and his passion for education equity was ignited.

Chase also found peace in shared efforts, especially in moments of doubt. There have been days when the scale of problems, especially in education, felt too big. The idea that no matter how many classrooms you reach, another will always need help can feel overwhelming. In Florida, the emphasis on banning books put a stop to our deliveries in schools for more than a year. Chase saw this as a huge problem in helping kids have access to books. Studies show kids who have books at home are more proficient in reading, but the government was getting in the way of our community service work. Instead of allowing frustration to paralyze us, Chase took action. He spoke at a board of education meeting pleading with members to see the value in our book deliveries. Two members reached out following the meeting in support. Deliveries returned the following school year. Hopelessness lifts when we're reminded that we're not alone.

Zach learned early on that peace comes from purpose. Whether it's packing up books after a school event, sewing pet toys late into the night, or walking along a beach with a trash bag in hand, there's a calm that comes from knowing you're doing something that matters. That calm becomes peace. And it doesn't require recognition to be rewarding. Even though Zach has been honored with the President's Environmental Youth Award, the Action for Nature Eco Hero Award, and appeared on *The Drew Barrymore Show*, those accolades are not the source of his drive. The real reward is seeing the outcome of his service in the faces of others.

Zach was just seven years old when he started delivering books to schools. He was the same age as the kids choosing the books to take home and keep. Zach was deeply moved by a delivery when one girl asked him how he got the thousands of books he had set up on tables and was distributing for free. He simply stated that people like to share. He encouraged her to do the same when she finished reading her books. Can life be so simple? Help others? Share? Zach understood that everyone, no matter their age, can do simple acts of kindness as community service in their neighborhoods.

One of the most powerful sources of peace in our journey has been gratitude. Not just the kind we receive, but the kind we feel. Gratitude fills the air at our book drives, in the thank-yous from children clutching their new stories, in the smiles of tired volunteers, and in the satisfaction of a job well done. It's in the moment after a big event when the room is quiet, backpacks are heavier with books, and hearts are fuller than before. That's when we feel the most at peace, physically tired, emotionally full, and deeply grateful. Chase felt this gratitude in his first book delivery at the age of ten. A little girl his age told him she had never owned a book before. Chase had mountains of books at home, filling his shelves and toy chest. He helped her search for the perfect book, and when she found it, she beamed with excitement! She said she would "hold it, and love it, and keep it forever." That girl motivated Chase to continue his project. He later told her story and that of many others in grant applications for the NHL's Lightning Community Hero of Tomorrow Award, the prestigious Coca-Cola Scholarship, the National Honor Society Service Scholarship, and the NSHSS Claus Nobel Legacy Award and Be More Grant. Her story is the story of thousands of kids whose families are worried about affording food on the table, not prioritizing books on their shelves.. Her reaction to owning a book sparked hope.

At its core, peace is about connection. Chase often says that peace lives in the spaces between people—in conversations, in teamwork, in trust. It's watching others show up, knowing that even if you're holding only one corner of the puzzle, someone else is holding the next. This is true in our nonprofit work, in our partnerships with students and schools, and even in casual conversations that lead to mentorships, friendships, and inspiration. As high school student body president, Chase opened up the work of Eco Brothers to hundreds of kids in his school, offering more than 10,000 hours of community service and leading countless projects. Service doesn't feel like work when we can do it with friends.

When Chase opened our Eco Brothers Youth Council microgrant program and saw submissions from over a dozen countries, it reaffirmed that we are part of something global: a community of young people just as committed to creating change. Chase runs monthly meetings with more than 150 council members from nine countries. The coming together of young minds wanting change for this world inspires him. Peace is a shared mission.

Through more than 5,000 collective hours of service, we've learned that peace is not a destination. It's not something you find and then keep forever. It's something you build every day through small actions, shared missions, and deep connection. Whether we're organizing a cleanup, reviewing a grant application, answering a question from a curious student, or just showing up for someone in need, we try to do it in a way that makes others feel safe, seen, and supported. That's peace.

And the best part? Anyone can build it. You don't need a nonprofit, a big platform, or a long résumé. You just need a willingness to give—to show up, to try, and to care. The peace you're looking for might not be found in silence or stillness. It might be in the joy of community service.

We didn't set out on this journey looking for peace. We set out looking to help. But somewhere along the way, we discovered that the two are connected. Helping others helps us. Giving back gives us peace. And that's a gift we'll never take for granted.

It's Time to Percolate Peace—Your Call to Action

This is not the conclusion. It's the beginning.

You now hold the tools, the truth, and the choice.

Will you Percolate Peace in your life, your home, your work, and in the world?

We imagine a world where connection replaces separation, where the boundaries between us and others dissolve into one shared human experience.

What we are calling for is a shift in consciousness, where compassion transcends geography, where dignity isn't dependent on birthplace, and where we recognize one another first and foremost as human beings.

We're inviting a mindset shift—a reimagining of what peace and connection can look like. A return to something many of us understood naturally as children. That spark, that light, that said, *There is a light in you that burns in me. We are connected.*

We call this **The Point of Peaceful Connection**—the moment when you lift me, and I lift you, and together we lift the world. We hold a shared intention: to envision and embody a peaceful world. Yes, it may seem idealistic. But weren't all great changemakers once called naïve? We stand in bold, brave company. We are not asking for perfection. We are asking for participation. For presence. For compassion.

We are asking: **Can you help us hold this vision? What if, in every moment, we remembered peace to live peacefully?**

Preamble of Peace

We believe in honoring the dignity of all human beings.

We envision a world where all people are respected and valued— without labels, without fear.

We hold the hope of a future where borders of the heart no longer exist, and everyone feels safe, seen, and heard.

That's our vision of peace.

Let your presence be your practice.

Let your compassion be your cause. Let your life be proof that not only is peace possible, it is probable.

It begins with us. And it begins now.

A Call to Consciousness: Why We Wrote This

We will never stop worrying about the world.

And that includes you.

Why? Why us? Why this book? Why now?

Because peace cannot wait.

Because we need to believe peace is possible.

Each soul deserves dignity, safety, and love.

We, Elizabeth and Dr. Katie, were raised to believe that *all* souls matter.

We don't understand in our hearts why others think differently. But through the writing of this book, we've come to understand why in our minds: **We forget we are connected.**

And forgetting our connection is what unravels peace.

Collective compassion—directing love to all people, not just some—is the path forward.

It's how we stop the unraveling and begin the mending.

So many of us are asking questions in private that need to be asked aloud:

Why are we tolerating this?

Why are outdated systems still shaping our futures?

Why do we let cruelty, greed, and division be "the way things are"?

Why are we still made to believe that peace means silence?

We don't always "take it" or "let them."

Many of us are rising! We are speaking, leading, building, healing.

And yet we are often dismissed, labeled dramatic, or told, "Now is not the time."

Let us be clear:

Peace is not weakness. It's not passivity. It's not silence.

Peace is power.

Peace is participation.

Peace is a choice to show up, even when it would be easier to check out.

This isn't about politics or perfection.

This is about humanity.

We don't need more control. We need more connection. We don't need more power plays.

We need more peaceful people who are no longer willing to be quiet.

Not this time.

Not anymore.

Not on our watch.

Peace in Motion: Your Turn

So, what now?

Let's stop asking, *Why we keep allowing this?*

and start asking,

What can we do right now to change it?

Because we can.

Let peace begin with you.

Pause for Peace.

- Show up with love—for yourself and others.
- Lead with kindness.
- Listen with an open heart.

- Speak with honesty and compassion.
- Give generously, receive graciously.
- Heal forward.
- Live aligned.
- Choose peace again and again.

We hope you'll join us in creating a million peaceful moments. Because peace isn't a passive state, it's a powerful choice.

With peaceful love,
Elizabeth and Dr. Katie

ACKNOWLEDGMENTS

We would like to express our deepest gratitude to everyone who believes in us and supports our work through our books and work at The Best Ever You Network, The Percolate Peace Project, and Recreate Coaching and Counseling. You are the heart behind our mission, and we could not do this work without you.

To our husbands, John and Peter, thank you for your unwavering support, love, and encouragement. You lift us when it counts. To our children, Cali, Connor, Quinn, Cam, and Quaid, your presence grounds us in what matters most.

Thank you to our parents and extended family for encouraging and inspiring us with your never-ending support. We feel blessed to have friends and colleagues who mentor us, teach us, and hold us accountable, as well as show up for a walk, a dinner, or a quick cup of coffee to give us encouragement and wings to see our potential. Both of us also must mention most beloved cats and dogs, who remind us by sitting on our lap, resting at our feet, or even on our keyboards to play, rest, and stay present.

We are incredibly grateful to our agent, Steve Harris. You are not only our guide in the literary world, but also a soul-aligned supporter of our purpose. Your belief in this work means the world to us.

To the extraordinary team at Health Communications, Inc.—Christine Belleris, Christian Blonshine, Larissa Henoch, and Bob Land—thank you for being the dream team behind this book. Your expertise, creativity, and care have brought our vision to life in the most powerful way.

A special thank-you to all the contributors who generously shared their stories, insights, and hearts within these pages. Your lived experiences are threads of hope woven throughout this book, and we are honored to hold your words here.

Our contributors: Christopher Radko, Santosh Govindaraju, Christine Belleris, Jennifer Vaughn, Mariya Vynnytska, Lisbeth Cort, Jennifer Drews, Chad Stillwagon, Andy Archer, David Lukov, Shani Taha, Catherine Parrillo, Michael McGlone, Ameenah McCann-Woods, Rebeccah Silence, John B. Grimes, Sally Huss, Liz Olberg, Danielle M. Reiff, Chase and Zach Hartman, "The Dancing Ump" Vincent Chapman of the Savannah Bananas, and Grace Fraga.

A heartfelt thank-you to Christopher Radko. Your light and artistry inspire us and so many others to keep joy at the center of our lives.

We would also like to recognize and thank Mariya and everyone at the Ukrainian Circle. This initiative is deeply aligned with our mission. Formed by four brave Ukrainian women psychologists in the midst of war, often from bomb shelters, the Ukrainian Circle is a comprehensive mental health program dedicated to ending cycles of hate and promoting peace through posttraumatic growth. Their efforts to scale impact through the development of a transformative mental health app deserve global support. We are proud to lift up their work and invite you to help us help Ukraine.

While writing this book, we also discovered an inspiring group of spiritually motivated thought leaders at Humanity's Team. We are grateful for your work and shared vision.

Finally, our deepest appreciation to Rev. Mpho A. Tutu van Furth for gracing this book with her foreword. Your voice, wisdom, and unwavering commitment to peace elevate this work to new heights. Thank you for believing in our vision and blessing this book with your presence.

To all the peacemakers: Thank you to those of you who pick up this book and share it, and the messages within, around the globe.

With gratitude and peace,
Elizabeth and Dr. Katie

BOOK DISCUSSION POINTS

These discussion points are designed to deepen your reflection, inspire conversation, and encourage peaceful action. There are no right answers, only honest moments of awareness and shared learning.

1. Defining Peace

How does *The Peace Guidebook* define peace on both a personal and global level? How does this definition resonate with your own experiences of peace?

2. The Role of Hope

Discuss the importance of hope in creating peace. How does the book encourage readers to cultivate hope, even in challenging circumstances?

3. Healing as a Process

The book emphasizes healing as a critical step toward peace. What are some healing practices or perspectives shared in the book, and how can they be applied in everyday life?

4. Harmony in Relationships

How does *The Peace Guidebook* suggest we foster harmony in our relationships with others? What are the practical steps it offers for conflict resolution?

5. Personal Responsibility for Global Change

The book suggests that personal peace contributes to global peace. How does it explain the connection between personal actions and larger societal change?

6. Mindfulness and Presence

How does mindfulness play a role in cultivating peace, according to the book? Discuss any exercises or techniques you found particularly impactful.

7. Compassion and Empathy

The authors emphasize the need for compassion and empathy. How does the book challenge you to increase empathy in your interactions with others?

8. Forgiveness as a Pathway to Peace

What role does forgiveness play in achieving peace? How does the book help readers navigate the process of forgiveness?

9. Cultural and Societal Influences on Peace

How does the book address societal and cultural barriers to peace? What are some ways it encourages overcoming these barriers?

10. Inner Peace Versus Outer Peace

Discuss the relationship between inner peace and outer peace as portrayed in the book. Is one more important than the other, or do they work hand in hand?

11. Creating a Peaceful Mindset

The book offers strategies for cultivating a peaceful mindset. Which of these strategies do you find most useful or applicable in your life?

12. The Role of Leadership in Peacebuilding

How does the book view leadership in the context of peace? What qualities does it highlight as essential for peaceful leadership?

13. Your Personal Peace Project

The book asks readers to reflect on their own peaceful journey. What personal peace project or action step do you feel inspired to take after reading *The Peace Guidebook*?

14. The Importance of Community

Discuss how the book encourages community involvement in fostering peace. What role does collaboration play in creating lasting peace?

How might your group, community, or organization embody one of the Peace Points together?

REFERENCES

Burrows, Peter. "Steve Jobs: The Next Insanely Great Thing." *Business-Week,* May 25, 1998.

Eastman, Dr. Katie. *Uplifting: Inspiring Stories of Loss, Change, and Growth.* Bloomington, IN: Balboa Press, 2024.

Eastman, Dr. Katie, and Hamilton-Guarino, Elizabeth: *Percolate. Let Your Best Self Filter Through.* Carlsbad, CA: Hay House, 2014.

Eisler, Riane. *The Power of Partnership: Seven Relationships That Will Change Your Life.* Novato, CA: New World Library, 2002.

Frankl, Viktor E. *Man's Search for Meaning.* Boston: Beacon Press, 2006.

Gandhi, Mohandas K. *Non-Violent Resistance (Satyagraha).* Edited by Bharatan Kumarappa. New York: Schocken Books, 1961.

Goodman, Whitney. *Toxic Positivity: Keeping It Real in a World Obsessed with Being Happy.* New York: TarcherPerigee, 2022.

Goudsblom, Johan. *Fire and Civilization.* London: Penguin Books, 1994.

Hamilton-Guarino, Elizabeth. *The Change Guidebook: How to Align Your Heart, Truths, and Energy to Find Success in All Areas of Your Life.* Boca Raton, FL: Health Communications, 2022.

Hamilton-Guarino, Elizabeth. *The Success Guidebook: How to Visualize, Actualize, and Amplify You.* Boca Raton, FL: Health Communications, 2024.

Herman, Judith Lewis. *Trauma and Recovery: The Aftermath of Violence—from Domestic Abuse to Political Terror.* New York: Basic Books, 1992.

Huss, Sally. *A Lesson for Every Child: Learning About Food Allergies.* Colorado Spring, CO: Sally Huss, 2020.

Jeffers, Susan. *Feel the Fear and Do It Anyway.* New York: Ballantine Books, 1987.

Jobs, Steve. "You've Got to Find What You Love." Commencement address, Stanford University, June 12, 2005. https://news.stanford.edu/2005/06/14/jobs-061505/.

Kabat-Zinn, Jon. *Wherever You Go, There You Are: Mindfulness Meditation in Everyday Life.* New York: Hyperion, 1994.

King, Martin Luther, Jr. "Nonviolence: The Only Road to Freedom." Speech, May 4, 1966. In *A Testament of Hope: The Essential Writings and Speeches of Martin Luther King, Jr.* Edited by James M. Washington. New York: HarperCollins, 1986.

Mandela, Nelson. *Long Walk to Freedom: The Autobiography of Nelson Mandela.* Boston: Little, Brown and Company, 1994.

Millman, Dan. *Way of the Peaceful Warrior: A Book That Changes Lives.* New York: H. J. Kramer / New World Library, 1980.

Nietzsche, Friedrich. *Twilight of the Idols.* 1889. Translated by Walter Kaufmann and R. J. Hollingdale. New York: Penguin Books, 1990.

Orloff, Judith. *The Empath's Survival Guide: Life Strategies for Sensitive People.* Boulder, CO: Sounds True, 2017.

"Percolate." Oxford English Dictionary online.

Teilhard de Chardin, Pierre. *The Phenomenon of Man*. New York: Harper & Row, 1959.

Tutu, Desmond, and Mpho Tutu. *The Book of Forgiving: The Fourfold Path for Healing Ourselves and Our World*. New York: HarperOne, 2014.

Vivekananda, Swami. *Jnana Yoga: The Path of Knowledge*. New York: Ramakrishna-Vivekananda Center, 1953.

ABOUT THE AUTHORS

Elizabeth Hamilton-Guarino and Dr. Katie Eastman are internationally recognized leaders in personal growth, transformation, and peaceful living. Together, they blend science and soul to help individuals, families, and organizations navigate change with courage, compassion, and grace. Their collaborative work—including *Percolate: Let Your Best Self Filter Through* and *The Peace Guidebook*—invites readers to rediscover their potential, practice mindful presence, and create peace within themselves and the world around them. With decades of combined experience in psychology, coaching, writing, and leadership, Elizabeth and Katie are united by a single mission: to help humanity heal, grow, and live with greater love and understanding.

Elizabeth Hamilton-Guarino is one of the world's leading voices in personal development and peaceful leadership, inspiring a global movement toward authenticity, compassion, and change. She is a bestselling and award-winning author, certified Master Coach, and founder of The Best Ever You Network, a global multimedia platform reaching millions through its network, magazine, coaching programs, and internationally acclaimed podcast, *The Best Ever You Show*, which has more than 5 million downloads worldwide.

With a combined social media reach of over 500,000 followers, Elizabeth has built an engaged community dedicated to living with authenticity, purpose, and heart. For over two decades, she has helped individuals, teams, and organizations navigate change and cultivate resilience through her compassionate and practical approach to transformation.

Elizabeth is the author of several acclaimed books, including *The Change Guidebook, The Success Guidebook, Percolate: Let Your Best Self Filter Through* (coauthored with Dr. Katie Eastman), and numerous children's books. Her work redefines change, success, and peace as daily practices rooted in awareness, aligned action, and shared humanity.

With a degree in journalism from St. Ambrose University and leadership studies at Harvard Business School, Elizabeth brings both professional depth and lived experience to her work. She is a leading advocate for food allergy awareness, having survived multiple life-threatening anaphylactic reactions and serving as a spokesperson and board member for the Food Allergy & Anaphylaxis Connection Team (FAACT). She also coaches gymnastics at the Maine Academy of Gymnastics, encouraging young athletes to build confidence, courage, and joyful strength.

Elizabeth lives between Maine and South Carolina with her husband, Peter, and their two dogs and two rescue cats. They have four grown sons who continue to inspire their dedication to lead with love and leave a legacy of peace.

Learn more at ElizabethGuarino.com.

Dr. Katie Eastman is an internationally acclaimed grief and change expert, licensed therapist, Master Grief Coach, and cofounder of Recreate Coaching and Counseling. With over four decades of experience guiding individuals, families, organizations, and communities through life's most complex transitions, Dr. Katie Eastman is recognized globally for her unwavering presence, emotional depth, and ability to transform heartbreak into healing.

Trained and mentored by legendary psychiatrist and death-and-dying pioneer Dr. Elisabeth Kübler-Ross, Dr. Katie's work integrates the highest levels of clinical psychology with spiritual insight, compassion, and practical tools for peaceful living. Her approach empowers people, not only to navigate loss, but to rise from it. From pediatric palliative care to end-of-life transition planning and organizational trauma recovery, Dr. Katie has spent her life helping others access meaning, peace, and resilience even in the most uncertain of times.

She is the author of the award-winning book *Uplifting: Inspiring Stories of Loss, Change, and Growth*, and coauthor (with Elizabeth Hamilton-Guarino) of *Percolate: Let Your Best Self Filter Through* and *The Peace Guidebook*. Known for her ability to meet people in their most vulnerable moments with grace and grounded wisdom, Dr. Katie offers a rare and sacred space for reflection, reinvention, and inner peace.

As a speaker, coach, and consultant, Dr. Katie has impacted thousands around the world through her masterful teachings on anticipatory grief, emotional resilience, compassionate leadership, and the psychology of transformation. She is also a passionate voice in the global peace movement, reminding us that peaceful living is not the absence of pain, but the presence of love, self-trust, and human connection.

Dr. Katie lives in the Pacific Northwest with her husband, John. She is the proud mother of a strong, creative adult daughter. Whether guiding clients, mentoring professionals, or walking quietly by the shore, Dr. Katie leads by example, proving that peace and growth are possible, even after loss.

Learn more at DrKatieEastman.com.

Other Books by Elizabeth Hamilton-Guarino and Dr. Katie Eastman
Percolate: Let Your Best Self Filter Through

Other Self-Help Books by Dr. Katie Eastman
*Uplifting: Inspiring Stories of Loss, Change, and Growth Inspirited
by the work of Dr. Elisabeth Kübler-Ross*

Other Self-Help Books by Elizabeth Hamilton-Guarino
*The Change Guidebook: How to Align Your Heart, Truths,
and Energy to Find Success in All Areas of Your Life*
The Success Guidebook: How to Visualize, Actualize, and Amplify You
Best Ever You: 52 Week Journal to Your Bravest, Boldest You

Children's Books by Elizabeth Hamilton-Guarino
Blueberry and Jam: Adventures in Maine
I Love You, Pumpkin Spice
The Very Lucky Ladybug
Pinky Doodle Bug
Pinky Doodle Dance

Children's Books by Elizabeth Hamilton-Guarino and Sally Huss
A Lesson for Every Child: Learning About Food Allergies
Dream Big with Food Allergies
Max's Big Adventure: Traveling with Food Allergies
Dream Big
A Lesson for Every Child: Learning About Diabetes
Best Ever You
Self-Confident Sandy

IT'S TIME TO PERCOLATE PEACE!

If *The Peace Guidebook* spoke to your heart, consider this your invitation to take the next step from inspiration to action.

We invite you to log in your own Peaceprint at PercolatePeace.com. Each Peaceprint represents one act of peace, one choice of compassion, one person saying, "I choose peace."

Our collective goal is to reach one million Peaceprints around the world, a living tapestry of kindness, unity, and hope. Your single act matters. When we each leave our Peaceprint, we leave the world better than we found it.

Join us.

Add your Peaceprint.

Together, we Percolate Peace.

Join us at PercolatePeace.com.

Step forward. Be the example.

Let's unite, empower, and transform together. The world doesn't change by chance. It changes because people choose peace and act on it.